Sexual Animosity
between
Men and Women

Sexual Animosity
between
Men and Women

Gerald Schoenewolf, Ph.D.

JASON ARONSON INC.
Northvale, New Jersey
London

10 9 8 7 6 5 4 3 2 1

Library of Congress Cataloging-in-Publication Data

Schoenewolf, Gerald.
    Sexual animosity between men and women / Gerald Schoenewolf

    Bibliography: p.
    Includes index.
    ISBN 0-87668-933-0

    1. Sexual animosity. 2. Masculinity (Psychology) 3. Femininity
(Psychology) 4. Narcissism. I. Title.
    [DNLM]: 1. Hostility. 2. Interpersonal Relations. 3. Sex. BF
    575.H6 S356s]
BF692.15.S36 1988
155.3–dc19
for Library of Congress
                             88-19353
                              CIP

Manufactured in the United States of America. Jason Aronson Inc. offers books and cassettes. For information and catalog write to Jason Aronson Inc., 230 Livingston Street, Northvale, New Jersey 07647.

For my daughter,
Leah

Contents

Preface   xi

PART I: THEORY

Chapter 1   Sexual Animosity: An Overview   3

Chapter 2   The Etiology of Sexual Animosity   13

             Eros and Thanatos   13
             Critical Periods   17
             Mother and Child   20
             Freud and Oedipus   29
             A Schematic Review   36

Chapter 3   Male Narcissism   41

             Castration Fear   41
             Character Structures   46
             Manifestations   54

Chapter 4   Female Narcissism   59

             Penis Envy   59
             Character Structures   65
             Manifestations   73

Chapter 5   Sexual Animosity in Society   79

             Masculinism and Feminism   79
             The Masculinist Phenomenon   82
             Masculinism and War   85
             The Feminist Phenomenon   88
             The Attack on Freud   91
             Masculinism and Feminism in Conflict   95

Chapter 6   Sexual Animosity in Family Life   101

             The Family as a Microcosm of Sexual
                Conflict   101
             Narcissistic Parents and Their Children   104
             The Transmission of Animosity   107

Chapter 7   The Harmonic Couple   111

             Genitality   111
             Patriarchy, Matriarchy, or Egalitarianism   114
             Complementary Relationships   121

                    PART II: CASE STUDIES

Chapter 8   Lizzie the Brat   129

             Introduction   129
             The History   130
             Discussion   148

Chapter 9   The Loner   159

Chapter 10   Animosity in Africa: The Martyrdom
             of Dian Fossey   169

Chapter 11   An Analysis of *A Streetcar Named Desire*   181

Chapter 12   On a Rooftop in New York   193
             Background   193
             Caroline Isenberg before the Murder   196
             Emmanuel Torres before the Murder   202
             The Dance of Death   210
             The Aftermath   221
             Final Analysis   225

Postscript: Male and Female   233

References   235

Index   241

Preface

Sexual animosity between men and women lies at the root of family discord; it also forms the basis for much of our social pathology. Where does it come from? Classical Freudians claim that sexual animosity grows out of women's penis envy and men's castration fear. However, feminist psychoanalysts (both male and female) have created a revised theory of female development that largely dismisses classical Freudian concepts and attributes sexual animosity to cultural values that favor men and oppress women. To be sure, the subject of male and female sexual development and its effect on adult sexual relations is one of the more hotly debated in psychoanalysis, and the debate itself is often clouded in animosity. Many writings on the subject take on a moralizing tone, which, by its very nature, precludes calm and open discussion of the issues.

This book takes a centrist position between the poles of feminism and masculinism. It explores the origins of sexual animosity in childhood and its manifestations in both men and women; it defines male and female narcissism, from which sexual animosity springs; and it delineates the impact of sexual animosity on societal values and on the family. Part One offers an overview of the subject, while Part Two provides illustrative case studies that explore sexual animosity in childrearing and in adult life. Exploring the subject of sexual animosity can facilitate a return to the harmony between the sexes that is necessary for the survival of our species.

I would like to express my gratitude to the following people for their invaluable comments and assistance: Elizabeth Mulder, CSW, Mary E. Remito, CSW, and Richard C. Robertiello, MD. I would also like to thank Joan Langs for her expert editorial advice and Jason Aronson, MD, without whose encouragement this book would not exist.

PART ONE

Theory

1

Sexual Animosity: An Overview

Eastern sages saw life in terms of dualities. Life worked best, they thought, when there was harmony between the dual forces of masculinity and femininity, the spiritual and the material, the active and the passive, the creative and the receptive, the positive and the negative, and life and death. The authors of the *I Ching* and the *Tao Te Ching* regarded these dualities as differing facets of the same thing: Masculinity is activity is creativity is spirituality is positivity; femininity is passivity is receptively is materiality is negativity. These dualities were also seen as mirror opposites. Just as a negative of a photograph is the mirror reverse of the positive print, so the male is the positive of the female and the female is the negative of the male, and vice versa. This is what the ancients meant by the "great secret of the unity of existence and nonexistence." "All is one," Lao Tzu (Bynner 1944) asserts, "and whether a man dispassionately sees to the core of life or passionately sees the surface, the core and the surface are essentially the same" (p. 25). When all is one, and when the dualities are in harmony, nature follows its course smoothly and productively; but when these forces are in opposition, out of harmony, life becomes a struggle.

The ancients called these dual forces yin and yang and devised a symbol (shown below) to represent them, the *tai ji* (literally, the primal beginning). This circular figure, the "being within each other" of the positive and negative, played a major part in ancient Chinese thought.

Separately, the light and dark halves of the circle represent the positive, male light principle and the negative, female, dark principle; together they form the "all one."

Sigmund Freud was also fond of dualities. In the beginning of his career he conceived of libidinal energy as having both a sexual and an aggressive component. He later developed his dual-instinct theory, postulating separate sexual and aggressive drives, which he called *Eros* and *Thanatos*. Eros and Thanatos in their broadest sense might be viewed as Western equivalents of yin and yang. Eros is life, creation, order; Thanatos is death, destruction, disorder. Eros is peace and love; Thanatos is aggression and hate. Eros is expansion; Thanatos is contraction. Eros is positive; Thanatos is negative. Although Freud did not refer to Eros and Thanatos as symbols of the masculine and feminine, he did give to Thanatos a connotation of "back to the womb" (1920a), which would suggest a feminine meaning. Moreover, the fact that he built his clinical theories around the resolution of the Oedipus and Electra complexes—a dual concept if not a duality—is evidence of the significance he attributed to the relationship between men and women. In both the East and the West, leading thinkers have understood the centrality of male–female relations and the significance of dualities.

The harmony or disharmony between men and women is at the very core of the human predicament. Men and women, as the breeders of future generations, to a large extent determine the personalities of individuals and the collective personality of our society and of the world. A marriage in which the husband and wife are at odds, in which the harmonic balance is off, in which unconscious animosity in the form of misogyny and misandry are acted out, is a marriage that will produce children whose personalities will reflect this imbalance and who will perpetuate it in their adult lives. The ancients knew this. Freud knew this. Yet sexual disharmony—the so-called battle of the sexes—which is so frequently and graphically depicted in the popular media, has been relatively neglected by psychoanalysis. Various writers have considered aspects of the topic of aggression between men and women, but none has considered it in its entirety, from the development of aggression to its social manifestations in the lives of both men and women. And there has been only a partial attempt (primarily by feminists) to differentiate between aggression in general and the special type of aggression that occurs between the sexes. I call the latter type of aggression *animosity*.

This book synthesizes knowledge about the origins and manifestations of sexual animosity, defines and distinguishes between the various ways in which men and women express or act out animosity in their roles as parents and in their relations with each other, and explores the impact of animosity on society. Further, it attempts to find a middle ground between the more recent feminist position on sexual animosity, on the one hand, and the "masculinist" position, on the other hand, which has largely prevailed throughout history.

The masculinist position is the traditional male view of women as portrayed in works such as the *Bible*. Here, Eve, the first woman to inhabit the Earth, ate the apple from the tree of knowledge despite the warnings of both God and her husband; thus she committed the original sin and brought calamity and mortality to humankind forever after. This view of woman as the archetype of evil can be discerned even in the modern era, where it is evident in the thoughts, writings, and actions of men; it is an attitude about women that is deeply ingrained in the psyches' of both men and women. Some would put Freud's concepts about female moral development in the masculinist category.

Freud (1918, 1925, 1931) approached the subject of sexual animosity from the angle of psychosexual development, concentrating on the psychodynamics of the phallic stage, during which males and females first become attracted to their parents of the opposite sex. Accordingly, animosity stems from the man's castration complex and the woman's penis envy. Men fear women because of unconscious-preoedipal concerns about being devoured by the omnipotent mother, and because of oedipal guilt that forbids their getting too close to women lest they be contaminated by their physical inferiority (lack of a penis) or castrated by the phallic father. To compensate for, and defend against, these fears, they put women on pedestals or disparage them or suppress them. Women, on the other hand, resent men because of unconscious preoedipal feelings of narcissistic rage and inferiority surrounding the discovery that boys have penises and girls do not, and because of oedipal anger at both parents for not righting this wrong. To compensate for this resentment, women attempt to control and manipulate men and to castrate them psychologically. However, because women do not fear castration (on a primary level, they feel they have already been castrated), they are not as moral as men are, particularly when it comes to the battle of the sexes.

Feminist psychoanalysts Adler (1927a), Horney (1926), Thompson (1950), and, more recently, Gilligan (1982) have taken Freud to task for his concepts of penis envy, female masochism, and female moral development, and have countered by pointing to cultural inequalities between men and women. They have attempted to show how women's cultural disadvantages result from unconscious male subjugation of—and animosity toward—women. Over the years, feminists in general have provided numerous examples of male oppression of women.

Indeed, feminists have sought to refute Freud's theories about women through an attack on Freud himself: Books and articles have appeared, one after another, detailing his cocaine addiction, his distant relationship with his wife, his mother complex, his father complex, his sibling rivalry with his sisters, his supposed affair with his sister-in-law, his excessive attention to his youngest daughter, Anna, his desperate relationship with Wilhelm Fleiss, his deviations from classical psychoanalytic technique, his abandonment of the seduction theory, and his Victorian values. On the surface, feminists have psychoanalyzed Freud in order to invalidate his theories; on a deeper level, they have acted out their own sexual animosity by psychologically castrating the man who, it appears, gave them an interpretation they did not want to hear.

Freud (1931) himself noted the feminist attack—it had started soon after his *Three Essays on the Theory of Sexuality* appeared—and defended himself by suggesting that they were misusing psychoanalysis. In a footnote to his paper on "Female Sexuality" he anticipated that feminist analysts would say that his notions about female psychology "have their origin in the man's 'masculinity complex,' and are meant to justify theoretically his innate propensity to disparage and suppress women" (p. 230). He replied that proponents of the classical view might similarly analyze the feminist position, referring to Dostoyevsky's famous "knife that cuts both ways." Such a misuse of psychoanalysis could be of no service, he believed, in resolving theoretical disputes.

There was probably another reason for his feeling that psychoanalysis, misused or not, could be of little service in resolving these issues. As a colleague of mine jocularly put it, only a hermaphroditic robot from Mars could possibly examine either women's or men's psychological development without bias. The beliefs of men about women, and the beliefs of women about men, are usually an outgrowth of their development; neither gender can be objective about the other or about themselves. Feminism is for many women a vehicle for exacting revenge on men; masculinism offers men an excuse for depreciating and suppressing women. One can only try as best one can, within the limitations of one's constitution and character, to find the truth. This Freud did, and the present author continues that quest.

Jung (1951) was the first to use the word *animosity* with regard to the male–female dyad. He saw animosity as the expression of the anima–animus relationship between a man and a woman. The man's anima (the unconscious female component of his personality) and the woman's animus (unconscious male component) produce feelings of repulsion toward members of the opposite sex due to negative projections. "[W]hen the animus and anima meet," Jung says, "the animus draws his sword of power and the anima ejects her poison of illusion and seduction" (p. 153). Jung, like Freud, believed in the primary bisexuality of humans; this sexual duality affects the internal harmony of each individual and also the relations of men and women in general. Only a man who is in harmony with his feminine component can live in harmony with a woman, and only a woman who is in harmony with her masculine component can live in harmony with a man. However, since Jung traced the animus and anima to archetypes of woman and man transmitted via the collective unconscious of humankind (rather than to relationships with primary figures in early child-hood), this theory is more a genetic than a psychological explanation of male–female disharmony. If male–female animosity is inherited through the collective unconscious, there is nothing we can do about it. Psychoanalysis with patients suffering from neurotic or narcissistic symptoms (such symptoms always involving some degree of animosity) has proven otherwise; we *can* do something about it. It may well be that there is a collective anima and animus passed along from gener-ation to generation – a natural tendency toward attraction and repul-sion not unlike the attraction and repulsion of the two poles of a magnet; but this tendency would then be subject to modification by the environment. Therefore, the degree of animosity would depend on the environment.

Another aspect of sexual animosity that has been studied by psychoanalysis is sexual sadomasochism (termed by Freud "erotogenic masochism"). Nowhere is the animosity between men and women more apparent than in these rituals of punishment, sex play, and degradation. Lowenstein (1957) interpreted these rituals as symbolic repetitions of childhood situations wherein sexual fantasies, erotic games, and strivings toward sexual contact with the parents – partic-ularly of the opposite sex – have been met by real or imagined threat, teasing, punishment, or ridicule. In the sadomasochistic ritual, the sadist, who stands for the parent, joins in the sexual play instead of disapproving. By urging the sexual partner to participate in a scene of castration threat or punishment, the masochist forces the threatening, disapproving parent of his childhood to undo the early rebuff. This repetition then becomes a veiled, incestuous gratification for both sadist (who identifies with the parent-aggressor) and masochist (who identifies with the child). Those who engage in such games sometimes switch roles, since every masochist has the potential to be a sadist, and vice versa. Obviously there is much acting out of sexual animosity in sadomasochistic rituals, which may indeed be the most blatant form of its expression.

Numerous writers have described the genesis of aggression or rage (which later transforms into sexual animosity) during the earliest years of life – among them Freud (1918), Klein (1932), Ribble (1943), Erikson (1950), Kohut (1971), Mahler and colleagues (1975), Khan (1979), and Spotnitz (1985). Klein extensively explored the relationship between the infant and the mother's breast, attributing the beginnings of sexual ambivalence to the infant's feelings about the alternately gratifying and frustrating breast. All have studied the mother–child relationship during the first two years of life, describing how maturation becomes blocked by deprivation or hostility in their many guises, resulting in the infant's turning his aggression against himself, which in turn leads to the development of pathological object relations.

All have also been concerned with the duality between the libidinal and aggressive drives, recognizing the importance of the libidinal drive in modifying and neutralizing aggression, although there is disagreement about whether aggression is actually a drive and whether it is innately destructive, as Freud and Klein contend. It seems to me there *are* two drives, which I will call Eros and Thanatos. My definition of these dual entities differs from Freud's, however, and is more in line with Spitz's (1965). Unlike Freud's Thanatos, the aggressive drive as I see it is not destructive under normal operational circumstances. It becomes so only when the aims of Eros have been frustrated or if, due to trauma, it becomes fixated in a destructive mode. In my definition, this duality represents yet another form of the yin and yang—the aggressive drive being the male part, and the libidinal drive being the female, and vice versa.

"Women! Men! You can't live with them, and you can't live without them!" This popular saying poignantly expresses the interplay of libidinal and aggressive forces (love and hate) in the relations of men and women. When psychoanalysts speak about relationships, the word *ambivalence* inevitably comes up. From Freud to Klein to Spitz to Kohut—all have been concerned with ambivalence. In fact, it has become a truism in the profession that intimacy requires the mastery of ambivalence. Mastering ambivalence is not easy; however. When there has been a pathological build-up of aggression (some would say narcissistic rage), the capacity for love is diminished. Male and female narcissism prevents the working through of ambivalence, resulting in a psychic stalemate. This in turn leads to marriages in which one or both partners are not truly there emotionally, marriages in which resistance and transference behavior block sexual harmony. And when a husband and wife cannot be there for each other, they also will not be there for their children. Indeed, children are the ultimate targets of sexual animosity.

The signs of sexual animosity are all around us, and they appear to be on the rise in American society. Nearly 50 percent of all marriages end in divorce. The incidence of rape is increasing, as is the incidence of sexual crimes against children. Sex-related murders are also on the rise. Other more subtle signs of animosity include an increase in homosexuality among both genders and a greater emphasis by both men and women on careers rather than relationships, all of which has left more and more of our children in daycare centers or with baby-sitters.

Victimology is a new area of research that has recently sprung up, out of concern about some of these issues. Unfortunately, much of this "research" is biased, its goal being foreordained: to absolve victims of any responsibility for their victimization. In this respect it is a propaganda effort on behalf of one side of the "battle of the sexes," a quasi-science whose aim is to rally public opinion against victimizers (mostly men) and obtain public sympathy and absolution for victims (mostly women). The destructive aspect of such research is that it creates a paranoid view of male–female relations in which men are viewed as potential persecutors; at the same time, it rewards women for being victims, thereby fostering masochism. If a woman can get sympathy and attention and sometimes even praise for being a battered woman, and if, at the same time, she does not have to take responsibility for her contribution to an unhealthy relationship, there will be no motivation for her to grow. On the contrary, there will be a motivation for her to repeat the pattern that evokes so much sympathy and support, and from which she comes out "smelling like a rose" while her male counterpart is castigated as a villain.

On the other hand, research on gender roles seems to offer valid findings on how the role one is accorded in a society, and the value society places on that role, affects one's self-esteem and general attitude. The traditional roles of wife and mother have not been given the same respect as the traditional roles played by men. Thus, when public opinion surveys are conducted in which people are asked to rank occupations according to prestige and importance, the profession of "surgeon" (a traditionally male preserve) ranks first, while "homemaker" or "mother" is usually ranked near the bottom. Nor are traditional women's roles portrayed as heroic in the popular media, as traditional men's roles are; we have been deluged with novels, plays, movies, and television shows about physicians, while there have been few works about the heroics of homemaking or motherhood. Such cultural influences cannot help but affect the relationship between the sexes and contribute to sexual animosity. They reinforce feminism and masculinism and bring about a competitive atmosphere between men and women—who vie for the same roles—rather than a complementary atmosphere. They have also had a destructive impact on the family and on child rearing, since a disgruntled mother, unhappy with her role, is less likely to care for her children with the same enthusiasm as a mother who is happy with her role.

It is unfortunate that the role of mother is not given more prestige as an occupation in our society, for it is perhaps the most important role in any society. Actually, just the opposite has occurred. The status of motherhood has decreased in recent years as more and more women have chosen the workplace rather than the home. Paradoxically, the realm of motherhood is at the same time enveloped in a veil of sanctity; mothers (be they male or female caretakers) are not required to undergo any training before raising children, while psychotherapists are required to undergo an average of ten years of training in order to be qualified to correct the effects of errant parenting.

The philosopher Schopenhauer (1896), perhaps more than anyone except Freud, underscored the importance of male–female relations and the impact of sexual animosity on society. He wrote that the relation of the sexes is really the invisible central point of all action and conduct, whether between women and women, women and men, or men and men. It is the cause of war and peace, and the basis of all jests, the source of all wit, the key to all allusions, and the meaning of all hints. The relation of the sexes lies behind the daily meditation of the young, and often also of the old, and it permeates the thoughts of both the chaste and the unchaste. Sexual passion, Schopenhauer believed, is the most perfect manifestation of the will to live, and the origin of an individual's identity. Sexual discord, on the other hand, is the cause of all misery.

It is likely that the causes of animosity are overdetermined. However, it is not inevitable for animosity to become so prevalent that it brings about the breakdown of families, erects a barrier of distrust between the sexes, and leads to an array of social pathologies. These are the symptoms of a society in which animosity is the rule, love is the exception, and cooperation is rarely mentioned. Only by understanding the environmental contribution to this problem and its ramifications can we do something about it.

Yin and yang. Male and female. Love and aggression. Harmony and disharmony. Is there really a natural way, as Lao Tzu suggests, that will lead to harmony between these dualities? Is such a way attainable in our modern civilizations with their "discontents"? Freud (1930) apparently did not think so. His notion that civilization requires repression and fosters neurosis seems to imply that resignation to sexual discord is the price of progress. I hope not.

2

The Etiology of Sexual Animosity

EROS AND THANATOS

The duality of Eros and Thanatos is basic to human existence. To understand the operation of this duality, one can use the analogy of a growing plant. Plants need certain nutrients from their environment in order to survive and flourish, including just the right amount of water, minerals, sun, and carbon dioxide. They also need to make contact with animals who assist in the pollination process. If a plant does not get these needs met, it is likely to rot and die. Humans (and other animals) also have primary needs. As a plant reaches out toward the sun and its roots drive ever further into the soil in search of nutrients, humans also reach out to satisfy their needs for survival and growth. Eros represents the drive toward the satisfaction of these needs.

What are these primary needs? There are the obvious needs for oxygen, food, and water, as well as warmth of the sun. In addition, there is a primary need for love—that is, for a supportive emotional and physical relationship with another human being. During certain critical stages of development, love is essential for survival. During other periods, its presence or absence can make the difference between merely existing and flourishing, and its chronic absence will lead to slow deterioration of functioning. In the first months of life, the breast-feeding relationship between mother and child constitutes the primary mode for obtaining love. During adulthood, the primary mode for experiencing love and bonding is sexual intercourse. In a broader sense, all social interactions provide sources of love.

When Eros, or the libidinal drive, is frustrated in its attempt to obtain primary needs, Thanatos, or the aggressive drive, springs into action. The aggressive drive, like the libidinal drive, is innate; all higher animals have aggression to help them hunt for food, establish dominance, defend territory, procure a mate, and obtain other needs. Aggressive energy is also utilized in the process of aging. The ultimate aim of life, as Freud (1920) states, is death, and Thanatos is the energy that drives the organism toward that aim—death being the last maturational stage, a return to disorder. However, when the environment frustrates an organism's primary needs (or threatens to), Thanatos goes into "fast motion." Its initial aim is to gain power and control over, or safety from, the frustrating element; if this cannot be done, it tries to destroy the element (that is, it becomes sadistic); finally, if this is unsuccessful, the organism destroys itself (becomes masochistic). Homicide and suicide are results of extreme frustration. Hence, under normal circumstances, Thanatos is helpful; under frustrating circumstances, it becomes destructive.

A clear example of suicidal behavior (self-destruction) following the frustration of Eros—as well as an illustration of the primary need for love during the early stages of an infant's development—is provided by Spitz (1965). In his observations of deprivation in a foundling home, he studied ninety-one infants who were separated from their mothers after the age of 3 months and fed by a succession of nurses. Thirty-four of the infants died by the second year. All infants showed symptoms of Thanatos: first angry crying and clinging (trying to control or destroy the frustrating element); then anaclitic depression (aggression turned against the self); then motor retardation, then marasmus and, very often, death. Bowlby (1979) observed a similar pattern in studies of children in nurseries. Similar responses to the frustration of Eros can be observed in adults as well, as when a husband or wife suddenly dies and the spouse dies quite suddenly a short time later, often without any warning signs. Thanatos is also in evidence when a man kills his wife and himself in a "blind rage." Indeed, all acts of violence against others or against the self are the result of the aggressive drive having become destructive due to the frustration of Eros.

The more an organism can live in harmony with himself and with others, the less frustration of Eros there will be; the less frustration of Eros, the less expenditure of Thanatos. Of course, there will always be frustration in life, but the healthy individual will handle such frustration in the most expedient way, with the least amount of aggressive energy. Every expenditure of aggressive energy would seem to speed the process of death. Thanatos is to animals what rotting and dying is to plants.

Manifestations of Thanatos range from the subtle to the obvious. More subtle signs of Thanatos include any pursuit in which the aim is power and control. While love is a primary human need, power is a secondary need. Humans who cannot obtain necessary love, will attempt to obtain power over the people and things around them. All relationships between men and women in which one partner is dominant and the other is submissive are power, rather than love, relationships. In such relationships, both the dominant and the submissive partner attempt to manipulate the other into supplying love—the dominant partner through intimidation, and the submissive partner through the induction of guilt. However, only the illusion of love, and not love itself, can be obtained in this manner; the safety of knowing that one controls the other person, and hence will not be hurt by him, passes for love.

Love, as Klein (1932) has pointed out, is an offshoot of gratitude. The original gratitude the infant feels toward the gratifying breast is later transferred to other intimate objects that are similarly gratifying. In an equal, mutually respectful relationship between two caring humans, each has an opportunity to give to the other voluntarily (not because of manipulation). This voluntary giving breeds gratitude and then, as it grows deeper, love. A mother's voluntary giving of love to her infant, who is too helpless to control her whether she does so or not, is the prototypical act of love. All resistance behavior, in and out of the therapy office, is an attempt to manipulate and control the environment, and is a manifestation of Thanatos.

Every form of pathology, whether behavioral or physical, is a manifestation of the degenerative process—of Thanatos. Thus, such symptoms as neurotic defenses, narcissistic grandiosity and rage, psychotic withdrawal, and character disorders, stem from frustrated Eros. Likewise, most organic diseases (except those that clearly have genetic origins) also have a psychological component; that is, they result, in part, from frustrated Eros. Psychiatric hospitals are full of individuals whose Eros has been severely frustrated and whose aggressive drive to control that frustration met with still more frustration; hence the aggression has been turned against the self. Prisons hold individuals whose aggressive drive has become stuck in the mode of trying to destroy the environment, which has failed to meet the needs of Eros. Cancer may be an example of the rotting process in humans, the final somatic result of aggression turned against the self. Wars are sometimes the result of the collective frustration of Eros (most often the acting out of collective narcissistic grandiosity and rage); paranoid projections of an infantile nature run high during times of war.

On a national level, we can see that the more a country spends on defense for war, the less it will have to spend on the improvement of social services. In individual terms, the more energy one expends on defense (the more the aggressive drive is activated), the less time and energy one will have to pursue the satisfaction of one's primary needs, particularly the need for love. The saying, "Make love, not war," is an expression of the duality of Eros and Thanatos.

The act of copulation is the ultimate victory of Eros over Thanatos. Klein (1932) notes that during intercourse an individual's aggression is neutralized:

> Libidinal satisfaction diminishes his aggressiveness and with it his anxiety. In addition, the pleasure he gets from such satisfaction seems in itself to allay his fear of being destroyed by his own destructive impulses and by his objects, and to militate against . . . his fear of losing his capacity to achieve libidinal satisfaction. Libidinal satisfaction, as an expression of Eros, reinforces his belief in his helpful imagos and diminishes the dangers which threaten him from his death instinct and his super-ego. [p. 201]

Unfortunately, most people make war rather than love. They control and manipulate rather than relate in a genuine way. The heros of our popular culture are invariably those who have learned to direct their aggression outward in socially acceptable forms, their value systems providing the justification for their sadism. By finding socially acceptable means of directing aggression outward, we maintain a feeling of well-being, often at the expense of others. Today's socially acceptable cause may be tomorrow's embarrassment. Aggression breeds aggression.

Sexual animosity is a particular form of the aggressive drive. More specifically, it is male and female narcissism. Here aggression is aroused, and then repressed, in connection with narcissistic injuries associated with one's sense of maleness or femaleness. How does it begin? Some would point to the discovery of one's maleness and femaleness somewhere between the first and third years of life. Others would trace the beginnings of its development to an earlier point. It might be said to begin during the merging of male and female in the process of reproduction.

Ideally, the act of love should be a pure expression of Eros. Since no one is without aggression, however, Eros and Thanatos are inter-mingled in the act, giving it a particular character. Every form of animosity is communicated in this act, and it may be that the spirit in which one is conceived carries over to life in the womb.

CRITICAL PERIODS

A newborn comes into the world with certain character traits. Some infants are criers and need more comforting from the beginning; others are more placid and require less comforting. Some are outgoing and aggressive; others are shy and reclusive. Some traits are considered predispositions to various forms of illness; others seem to bode for healthy development. These traits reflect the interplay of the libidinal and aggressive drives at birth. Many psychiatrists are of the opinion that these initial character traits are mainly genetic; analysts, for the most part, believe that a number of traits, particularly temperamental ones, are transmitted by the mother during pregnancy. Those who stress the connection between life in the womb and life in the crib point to observations by analysts and psychologists relating the mood of the mother during pregnancy to the mood of the newborn (Ribble 1943, Spitz 1965, Mahler et al. 1975, Stern 1977).

It seems that the environment is the key variable in determining normal or abnormal development. An infant may be a crier and may be particularly vulnerable to stress, but if the caretaker is able to meet his specific maturational needs and help him travel smoothly through the normal stages of development, he will become a healthy adult. If, on the other hand, the caretaker is unable to meet the infant's needs, he will become fixated at one or more stages.

Whether viewed from the perspective of ego psychology, object relations, self psychology, modern psychoanalysis, or any of the other schools of thought, the first six years of childhood are considered the breeding ground for normal and abnormal development. Research has validated this notion.

Coles (1982) reports "critical periods" in humans akin to those attributed to lower animals—developmental stages during which individuals are particularly sensitive or receptive to certain events and experiences. The term *critical period* was first used to explain imprinting in geese. Researchers discovered that for geese and other birds, there was an optimal time for imprinting (the formation of emotional bonds and social behavior) to occur, and if it hadn't occurred by that time, it wouldn't occur at all. It was also demonstrated that there are optimal periods for the formation of emotional bonds between puppies and their trainers. Work with monkeys has demonstrated a critical period for learning adequate sexual and maternal behavior.

Coles points to studies with orphans who grew up "incurably unsocialized" because they did not receive adequate social interaction during a critical period. Spitz (1965) used the term *critical phases* with respect to hospitalized and institutionalized infants, noting that there were three developmental turning points, or "organizers," in the first year of life. Mahler and co-authors (1975) also spoke of critical phases, while Roiphe and Galenson (1981) stressed the rapprochement stage, pointing to the two important events that occur during this period: toilet training and the child's discovery of the anatomical differences between the sexes. Critical periods might also be shown to correspond to the psychosexual stages in general—the oral stage being crucial to the establishment of object relations, the anal stage vital to the learning of cooperative and social behavior, and the phallic stage essential to the development of mature sexual behavior.

Animal studies cited by Coles have demonstrated the connection between early childhood trauma and later mental illness. In one study, newborn monkeys were separated from their mothers a few hours after birth and put into bare cages in a large room where other newborns were similarly caged. Monkeys reared in this manner, without any maternal contact, manifested behavioral patterns similar to those observed in emotionally disturbed children. They would sit and stare into space, circle their cages in a repetitive manner, clasp their heads in their hands and arms and rock, and often develop compulsive, self-destructive habits, such as pinching the same piece of skin between their fingers a hundred or more times a day. Furthermore, their social behavior with other animals was noted to be markedly impaired. Early separation of mother and newborn had apparently not only produced abnormal behavior, but had also resulted in an impaired ability to form effective social relationships.

In another experiment, a litter of dogs was divided into two groups at the age of four weeks (immediately after weaning). One group was raised normally while the other group was confined to cages, one dog per cage, with severe restrictions on sensory experiences and contacts with other living things. After seven months the dogs were released from the cages and were observed in a variety of experimental situations. Four of the experiments demonstrated that the dogs who had been deprived of normal sensory experiences responded abnormally to pain at maturity; they didn't appear to be affected by painful stimuli—which is commonly cited as a characteristic of psychopathic or sociopathic personality. Some were even attracted to the painful stimuli—a characteristic of masochism. In a fifth experiment, each dog was released into a large room in which two other dogs were contained in pens, one in each corner. The control dogs—those raised normally—typically approached one of the pens, stared at the dog inside, wagged their tails, and barked. The experimental dogs tended to ignore the occupants of the pens and sometimes even urinated on the pen.

Montagu (1976), an ethologist, examined the way in which

aggression is nurtured in various environments and found that the incidence of aggressive (destructive) behavior by parents is much higher for delinquent than nondelinquent boys. A longitudinal study of child abuse over three generations showed that children who were abused by their parents from infancy become abusers of their own children. In addition, he cites anthropological studies showing that where aggressive behavior is strongly discouraged—as it is among the Hutterites, the Amish, and the Hopi and Zuni Indians—it is almost unknown.

MOTHER AND CHILD

Analysts from differing schools have variously observed the mother-child dyad, each viewing the relationship from a different angle and explaining the transmission of animosity in different language. There is general agreement that this first relationship between the infant and his mother's breast, and later between the infant and the mother herself, sets the precedent for all future relationships. It is also generally agreed that trauma results from the damming up of aggression in the infantile ego. Spotnitz (1985), writing about the development of narcissism in schizophrenics, notes that in some cases aggression seems to have been mobilized by too much sensory deprivation and in other cases by undue excitation. "In either event," he concludes, "more aggression was mobilized than the infantile ego could cope with healthfully" (p. 69). Kohut (1971) approaches the problem from the angle of empathy but reaches similar conclusions. He explains that, due to her own narcissistic fixations, a mother's self-absorption may lead to her projecting her moods and tensions onto the child, or to her responding hypochondriacally to his moods when they mirror her own and uncaringly when they seem opposite to hers. He concludes: "The result is a traumatic alteration of faulty empathy, overempathy, and lack of empathy, which prevents the gradual withdrawal of narcissistic cathexes and the building up of tension-regulating psychic structures: The child remains fixated on the whole early narcissistic milieu" (p. 66).

Although Spotnitz and Kohut are writing about the development of pathological narcissism, I believe that their observations apply to the development of psychopathology in general. Both appear to express the same ideas in different language. Spotnitz speaks about the alternation of "sensory deprivation" and "undue excitation," and Kohut refers to the alteration of "faulty empathy, overempathy, and lack of empathy"; Spotnitz writes of "more aggression" being mobilized than "the infantile ego could cope with," while Kohut talks about the prevention of the "building up of tension-regulating psychic structures."

Winnicott (1965) expresses a similar idea when he speaks about "traumatic impingements" at the "stage of absolute dependence." Winnicott asserts that in order for infants to develop normally, they must receive "good-enough mothering," particularly during the earliest stage of life, when they are absolutely dependent. The mother sets up a "holding environment" in which the infant establishes a continuity of being, resulting in healthy maturation. When this holding environment is inadequate, there will be too many traumatic impingements for the infant to handle. "Traumatic impingements" refers to disruptions in the mother–infant relationship that require the infant to react rather than to just be. If the mother does not come when he cries, or if there are repeated changes in techniques or changes of caretakers (such as when several nurses take care of an infant), or if the mother's mood changes from day to day, these will become traumatic impingements, disruptions in the flow of continuity, requiring the infant to react. This in turn will arouse in the infant a desire to annihilate the mother, for during these moments when the environment is inadequate and he must react, he himself fears annihilation. An accumulation of such impingements, Winnicott observes, sets up a pattern of fragmentation and loads the infant in the direction of psychopathology.

Klein (1932) contends that the seeds of gender aggression, or sexual animosity, are laid during the initial relationship between the infant and the mother's breast. According to Klein, the first objects that an infant introjects are the good mother and the bad mother, as represented by the mother's breast. When the breast is gratifying, the child thinks of it as good. If the breast is not there when the child wants it, the child thinks of it as bad. For the girl, the desire to suck or devour the penis is directly derived from her desire to do the same to her mother's breast. If she experiences the breast as a good breast, she will have positive feelings about it and feel grateful. If, due to repeated frustrations, the child experiences the breast as bad, she will have negative feelings about it and will envy its power over her and want to devour it. Thus Klein finds that the predisposition to penis envy begins at this stage. "Not only do the envy and hatred she feels towards her mother colour and intensify her sadistic phantasies against the penis, but her relations to the mother's breast affect her subsequent attitude towards men in other ways as well" (p. 207). Klein places the beginnings of the masculinity complex at this stage.

For the boy, the breast is the precursor of the castration complex, which in turn leads to animosity and fear of women. If the boy experiences the breast as gratifying, he will think of it as a good breast, and through a process of identification and then introjection, he will think of his penis as a "good penis." On the other hand, if he experiences the breast as frustrating, he will perceive it as a bad breast and will then think of his penis as a "bad penis." At the same time, he also imagines that his mother has a penis, or several penises, inside her (these penises originally belonging to the father); if the boy experiences the breast as a bad breast, he then assumes that the penises inside the mother are also bad, and he will then turn away from her and later from women in general, not wanting to assault them with his bad penis or to risk being assaulted by their internal bad penises. Thus the initial relationship between the male infant and the breast lays a primitive superstructure in the unconscious that affects all his future relationships with women.

Winnicott (1964) alludes to sexual animosity when he talks about the social consequences stemming from the fact that every man and every woman came out of the womb of a woman, and that everyone was at first absolutely dependent, and then relatively dependent, on a woman. Therefore, all individuals, men and women, have in reserve a certain fear of Woman—that is, the unacknowledged mother of the first stages of life. This fear of Woman is in reality a fear of dependence, of regressing back to the stage of absolute dependence experienced in infancy. Dependence implies powerlessness and impotence; independence implies powerfulness and potency. When a mother interferes with this striving toward independence, however, the boy retains a fear of her interference, domination, and power; this fear is evidenced in nightmares of witches. Winnicott feels that men and women deal differently with this fear. Women are better able to identify with Woman, as they can become mothers themselves; hence they can allay their fear through an identification with Woman and a separation from men. These forces tend to reinforce feminism. In men, the fear of Woman can lead to the suppression of women. "In very few societies does a woman hold the political reins" (p. 132).

Khan (1979) attributes the development of perverse sexual practices (heterosexual as well as homosexual) to mother–infant relationships in which the mother lavishes intense body-care on the male infant, but in a rather impersonal way. The child is treated by the mother as her "thing creation" rather than as an emergent growing person in his own right. In essence, the mother idolizes the infant. The child very early on begins to sense that what the mother idolizes is at once something very special in him and yet not him as a whole person. He learns to tolerate a dissociation in his experience of self and gradually turns the mother into an accomplice in maintaining this created object. In the oedipal phase, however, these mothers suddenly become self-conscious about their strong attachment to their boy children and abruptly withdraw; the children endure a belated separation trauma and develop internalized idolized selves that choose perverse sexual practices. Because this rejection by their mothers occurs during the oedipal stage, when feelings have become consciously sexualized, such boys feel sexually rejected and, indeed, annihilated. A rage reaction ensues.

In studying female homosexuality, Khan found a similar mother–infant relationship. He noted a form of pathogenic mothering in which the latent depression or overt hypochondriacal anxious depressiveness and lack of true affectivity toward the infant girl results in a kind of symbiosis. As was the case with male children, these mothers do not relate to the girl's whole self; instead, they bind them in a symbiosis in which the infant is required to respond to the mother's needs rather than the reverse. A split then takes place: Mental-ego development becomes dissociated from body-ego development. The body ego becomes allied with the mother and her mood, while the mental ego tends to exploit the erotogeneity of the body orifices and body surface out of an attempt to make restitution to the mother, to the deprived body ego, and to compensate for inner anxieties provoked by muted rage and anger. Such a child will develop a precocious form of masturbation as a self-consoling technique, which the mother will attempt to prohibit; this prohibition will only intensify the conflict and guilt and at the same time turn these activities into an omnipotent means of provoking a response from the mother. "The sadomasochistic vicissitudes of these processes," Khan states, "can lead to a very profound predisposition towards pathological object-relations and distortions of both the instinctual life and ego-functions later" (p. 96).

Spitz (1965) points out that an infant will become fixated at the preambivalent stage of development unless he is able, at around the sixth month of life, to fuse his aggressive and libidinal drives and direct them simultaneously at his mother. This fusing of the libidinal and aggressive drives corresponds with the fusing of the "good" and "bad" mother. In research observations conducted in hospitals and institutions, Spitz noted that children who were not able to make this transition were invariably children dominated by their aggressive drive, which had turned against the self. Hence the mother never really became "the love object," usually because she had not been the "good mother"—at least not enough of the time.

Mead (1935, 1949) writes of the development of sexual animosity in the Mundugumor, a tribe that lived in New Guinea near a tributary of the Sepik River. The Mundugumor women actively disliked child-bearing, and also children themselves. Infants were carried in harsh opaque baskets that scratched their skin; later they were carried high on mother's shoulders, well away from her breasts. Mothers nursed their children grudgingly, walking as they did so and pushing them away as soon as they were minimally satisfied. Breasts were shoved into the mouths of adopted children in an aggressive, angry fashion. In later life, lovemaking was conducted "like the first round of a prizefight, and biting and scratching are important parts of foreplay" (1949, p. 70). The men and women of this cannibalistic tribe bickered constantly, every man's hand against every other, with the women as assertive and vigorous as the men. When they captured an enemy, they ate him and "laughed as they told about it."

Erikson (1950) links sexual animosity with the establishment of basic trust or mistrust of the world, which hinges particularly on the events of the oral-sadistic phase of development. When the infant's teeth begin to emerge, he is thrown into a dilemma. Now, for the first time, he has the means to hurt the breast and the mother who owns it. Sometimes he may not mean to hurt her but is simply trying out the new teeth; at other times, when he has felt frustrated by the breast, he wants to destroy it. If the mother becomes angry, or if she decides to wean the child at this time, the infant may withdraw into a sadomasochistic confusion. The confusion leaves an impression of loss of paradise, which Erikson relates to the story of Adam and Eve, speculating that it "is probably the ontogenetic contribution to the biblical sage of paradise, where the first people on earth forfeited forever the right to pluck without effort whad had been put at their disposal; they bit into the forbidden apple, and made God angry" (p. 79).

Mahler and co-authors (1975) confirm what Klein had previously asserted about the development of sexual animosity during the anal phase: that the phallic phase—or at least a part of the phallic phase—begins much earlier than Freud had thought. In observing thirty-eight children and twenty-two mothers over a period of four years, Mahler and colleagues noted the importance of the "rapprochement subphase" of the separation–individuation process. In the rapprochement period, which begins at the age of 15 or 16 months, there develops in the toddler the definite awareness of his own separateness, in the face of which he is no longer able to maintain the delusion of his omnipotent grandeur. He must gradually give up both the delusion of his own grandeur and the belief in the omnipotence of his parents. Moreover, he is now required to give up the free-spirited, pampered life of the infant and begin the process of socialization, via toilet training. The result is a heightened separation anxiety and an ongoing fight with the mother. Then, to complicate matters, it is also at about this time that children first discover the anatomical difference between the sexes. During this period, boys are initially prone to quiet masturbation; then upon noting the difference between themselves and girls, they tend to clutch their penises for reassurance. Girls, upon discovering their lack of penises, tend to masturbate desperately, aggressively, and this discovery "coincides with the emergence of the affect of envy." The authors describe a typical response by a 14-month-old girl. One day, instead of sitting on the toilet, she began to whine and hold her genital area. A period of extreme crankiness followed. This following scenario ensued:

[This] charming little girl became impossible to satisfy in our nursery group. A while later, Cathy started to become not only cranky but aggressive toward the other children. Her particular form of aggression (from which nothing could deter her) was pulling the hair of boys and girls alike. Eventually, the mother told us that because Cathy hated to have her hair washed, she had been taking her into the shower with her to wash her hair. In the shower, Cathy had grabbed at her mother's pubic hair, obviously searching for the "hidden penis." [p. 106]

This stage seems to be more difficult for girls than for boys. The authors explain that, upon the discovery of the sexual difference, girls "tended to turn back to mother, to blame her, to demand from her, to be disappointed in her, and still to be ambivalently tied to her. They demanded from mother that she settle a debt, so to say" (p. 106). Boys, on the other hand, can turn to father as someone with whom to identify—their severest castration anxiety still to come during the phallic phase. The authors conclude that the rapprochement crisis often remains an unresolved intrapsychic conflict that may later interfere with oedipal development.

The findings of Mahler and co-workers have been confirmed by Roiphe and Galenson (1981), who worked with infants and their parents for many years, conducting an intensive study of about seventy infants. Like Mahler, they point to a definite genital awareness and the beginning of a sense of gender identity by the end of the second year. They assert that girls universally react quite strongly to the discovery of their lack of a penis, which brings about the "recrudescence of fears of object loss and self-disintegration." Boys show far less overt disturbance as they defend against castration anxiety "by a more profound denial and displacement" and through an emotional involvement with the father, particularly "in connection with the development of exhibitionistic pride as well as the urinary technique" (p. 273). In boys with severe preoedipal castration reactions, there was a tendency to develop a negative oedipal attachment. In girls with severe penis envy, the hostile ambivalence toward the mother becomes very intense, the maternal attachment is heightened, and the turn to the father does not occur.

Roiphe and Galenson describe a typical boy's response to the anatomical difference. Jeff, at the age of approximately 28 months, saw both his uncle's penis and a girl playmate's genitals. He was quite startled in both instances and proceeded to question his mother continually. Where was the girl's penis? Did his mother have a penis? Could his own penis be flushed down the toilet? For days he questioned her persistently about whether all the people he knew did or did not possess a penis. The boy then seemed to forget about the difference between the sexes for several months, only to bring it up again in another connection later. This sort of waxing and waning of the recognition of the sexual difference, which is common in boys, is explained by the authors as a way of denying the genital difference in order to allay castration fear.

Another boy, Billy, discovered the difference at 15 months of age and began sleeping with his bottle under his penis. For several months he masturbated in a driven manner. On a number of occasions he would straddle his mother's leg and vigorously rub himself back and forth. His mother viewed this as boyish horseplay. She was later alarmed, however, when he took hold of her hand while she was changing his diaper and placed it on his penis. On yet another occasion, as she was tickling him under his arms and chin, he took her hand, placed in on his penis, and began to rock "in a state of obvious arousal" (p. 84). Because Billy's father was absent for a year, he was not supported by a growing identification with the father. His subsequent castration reaction was more severe than normal, so that whenever he became frustrated in an activity or angry with his mother, he would clutch his penis. His "erotization of aggression" would form the basis "for a sadomasochistic object relationship" (p. 86).

Roiphe and Galenson supply numerous such case histories. Typical of those about girls is one describing Suzy's rude awakening. She first showed an interest in her genital area at about 15 months of age—at the time she first saw a boy's penis. With her eyes "riveted on his penis," she pointed at it and then touched her own genital area. For the next few months she often tried to lift the skirts of the women in the nursery (looking for penises). She did the same at home with her mother, who became upset by this behavior. The authors speculated that she might also have tried to touch her father's penis, during her showers with her parents. When she was 20 months old, she had a guest in the house, a little boy; after following him into the bathroom, she reached out and touched his penis. "Pee-pee," she said. This event initiated a period of intense masturbation and lifting of her skirt and the skirts of women around her. At the same time there was a complete deterioration of her toilet control, which persisted over the next few months. Again her mother was upset by this behavior. "Michael has a pee-pee. I have no pee-pee. Why?" she asked her mother.

The deterioration of toilet control was followed by a profound general behavioral regression and negativism. When she came to the nursery, she refused to leave her stroller. "Sitting there for a considerable time looking sullen and distressed, she screamed if any of the children tried to touch her" (pp. 144–145). She would cling to her mother, who, feeling perplexed, frustrated, and angry, "reacted as if her self-esteem had been wounded." The authors interpreted that the child's anger with and disappointment in her mother were reflected in an almost paralyzing hostile dependence on her. "This accretion of aggression tends to threaten the cohesiveness of the ego, tends to threaten the integrity of the crucial self and object representation," which in turn calls forth "the early defense mechanisms of splitting the good and bad mother images and turning the aggression against the self " (p. 145).

Roiphe and Galenson find that while parents tended to give little boys words—sometimes pet words—for their genitals from a very early age, only a few parents did the same with their girls. They interpreted this omission as a cultural manifestation of the castration complex. They also pointed to the interplay between toilet-training conflicts and the castration reaction following early genital arousal. Finally, they stated their unequivocal agreement with Freud on the effect of penis envy on women's personality formation, asserting that Freud's original position is correct "in so far as his premise that penis envy and the feminine castration complex exert crucial influences upon feminine development" (p. 285).

Other studies of early sexuality by Stoller (1968), Money and Ehrhardt (1972), and Socarides (1979) have also identified the second half of the second year as a critical period for establishing gender identity. Stoller placed the beginnings of feminine identification among transsexuals in the preoedipal phase, explaining that the mothers of such individuals had the common psychological feature of having treated their sons in a way that interfered with the development of "core gender identity." Money and Ehrhardt designated the eighteenth month or so as the critical age beyond which successful sex reassignment is not possible. Socarides, in his research on perversions, concluded that the nuclear conflicts of all sexual deviants derive from the preoedipal period, especially the years between 1½ and 3 years of age. He noted that sexual deviants were unable to pass successfully through the separation–individuation phase.

The so-called anal stage is, in reality, both anal and preoedipal. Castration reactions that begin in this period, intermixed with the power struggles over toilet training, have a profound influence on drive and ego development, as well as on future object relations. In short, from the time of the recognition of genital differences—between the first and third years—there is a marked divergence between the development of boys and that of girls. Freud himself was the first to understand this, although he did not know just how early the divergence occurred.

FREUD AND OEDIPUS

As previously stated, Freud traced sexual animosity to castration fear and penis envy. Upon discovering that they have penises and their mothers do not, little boys imagine that females are castrated; hence they begin to fear that they will be castrated too. This fear is reinforced when their oedipal conflict—their desire for mother and rivalry with father—is not adequately resolved. If this conflict remains unresolved, it can lead to animosity and condescension toward women. As Freud (1931) points out, "one residue of the castration complex in the man is a measure of disparagement in his attitude towards women, whom he regards as having been castrated" (p. 229). Elaborating on this fear of women, he writes:

> Man fears that his strength will be taken from him by woman, dreads becoming infected with her femininity and then proving himself a weakling. The effect of coitus in discharging tensions and inducing flaccidity may be a prototype of what these fears represent; and realization of the influence gained by the woman over a man as a result of sexual relations, and the favours she extorts by this means, may all conduce to justify the growth of these fears. [p. 198]

The idea to which Freud is alluding was later termed "fear of re-engulfment" by Mahler and colleagues (1975) and others. It is not only the fear of castration that arouses animosity, but also the fear of "becoming infected with her femininity" and of "the influence gained by the woman over a man as the result of sexual relations." These last phrases suggest the fear of re-engulfment—that is, of becoming dependent once again on Woman (Winnicott 1964), which is the forerunner of the castration fear.

For girls, the castration complex (penis envy) involves the awareness that little boys have something they do not: a penis. Freud (1918) agrees with Klein and others that penis envy begins at an earlier phase of development—that is, before the age of 3—and is "more closely allied to primal narcissism than to object-love" (p. 204). In other words, little girls feel the lack of a penis as a blow to their self-esteem. Hence it is a narcissistic injury. They feel cheated, first by their mothers, then by their fathers. For little girls it is a shock, the effect of which is difficult to overcome; it is comparable perhaps to the shock of discovering one's own mortality. Freud explains: "From the analyses of many neurotic woman we have learned that women go through an early phase in which they envy their brothers the token of maleness and feel themselves handicapped and ill-treated on account of it" (p. 205). He goes on to say a mother's favoring of a brother over a sister can lead to an exacerbation of penis envy and resentment of the brother, which in turn leads later to an animosity toward men in general. In addition, Freud describes a link between penis envy and feminism:

> Now, upon this penis envy follows that hostile embitterment displayed by women against men, never entirely absent in the relations between the sexes, the clearest indications of which are to be found in the writings and ambitions of "emancipated" women. [p. 205]

Freud (1925) further asserts that the difference in the way the oedipal conflict develops for boys and girls leads to a corresponding difference in the formation of the superego. The oedipal conflict forces boys—out of a fear of castration—to develop a sense of morality, while the oedipal triangle often arouses even more resentment in girls. On the one hand, they may end up angry at both parents as they turn from mother to father and feel frustrated by both, since their primitive desire is to be given a penis and male potency by each parent. On the other hand, they do not fear castration—in fact, they feel they already have been—so they have less motivation to be moral; hence their superego development is, according to Freud, faulty. "I cannot escape the notion (though I hesitate to give it expression) that for women the level of what is ethically normal is different from what it is in men" (p. 259).

Finally, Freud and his followers, namely Deutsch (1944) and Bonaparte (1953), posit the concept of feminine masochism: That is, in their normal sexual development, females resolve their penis envy by giving up the clitoris in favor of the vagina, after which they are said to "masochistically" welcome the penetration of the penis, and then to desire babies as a substitute for the originally coveted penis. In fact, recognition of her "castration" is the female child's entry into the oedipal phase. After this recognition, the girl will proceed through the oedipal conflict along one of three developmental lines, one of which involves the resolution of her penis envy. The second possibility is that because her self-esteem has been shattered by her lack of a penis, her hostility to her mother, who was supposed to be phallic but was discovered to be castrated, can cause her to turn away from women and womanhood altogether and forgo all sexuality. The third possibility is that she will cling in obstinate self-assertion to her "threatened masculinity" and cherish the hope of someday getting a penis, while her fantasy "of really being a man, in spite of everything, often dominates long periods of her life" (Freud 1931, p. 230). This "masculinity complex" may also result in a homosexual object choice.

Meanwhile, males resolve their castration fear and their Oedipus complex in a simpler fashion: By relinquishing their desire for mother, and identifying with father and deferring to the castration threat from him, they advance to the stage of genital potency with the hope of future possibilities. If they do not resolve their oedipal conflict and castration fears, they may opt to deny the difference between the sexes, feel a triumphant contempt for women, or compensate for castration fears by disparaging women or by retreating to homosexuality or perversion.

Thus, in Freud's scheme, castration fear and penis envy—mis-

andry and gynophobia—are seen as engendering the age-old conflict
between the sexes. Women smitten by penis envy resent men for
having what they lack and seek vindication; men with castration fear
despise women for lacking what they possess and seek subjugation.
Indeed, this would appear to be another case of the "haves" against the
"have nots."

The psychoanalytic community has become somewhat polarized
over Freud's theories of female development. Those who basically
support Freud's position include Deutsch, Bonaparte, Klein, Abraham, Lampl de Groot, Fenichel, Mahler and colleagues, Roiphe, and
Galenson. Opponents of Freud's position—those who have taken a
feminist psychoanalytic position—include Horney, Thompson,
Adler, Zilboorg, Sherfey, Marmor, Moulton, and Gilligan. Over the
years these two sides have fought the "battle of the sexes" in the
psychoanalytic arena. However, neither position appears to represent
the whole truth (if there is such a thing) about female or male
development, because each is influenced by gender narcissism. Classical analysts tend to lean in the direction of male narcissism (masculinism) or, if they are women, in the direction of identifying with the
aggressor (Freud) and agreeing with his views. Feminist analysts are
influenced by female narcissism (a female inferiority complex) or, if
they are men, tend to allay castration fear and phallic guilt by
championing feminist causes.

To be sure, there are parts of Freud's theory that smack of male
narcissism. Superego development is undoubtedly different for men
and women. Therefore, it may be that women are more likely than
men to develop feelings of jealousy, as their unresolved penis envy is
converted to jealousy; at the same time, men may be more likely than
women to behave in an angry brutal way, due in part to their larger
physical size and to hormonal differences. Freud's assertion that "for
women the level of what is ethically normal is different from what it is
in men" may reflect a degree of male narcissism, however. Freud was
alluding to the fact that women have traditionally been allowed to be
more emotional than men and have taken advantage of society's
permissive attitude toward their behavior. Whether this fact stems
from penis envy or from cultural conditioning is arguable. But to infer
from this phenomenon that women are less moral than men seems
specious. The pathological, narcissistic (animus/anima) component of

each sex's personality continually tries to make the other sex the scapegoat for its troubles, to make it out to be the moral culprit. Where Freud impugns the morality of women, he is guilty of that excess. In actuality, each sex can be moral or immoral in varying degrees and circumstances. Since each plays off the other, there is correspondingly equal animosity in each sex. Each can be pathological in its behavior, but in different ways, based on male and female styles.

Female masochism as a concept of normal development would also seem to be an expression of male narcissism. It is a contradiction in terms to label the woman who has undergone "normal" development – has reached the genital stage – masochistic if she welcomes the penis during the act of sex. How can a woman be both normal and masochistic? If a normal female is masochistic, then is a normal male sadistic? Instead of using the term *masochism*, Freud might have used *receptive*. A normal female would be receptive (not masochistically passive) to the penetration of the penis. It is not an act of masochism for a normal female, since for her intercourse is not a punishment, but rather a pleasurable activity associated with love and tenderness. Only for an "abnormal" female – one who is fixated at a pregenital stage of development and who has a masochistic personality structure rooted in unresolved conflicts at the anal-rapprochement level – would intercourse be said to be masochistic.

Unfortunately, Freud used provocative language throughout his writings about female development. He writes that the effect of the castration complex on the girl is that she "acknowledges the fact of her castration, the consequent superiority of the male and her own inferiority . . ." (1931, p. 320). Freud means here that the girl acknowledges the *apparent* superiority of the male's sexual organ, and in her mind the male himself then *appears* superior as well. He also writes, "There is yet another surprising effect of penis envy, or of the discovery of the *inferiority of the clitoris* . . ." (1925, p. 257; italics added). Here again, he means the *apparent* inferiority of the clitoris. This kind of language lends itself to misinterpretation.

Feminist analysts tend to go to the other extreme, bent upon dismissing – and in some cases discrediting – Freud's theories about female development. Horney (1926), Adler (1927a), Thompson (1943), Sherfey (1966), Mitchell (1974), and Gilligan (1982) are among those who have taken a dim view of Freudian theory about women, particularly regarding penis envy. They contend that penis envy has nothing to do with the anatomical differences between the sexes. It is not the phallus that women envy, but rather men's privileged position in society. It is not the penis they resent, but male domination. "I believe," Thompson states, "that the manifest hostility between men and women is not different in kind from any other struggle between combatants, one of whom has definite advantage in prestige and position" (p. 53). She and other feminists assert that male narcissism is behind the concept of penis envy. It is men who overvalue their penises, not women. Men project their narcissism about their penises onto women, and use concepts such as penis envy and female masochism to keep women in their place. It is the man who experiences the penis as a valuable organ, Thompson concludes, and she—along with Gilligan and Sherfey—emphasizes that only women can understand female psychology. Freud and other male analysts are biased.

In our society, the traditional roles of women have not been accorded the same prestige as the traditional roles of men. Our society has been a patriarchal society in which men are favored for leadership positions and entry into the professions. Whether this constitutes oppression of women, or is a natural evolution of civilization from an agrarian to an industrial operation in which the roles of males and females have changed according to the situation, is a matter of debate. "Social injustice" is often used as an excuse in order not to take responsibility for one's individual plight—a situation often observed by clinicians who work with paranoid personalities. For feminist analysts to attribute female sexual animosity solely to cultural factors is, in effect, to absolve themselves of responsibility and make men the scapegoats of female misery. This is an expression of female narcissism. Although some female discontent may indeed result from cultural inequalities, the deepest layers of bitterness toward men, the feelings of inferiority (often projected onto men), and the narcissistic grandiosity (the women-can-do-anything-better-than-men attitude) stem from unresolved penis envy. The attempt to blame the male system rather than penis envy for their animosity also sets up a double standard. Men can have castration complexes and be sadomasochistic, but women cannot.

The feminist focus on separation issues and denial of the importance of the castration complex for women (Gilligan 1982) is not borne out by the observations of analysts, most notably Mahler and co-workers, Money and Ehrhardt and Roiphe and Galenson. They and other researchers have shown that there is a period of development in which children discover with shock, and often with intense reactions, the difference in sexual anatomy. Gilligan and others are inattentive to this research; their attempt to deny its importance and to disparage and reject male thinkers (insisting that men cannot understand women; only women—particularly feminist women—can understand women) is an expression of female narcissism. Their need to focus on separation issues likewise excludes men. Men—fathers—are not important enough to be crucial influences on female development. In essence, feminist psychology excludes men, just as the father is excluded by mother and daughter in some family systems. Psychodynamically, this process of excluding men is an acting out of unconscious animosity and narcissism. It *is* important for daughters to separate from mothers, and it is *also* important for them to achieve satisfactory intimacy with their fathers and with other men.

Implied in the feminist attack on Freud is a moral indictment of his character. An article typifying this indictment appeared in the *Journal of the American Academy of Psychoanalysis*. In this article, Freud's concepts of female masochism and penis envy are debunked; Kanefield (1985) proclaims that "Freud's view of women as castrated men, reconciled to inferiority due to their biological lack, is misogynous." She proceeds to criticize what she sees as Freud's presumption that "women are lesser because they are different from men," calling it "deeply sexist and unfounded." She concludes that "the fact remains that patriarchal society has devalued women's bodies, minds, and contributions, and that women themselves have learned to disqualify their own experiences" (p. 352).

Although Freud was to some degree a male narcissist, he did not believe that "women are lesser because they are different from men"; nor did he view them as "castrated men, reconciled to inferiority due to their biological lack." These are exaggerations. What Freud said was that *some*, not all, women *feel* inferior to men—women who have not resolved their castration complexes. Much also has been made of Freud's Victorian attitude toward women—his protectiveness toward his younger sisters, for instance, and his authoritarian stance toward his wife; these and other personal data are used to prove his so-called sexism, and to disprove his theories. To disagree with Freud's theories is one matter, but to distort his views and attack his character is a manifestation of female narcissism.

There is a middle ground between the narcissistic aspects of both Freudian and feminist positions. Castration fear and penis envy remain valid concepts, while the term *female masochism*, when applied to female sexual development, might well be replaced by *female receptivity*. The term *masochism* might then be applied to both men and women when appropriate. Neither Freud's view that females are less moral than males, nor the feminist contention that males are less moral (more biased) than females, is defensible. There is a cultural factor, but to attribute female animosity to this factor and deny the influence of developmental impacts is ungrounded. Freud's formulations about the three potential paths of female sexual development, and the various paths of male development, remain basically valid.

A SCHEMATIC REVIEW

The development of sexual animosity begins during earliest infancy, if not in utero. The infant's relationship with the gratifying or frustrating breast (or bottle) lays the seeds of the castration complexes of both men and women.

The early mother–infant relationship is a period critical to healthy social functioning. The mother serves as the child's introduction to the world; through her the child learns about the culture, values, and customs of society. Through his relationship with her breast and then with her, he has his first experience of intimacy. The mother–infant relationship is a prototype of all future relationships and of all subsequent sexual experiences. The relative harmony or disharmony of future relationships depends on the outcome of this first one. If the mother, during the infant's oral stage, is depriving or smothering, anxious or hostile, distracted or depressed, the child may become fixated at that level.

The sucking of the breast is not only the child's first act of self-preservation, it is also the child's first act of love. Love and aggression merge here for the first time, and the balance of these forces is set in motion. Undue frustration or eros will result in a rage reaction. This rage is aroused, as Spotnitz (1985) points out, whenever "the totality of his environment" fails to meet the child's "specific maturational needs" (p. 68). When the environment repeatedly fails to meet the child's needs, and when even the rage is responded to inappropriately (if the mother turns her back on the child, for example) there will be a damming up of the aggressive drive, and it will become a force of destruction. This destructivity will then predispose the child to complex formation during the anal-rapprochement and phallic phases.

The harmony between the mother and father is also important for the child's development. In a sense, the husband's relationship with his wife sets the tone for her relationship with the infant; if he deprives her, she may in turn deprive the infant. During the anal and phallic stages, the father's active participation becomes more important. Disharmony between a husband and wife may take the form of a competition over who controls the child. Some mothers will exclude the father from the child-rearing process; the father may fight with the wife over control or retreat to passive-aggressive rejection of mother and child. Some fathers will attempt to take over or intrude, in an effort to invalidate the mother's relationship with the infant. If both parents have careers outside the home, there may be a conflict over who will take primary responsibility for the child.

Looking at it schematically, a mother who carries unconscious or ego-syntonic animosity toward men will convey that animosity to her infant. If the child is a boy, she may tend to be physically depriving; she may be unable to relax when she holds him; she may gaze at him with an expression of resentment; or she may develop a close-binding, symbiotic, and sexualized relationship which stifles his quest for independence and his search for a masculine identity. If the child is a girl, she might tend to be overprotective and close-binding, or she might reject the child because she unconsciously views the girl as an inferior product, like herself. In either case, both the girl and the boy will be unable to successfully complete the separation–individuation process, as Mahler and co-authors (1975) and Roiphe and Galenson (1981) observed. They will enter the anal-rapprochement phase with a predisposition to forming a castration complex. If the initial caretaker of the infant is the father or another male carrying sexual animosity, the reverse will happen.

A father who has unconscious fear and hatred of women (due to an unresolved castration complex) may be inclined either to sexually tease, reject, and emotionally distance himself from his preoedipal and oedipal daughter or to be overly sexual, sometimes to the point of committing incest. This interaction usually begins during the rapprochement phase, when the little girl turns to her father. It is quite normal for girls of this age to ask to see their father's penis, and they can be very adamant about it. A father's sexual rejection (vehemently refusing to show her his penis in a tone that suggests that she is naughty) or incestuous advances (from mild flirtation to actualized sexual relationships) become either narcissistic wounds or complexes of guilt and anger. If the father denies that he has done anything to hurt her, despite her protests, she may repress her feelings about her father's inappropriate response to her sexual curiosity, including the shock, hurt, rage, and guilt that accompanied the event.

The picture can become more complicated. If the mother has unconscious feelings of inferiority about being a woman she may behave so as to reinforce the father's sexual rejection or incest, while also reinforcing the development of penis envy in the daughter. She may do so by (1) reacting inappropriately to the child's discovery of the anatomical difference, (2) favoring a brother, (3) intruding on the child's relationship with her father and keeping her dependent on herself, or (4) turning her back to the father's inappropriate responses and becoming a silent conspirator. Depending on the degree of maternal reinforcement of penis envy and the nature of the father's contribution, the girl may develop an envy and animosity toward her brother, father, and all males.

On the other hand, a mother who has an unresolved castration complex will tend to sexually tease, psychologically castrate, or emotionally distance herself from her oedipal son. In other cases the mother is flirtatious, sometimes to the point of having a romance with the child—that is, a highly sexualized relationship that may or may not include incest but may be psychologically experienced as incest. Such a relationship can be psychologically castrating and, as documented by the research of Khan (1979) and Socarides (1979), can block the child's sexual and emotional development, engendering a dependency on the mother, animosity toward and fear of women, inadequate sexual identity, and perverse sexuality.

The mother's castrating behavior is actually the equivalent of a father's incestuous behavior, particularly if it continues from early childhood through adolescence; and it can have the same effects as a father's incestuous behavior. To a boy, a mother's sexual castration (as when she binds him to an alliance with her against the father) may lead to narcissistic wounds comprising varying degrees of unconscious hurt, rage, and guilt. If the mother denies, in the face of the boy's complaints, that she has done anything wrong, the boy's sexual and emotional development will be even further blocked.

If a boy has both a castrating mother and a rejecting father, so that he has no male with whom to identify during the rapprochement phase, and then he is unable to resolve the castration or Oedipus complex, there can be so much castration fear and narcissistic rage that he will develop a fear and animosity toward his sister, mother, and all women.

Related to this transmission of sexual animosity in childhood are the value systems that underlie the way in which parents relate to their children and to each other. Male children have traditionally been favored over female children by parents. As a result, girls are treated as though they are inferior, usually by both parents; this has a damaging effect on both boys and girls. Such a value system might be termed masculinist. On the other hand, children raised under the feminist value system, which due to overcompensation, tends to favor females over males, suffer a similar kind of damage.

The transmission of animosity by either parent, be it through an incestuous father–daughter relationship or through a castrating mother–son relationship, is equally damaging. *Neither sex is more culpable than the other, and any thinking to the contrary is both erroneous and destructive.* The development of sexual animosity leads to male and female narcissism—an accumulation of unconscious (or conscious) feelings of grandiosity, self-loathing, rage, and identity confusion all centered around gender. In adulthood, animosity may be manifested in a variety of ways and may have a multitude of influences on male–female relationships, child rearing, and society in general.

3

Male Narcissism

CASTRATION FEAR

Margaret. Mr. Adolf, what is the trouble now?

The Captain. I don't know, I don't know. But can you tell me why you women must treat a grown man as if he were a child?

Margaret. Well, I can't tell you exactly why, but I suppose it is because you are all children of women—all of you men, big and small. [August Strindberg, *The Father*]

These lines make a point about male–female relations: that all men are psychologically influenced by women. Winnicott (1964) said it differently, noting that every man and every woman is born of Woman and that each retains a fear of Woman, a fear of being lured back into a state of infantile dependency. Women are able to mitigate this fear through identification and by actualizing their femininity— by becoming mothers; and to some degree their behavior toward men always contains an element of Woman—that is, an element of the maternal. Men cannot become mothers, cannot become Woman—a reality they gradually experience during the early years of life. It hits them "squarely between the legs" upon their discovery that they have penises and their mothers do not.

Mahler and colleagues (1975) speak of the fear of re-engulfment that can be observed in girls and boys during the various subphases of the separation–individuation process. The fear is stronger in boys than in girls because the gender difference heightens separation anxiety.

Mead (1935, 1949) writes of womb envy among boys, describing several South Sea societies in which boys grow up among women, identifying with women, envying their ability to give birth and to suckle an infant, and then are suddenly yanked out of the women's milieu and into the initiation rites reserved for men. Mead notes how male separateness from women has developed into an institution in these societies, with men's houses and male initiation ceremonies to bolster a boy's fragile masculine identity and to compensate for the womb envy. In a sense, all male strivings for achievement are a compensation for their feelings of inferiority because of the inability to give birth—the ultimate act of creation and achievement. As Mead observes, women do not have to prove their femininity; upon reaching maturity, they simply do what comes naturally. Men need to prove their masculinity through other kinds of achievements, some of which involve years of work and struggle. Yet no matter what they achieve, women continue to exert psychological influence on them.

Freud (1909) referred to womb envy in his case history of Little Hans, commenting that the 5-year-old boy had a wish to bear and nurse infants and that "in phantasy he was a mother and wanted children with whom he could repeat the endearments that he had himself experienced" (p. 93). This identification with mother and her gender role is a normal development in boys; if it continues beyond the anal-rapprochement stage, however, it may interfere with the establishment of male gender role identification. Such was the case with Little Hans. At the age of 5, well into the phallic phase, he was still clinging to his identification with his mother, so that it had become more than identification: It had become womb envy. Womb envy is the precursor of castration fear. Therefore, by the time a boy reaches the anal-rapprochement stage, in which he discovers that his penis performs "magic tricks" (goes up and down of its own accord) and is a source of autoerotic pleasure, he has already developed a fear of Woman, a womb envy. Added to this womb envy is this discovery of the importance of his penis and an intense separation anxiety with respect to the independence he has gained from his mother. And then the final blow: He discovers that his mother does not have a penis. His very existence seems suddenly threatened.

Throughout infancy, a boy believes that he and his mother are alike. At first he believes that they are one; then he believes that they are separate but similar. Increasingly he must face the fact that he and his mother are different. The final piece of evidence, and the most shocking, is his discovery that she and other females do not have penises. He will at first imagine that his mother has been castrated. He sees something between her legs resembling a wound: a mound of hair with a reddish hole in the middle. This observation is so shocking that he becomes obsessed with the loss of his own penis.

It is at this time that his mother suddenly begins making demands on him. First there are those associated with his new mobility: He can walk and explore. "No!" she is continually saying to him as he walks around, putting this into his mouth and that into his anus. He is now required to use the potty; he can no longer be a hedonist. Feces are dirty. Masturbation is dirty. By implication, *he* is dirty. He begins saying "No!"—imitating her. He gets into a power struggle with her. Sometimes he loves her; sometimes he hates her.

Depending on how sadomasochistic or obsessive-compulsive his parents are, the boy may develop a sadistic-defiant, masochistic-compliant, or obsessive-compulsive mode of operation during this period. When the parents are permissive to the point of being masochistic, a boy may become not only sadistic toward them, but also psychopathic. When the parents are cruel, to the point of inflicting punishment in the form of beatings or enemas, the boy may become masochistic, with or without anal-erotic tendencies.

Miller (1983) has written about the cruelty in child rearing, usually beginning in the toilet-training period, that leads to violent behavior in adults. In a study of Adolf Hitler, she demonstrates how his father's tyrannical cruelty during Hitler's early childhood, combined with his mother's weak (uncaring) acquiescence to the father and to him, led to Hitler's extreme cruelty. In Hitler's case, one parent was sadistic and strict, while the other was masochistic and permissive, so that he became both sadistic and masochistic—as well as psychopathic.

A boy is being assaulted from all sides during the anal-rapprochement phase, attacked by changes, all of which are stressful; and on top of everything else, he has to cope with his mother's "castration." He wants to be like her, for she has been his first model. The shock of not being like her, and of finding out that this great omniscient, omnipotent maternal being has, in fact, been castrated, is too much for him. He is filled with dread—the fear of castration—and with guilt about possessing something that gives him so much pleasure and of which his mother is deprived. He despises her for being castrated, for disappointing him, and, by way of the talion principle, he then imagines that she also despises him and wants to castrate him. In some cases, the mother may harbor feelings of envy and wishes of castration toward her son, which she will act out, primarily by interfering with his quest for independence. Because she has literally had her hands on his genitals from birth onward, he feels that his body is as much her property as his, to do with what she will; he feels vulnerable. His castration fear is thus further exacerbated.

If he is then able to turn to a father who has a healthy masculine identity, the boy can grab onto him as to a life buoy, and begin to establish an identity separate from mother. If the father is distant, hostile, or weak, however, or if the father is not present, the boy's fate is sealed. Roiphe and Galenson (1981) note that urination while standing with father represents a turning point in his sexual development, a "ceremony" that serves to bolster the boy's masculine identity. Tyson (1986) emphasizes that urination with the father is an important step toward the establishment of "core gender identity elaboration and consolidation" (p. 8).

The degree to which castration fear and phallic guilt develops and is repressed depends on the boy's relationship with his parents (and siblings). A mother who has a great deal of unresolved penis envy and animosity will create in her infant boy a corresponding castration fear and phallic guilt; he will sense in her handling of him, in her attitude toward his penis and toward masturbation, her animosity, and he will react to it. Likewise, a father with a great deal of castration fear and phallic guilt will offer little in the way of a strong masculine model, and will thus add to the boy's confusion. In cases in which the father has murderous wishes toward the boy, his castration fear will be tremendous. Tyson relates working with Davy, age 4, who suffered from castration fear of both parents. While playing one day he talked about his mother biting off his penis and his father chopping it off, and expressed the wish to have eight penises (p. 11).

During the oedipal stage, a boy will be tempted to allay his combined womb envy, castration fear, and phallic guilt by possessing and merging with the mother sexually. Because of phallic identification with his father, he desires to emulate him. He thus makes his father his rival; if he can possess his mother and conquer his father, he will no longer need to fear either of them. During this stage, the fear of castration gets displaced primarily onto the oedipal rival: It is the father, brother, and other men who now threaten to castrate the boy conqueror. If a boy succeeds in this conquest, or partially succeeds and then is suddenly rebuffed by mother, he may remain fixated at the phallic narcissistic stage while adopting either a heterosexual or homosexual orientation, depending on his relationship with his father. If the boy fails, he either resolves the Oedipus complex by identifying with father and giving up his desire for mother, in which case he will have a relatively healthy sexual attitude towards women, or he becomes fixated at one or more pregenital stages, utilizing one of several narcissistic defenses.

The narcissistic defenses serve to protect a boy from his unconscious womb envy, castration fear, and phallic guilt, which, if he felt them consciously, would arouse intense anxiety. They also serve to protect him from the animosity he has come to expect from mother and other women, and from the competition with other men. These defenses are gradually developed during the boy's passage through early childhood, particularly at those points when his maleness is at issue. The boy's ideal image of himself—part of the newly formed superego—may also contain narcissistic features pertaining to his maleness, such as grandiose views of his phallic prowess.

Male narcissism is a kind of character formation that evolves as a defense against the frustrations of a boy's normal masculine strivings. These strivings represent a masculine Eros; that is, they represent a drive to obtain the satisfaction of his masculine "love" needs. These needs include the establishment of loving independence from mother and identification with father, leading to the resolution of his fear of Woman and his envy of mother's capacity to create new life and nurture it. They also include the gaining of acceptance and approval of his penis, as well as the thoughts attached to it, from both mother and father, and also acceptance and approval from both parents of his oedipal urges (without, obviously, allowing such urges to be acted out). This acceptance and approval is crucial to the resolution of castration fear, phallic guilt, and the Oedipus complex.

On its deepest level, forming the core of male narcissism, is rage. This rage is generally the result of the parents' and siblings' accumulated frustration of the boy's maturational needs in the psychosexual arena. More specifically, it is a gender rage, connected primarily with his mother's attitude toward his penis and his masculine strivings; hence it is manifested as sexual animosity toward mother and toward women. The boy defends against the inner core of rage and the outer core of womb envy, castration fear, and phallic guilt by withdrawing his libido from the mother and later withholding it from all women. As in all forms of narcissism, the libidinal drive is turned back upon the self, creating a defensive bubble of masculine pride or masculine self-love. The sexual animosity resulting from this character structure is played out overtly or covertly. A man may appreciate women as ornaments, sexually conquer them, degrade them, molest them, idealize them, rape them, emulate them, acquiesce to them, or avoid them entirely. He may pretend to be their best friend or make them his worst enemy, but he will never again give his heart to a woman. He withdraws into a narcissistic shell.

CHARACTER STRUCTURES

Horney (1950) was among the first to use the term *male narcissism*, alluding to the phallic pride exhibited by many men. Male narcissism can take many different forms, however, and the pride may be obvious or not so obvious. These forms described here are the most notable examples; they roughly correspond to psychoanalytic character types or to psychiatric categories. In actuality, most men are fixated at more than one point of development; hence they exhibit a mixture of narcissistic defenses. In order to capture the great variety of such

defensive permutations, one would have to extend this list indefi-
nitely. The following will therefore suffice to demonstrate the range of
male narcissism.

Phallic Narcissism

This is the most blatant form of male narcissism, and the one that is
most often reviled by feminists. The phallic narcissist is primarily
fixated at the early oedipal stage, in which the penis is highly valued as
a source of power. The phallic narcissist usually has a mother who is a
hysterical narcissist (see Chapter 4). In effect, the mother acts out her
sexual animosity on the boy by sexually conquering him. Until the
oedipal phase, she appears to be available to him, relating in a loving
but flirtatious manner. During the oedipal phase, however, when he
attempts to take her away from father, she suddenly spurns his sexual
advances—sometimes treating him as though he were being ridiculous
to expect any such thing from her. The boy feels humiliated, and later,
in adulthood, he tries to turn the tables on the women he meets, his
aim being to sexually conquer them with his powerful penis, proving
the "manhood" that his mother rejected, and then abandon them, just
as his mother once abandoned him.

The phallic narcissist is proud of his masculinity (of his penis) and
is apt to exhibit a macho persona. Phallic narcissists can range from
the heroic man of action, such as John F. Kennedy, to the multiple
rapist, depending on the degree and form of animosity to which they
were exposed as children. They defend against womb envy, castration
fear, and phallic guilt through aggression: *Castrate them before they
castrate you.* All women are regarded as potential teasers and humilia-
tors. The phallic is generally quite skilled at sexual manipulation,
either by way of "sweet talk" or by other, less subtle methods. When all
else fails, they may resort to brute force. Once they have seduced and
abandoned a woman, their contempt for her becomes more overt.
They condescend to both males and females; since they are usually
grandiose about their sexual exploits, they must be always on guard,
always on the defensive to both sexes, lest they get knocked off the
"mountain." They are as manipulative toward men as toward women.

The phallic narcissist consciously and deliberately expresses his
animosity toward the female. Perhaps that is why this form of male

narcissism meets with the most female censure; it is the type that is most often labeled male chauvinism. In reality, however, phallic narcissists often have less animosity toward women than do preoedipal types who appear to be more loving. Because they can express their animosity in an active, conscious manner, they are sometimes able to overcome their ambivalence and feel genuinely tender feelings toward women. In addition, they are one of the two types of male character types (the other being the genital character) who have the capacity to stand up against the excesses and manipulations of the masculine-aggressive and hysterical forms of female narcissism.

Passive Narcissism

This is probably the most common variety of male narcissism, roughly corresponding to what is called the "passive-feminine" or "passive-aggressive" character in psychoanalytic literature. This type of male is well known to family therapists, for he is usually married to a dominating woman who brings him into therapy because she has become frustrated by him. Passive narcissists appear to be submissive to the women they marry, and sometimes they even proclaim themselves to be "new men" or feminists. On an unconscious level, however, they are acting out sexual animosity by withholding their feelings and driving their spouses to fits of anger and sometimes violence through their double messages. These men will act as though they do not understand why their spouses are behaving in such a "crazy" way. Their facade is that of the perfect gentleman. They will promise anything verbally, while nonverbally communicating a quite different message. For example, they may promise to pick up tickets to a play or to cook a dinner, but whether or not they remember to do so is another matter. They are sexually withholding, often prone to premature ejaculation or lack of interest. It is as though they were saying, "I'll do and say whatever you want, but you'll never get to my real feelings."

For the most part, passives are not conscious of their real feelings, particularly their animosity. They have mothers who are dominating and who cannot tolerate any expression of anger or aggression. The sons are forced to develop a passive-aggressive masculinity — they learn to keep their masculine pride and assertiveness hidden — and to act out their animosity in ways that are hard to detect. Such mothers leave their sons little choice but to develop an overtly compliant but covertly defiant mode of operation. Meanwhile, the fathers of passives are often passive themselves (or nonexistent), modeling passive behavior in their relationship with the boy's mother. Hence the boy does not have a healthy masculine figure with whom to identify. On a symbolic level, passives are holding back their feces and keeping their mother's intrusive hands away from their genitals. Like the phallic, the passive also wants to turn the tables on mother via the women he later becomes involved with, by frustrating their attempts to relate to him.

Like the phallic, the passive has contempt for women, but he may or may not be conscious of it and will never admit it. He manifests a gentle, intellectual, or spiritual persona: He is a "good boy." There is usually an obsessive-compulsive component to his personality, and out of this arises a reaction formation that defends against the conscious acknowledgment of his animosity: He firmly believes himself to be a loving progressive individual concerned with women's rights and social justice. He fits Vilar's (1972) description of men in general—"A man needs a woman because he needs something to which he may subject himself" (p. 20). This helps him manipulate the women in his personal life: He seems to be the perfect man, always deferring to the woman; yet he seldom gives them what they really want—his genuine feelings. Castration fear and phallic guilt, although repressed, nonetheless cause him to be always on guard with women. His fear of their disapproval will not permit him to establish independence from them. He can be dominated by women, and his political stance and philosophy is usually a reflection of what he thinks women want of him rather than of what he really feels.

Anal Narcissism

Anal narcissists tend to have sadomasochistic relationships with women. They are fixated primarily at the anal-rapprochement phase, during which time toilet training and anal eroticism is intermixed with the discovery of masturbation and the difference in the sexual anatomy. If a mother is sadistic during this period (humiliating him into masochistic submission), he is likely to become a masochist; if she is masochistic (allowing him to sadistically defy her out of a need to play the martyr), he may retain a sadistic orientation. The fathers in such cases are generally also sadistic or masochistic, when they are not literally or figuratively absent; and they often take an obsessive or sadistic interest in the boy's training at this point.

Basically, the anal narcissist corresponds to the anal character described in the psychoanalytic literature, most notably by Fenichel (1945), who points out that such characters tend to be stingy, stubborn, and orderly, such traits being an outcome of anal retentiveness begun during the toilet-training period as a defense against the sadistic domination or permissive masochism of anal narcissistic parents. However, the anal narcissist is the product not only of the frustrations of his anal eroticism, but also of his urethral eroticism and sexual strivings. His withholding from women is therefore a symbolic refusal to give mother his feces, his urine, and his sperm. Further, his withholding differs from that of the passive narcissist in that he is much more aware of the withholding and of the animosity behind it; the anal narcissist's fixation is firmly rooted in the anal period, while the passive's fixations are spread out over the oral, anal, and oedipal periods.

The anal narcissist may be sadistic or masochistic, and there is always a strong obsessive-compulsive substructure. The sadist views women as unloving guilt-inducers who want to try to make him feel negative about himself as a man; he therefore sets about humiliating and degrading women in any way he can. He will select a mate whom he perceives as inferior to him—from a lower class or a racial minority—and he will attempt to dominate and control her until she is robbed of any independence or initiative. He often sees women as witches who need to be tamed. The degree of animosity administered to him in his childhood will correspond to the degree of humiliation and degradation he will administer to the women in his life; his sadism can range from subtle mental cruelty to battering, torture, mutilation, sexual degradation, rape, and murder. The masochist sees women as potential persecutors who, if he is not careful, will sadistically humiliate and degrade him (as his mother did). He will be drawn to sadistic women and will provoke them into being sadistic toward him. His repetition compulsion drives him into a vicious circle in which he continually attempts, unsuccessfully, to undo the trauma originally inflicted upon him during the anal-rapprochement period. He will have to settle for secondary gratifications: By playing the martyr and inducing guilt in his sadistic partner, he may obtain some semblance of love in the form of appeasement or pity, while maintaining a lofty sense of moral superiority over his persecutor. Sexually, sadomasochists tend to be retarded ejaculators (withholding their sperm), and whether or not they actually engage in sadomasochistic sexual practices, their sexuality is always tinged with dominance and submission.

Womb envy, castration fear, and phallic guilt are warded off through these sadomasochistic activities and through obsessive-compulsive armoring. By sadistically degrading and suppressing the women in his life, or masochistically taking it on the chin, or obsessively guarding against the eruption of archaic feelings that might result in his being made vulnerable and susceptible to a woman's "charms," he keeps Woman at a distance and allays castration anxiety and phallic guilt.

Oral Narcissism

The oral narcissist is fixated primarily at the breast-feeding stage of development. He is dependent on women for the maintenance of his self-esteem, and he is simultaneously enraged at them (at his mother) for either smothering or depriving him. His attitude toward women is marked by splitting: They are either good breasts or bad breasts. As Klein (1932) pointed out, this feeling becomes introjected and affects his masculine core identity: Having experienced the breast as bad, frustrating, or smothering (another kind of frustration), he thinks of himself as bad, and of his penis and his masculinity as bad. As his attitude toward women is ambivalent, his behavior toward them swings from infantile submissiveness and dependency (like a baby at the breast) to infantile rage (during which time his demand for narcissistic supplies may be vampirelike), with fits of temper and sometimes violence.

The oral narcissist tends to be an addictive personality. He will be addicted to—or phobic about—food, or he will be addicted to—or phobic about—alcohol or other drugs. He is more in love with his addictive substances (his transitional object) than with his spouse; spouses are interchangeable, used primarily as vehicles for acting out oral rage, while the substances are his nourishment—symbolically, the milk which the frustrating breast either deprived him of or smothered him with. In general, orals have mothers who either stunt their growth through lack of support or thwart their independence by doing everything for them and not allowing them to set their own pace or learn to do for themselves.

Orals are drawn to oral sex. They defend against the fear of Woman by always being on the take, or by allowing themselves to be "re-engulfed" by a woman—that is, by becoming passively dependent on them for everything, like an infant. They tend to project their rage onto women, and the fear, rooted in the archaic fantasies of infancy, of having their penises devoured by the vagina dentata looms large. Genital sex therefore is avoided.

Psychopathic Narcissism

The psychopathic narcissist has no moral standards in dealing with women. He might marry a succession of wealthy women and take their money and run; marry several women at once; rape a woman on Tuesday and go home to his wife on Wednesday and ask what is for dinner; and, in extreme cases, perform acts of murder or mutilation. He will not feel any guilt.

The psychopath usually has parents who are psychopathic—at least in the way they relate to him in early childhood. Indeed, psychopaths often have parents who are church-going, upstanding citizens, or concerned political activists, who make a public show of social concern, but who behave abominably toward their children. Lindner (1955) asserts that mothers of psychopaths are unconscious seducers of their sons. Spitz (1965) coined the term "primary anxious overpermissiveness" for certain mothers who compensate for unconscious feelings of hostility toward their sons by being overpermissive, with the result that such infants become colicky. Mothers of psychopaths may be both seductive and anxiously overpermissive; meanwhile, fathers of psychopaths are generally psychopathic themselves, or are figuratively or literally absent; they are also frequently abusive.

The psychopath acts out animosity toward women almost as a way of life. He defends against womb envy and castration fear by keeping women under his control, using seduction, intimidation, deceit, force, or whatever method works best. Because of his need for control, he often does not achieve orgasm during intercourse. Phallic guilt is alien to him.

Perverse Narcissism

Perverse narcissists are men who have so much animosity toward women that they can no longer engage in sex with them. Socarides (1979) points out that perverse narcissists fail to successfully pass through the separation–individuation phase and have a common "fear of fusion and merging with the mother, a tendency to lose ego boundaries, and a fear of loss of self or ego dissolution" (p.183). Their mothers are generally close-binding but hostile, while their fathers are either hostile, distant, weak, or absent. In many cases, parents of perverse narcissists are perverse themselves.

In perverse narcissism, the boy does not want to accept that his mother is "castrated," and there is a primary identification with her. There is usually a tremendous oedipal fear of father, because of the close-binding nature of the relationship with mother. Perverse narcissists defend against womb envy, castration fear, and phallic guilt in various ways: homosexuals by achieving "masculinity" through identification with the male sexual partner; transvestites by achieving "femininity" through cross-dressing (if they are female nobody will try to castrate them); transsexuals by actually becoming female through surgery; pedophiles by having sex with children (who are less threatening than adult women); exhibitionists by achieving "masculinity" through the visual reassurance that their penises can have an effect on women; voyeurs by reinforcing "masculinity" through visual reassurance in viewing the female body without being swallowed up by its orifices; and fetishists by taking as their sexual partner an object, which Freud (1927a) first described as "a substitute for the women's (mother's) phallus which the little boy once believed in and does not wish to forego" (p. 153).

Psychotic Narcissism

Psychotic narcissism represents the most extreme form of withdrawal from the mother (and from women). In psychosis, frustration has been so great that the child is rendered nonfunctional by it. Animosity is taken out against the self; aggression floods the system and jams it, producing hallucinations, thought disorders, physical symptoms, impotence, and the like.

Attempts to use twins as research subjects in order to test the hypothesis that schizophrenia is hereditary are inconclusive. While there may exist a predisposition to mental illness (a low tolerance for frustration) in some infants, a predisposition can be mitigated by sound, healthy parenting. The environment remains an important variable. Further, studies of patients with multiple personalities have shown that schizophrenia can occur in one personality while hysteria, mania, or relative health may occur in others. Yet each personality is produced by the same environmental forces during different times and as the result of differing traumatic episodes. I contend that schizophrenia and other forms of psychosis are produced by the most frustrating impingements on the infant's growth process during the symbiotic stage of development.

MANIFESTATIONS

Many males, perhaps even the majority (according to my observation), suffer from narcissism. Their relationships to women are compulsive patterns devoid of authenticity or spontaneity; like a phonograph that recircles a particular groove on a cracked record, male narcissists go round and round the same cracked groove in their early development. Their fixations—the "cracks" caused by early frustrations of their maturational needs and masculine strivings—stay with them throughout their lives, unless they have some kind of transformational experience, such as psychoanalysis.

In male narcissism, Thanatos has gone into "overdrive" due to the frustration of Eros. The primary gratification of love needs has been replaced by secondary gratifications: obtaining power and control over the frustrating object (women), fleeing from the object, attempting to destroy the object, and attempting to destroy the self. The phallic narcissist tries to use his penis as a weapon of power and thereby gain control over women by conquest. The passive narcissist wants to control women through passive resistance. The anal narcissist strives to control women through obsessive-compulsive guardedness and by either humiliating her (degrading her femininity) or allowing her to humiliate him and proving he can survive it. The psychopathic narcissist is out to destroy women. The perverse narcissist flees from women, but still engages in secondary forms of sexual gratification. The psychotic narcissist withdraws completely, has no sexual outlet, and attempts to destroy himself. (See Table 3–1.)

Each form of male narcissism involves a degree of inflated or deflated masculine self-esteem in proportion to the degree of frustration of the masculine strivings of each during early childhood. Some character types, such as the phallic or the psychopath, may flaunt

Table 3–1
Forms of Male Narcissism

	Defense against Castration Fear	Mode of Aggression	Fixation Point	Character of Mother	Character of Father
Phallic	Sexual conquest	Control of object	Oedipal phase	Hysteric	Phallic or absent
Passive	Quasi-sexual surrender	Control of object	Oedipal, anal, and oral phases	Masculine-aggressive or hysteric	Passive or absent
Anal	Sexual dominance and submission	Control of object	Anal phase	Anal or hysteric	Anal, psychopathic, or absent
Oral	Passive dependence or "vampirism"; addiction	Control of object	Separation individuation phase	Oral	Oral, passive, or absent
Psychopathic	Sexual subterfuge	Destruction of object	Oral and anal phase	Borderline or oral	Psychopathic, anal, or absent
Perverse	Flight from (rejection of) women	Control or destruction of object	Symbiotic and oral phases	Homosexual or borderline	Perverse or absent
Psychotic	Total withdrawal	Destruction of self	Symbiotic phase	Psychotic or borderline	Psychotic, psychopathic, or absent

their inflated masculine self-esteem, while others, such as passives, may hide it. Some character types, such as the masochist, may flaunt their deflated self-esteem in order to elicit guilt or pity, whereas others, such as certain perverse types, may deny its existence.

A characteristic of all male narcissists is a tendency to repress all the tender feelings they may once have had toward their mothers, along with their memories of their early castration fear reactions and the events surrounding those reactions. Thus, males generally tend to avoid personal communication with women, always fearing that such communication will lead to castration—that is, to a rearousal of the traumatic feelings and memories surrounding the original discovery of the difference between the sexes. The popular notion that men have "fragile egos" and need to be protected and bolstered by women has a certain truth. Their egos may be fragile because of their anatomy, however. As Freud (1924) says, "anatomy is destiny" (p. 180), and this is true for men as well as women. The fact that men's genitalia are external, and the testicles are so vulnerable, causes them to be always fearful and guarded in a way that is not necessary for women. Many men defend against this fear by cultivating a macho attitude. The more narcissistic they are, the more they distance themselves from women.

Male narcissism is expressed in the workplace as well as in the home. Since men cannot give birth, they must use substitute gratifications such as scientific or artistic creations; such creations help to allay womb envy. Earning a great deal of money is an indirect way of gaining power and control over women, as is the attainment of fame or some other kind of elevated status, such as that of corporation president, professor, physician, or analyst. Power serves to allay castration fear and womb envy and provides the man with leverage for controlling women. Athletic achievements also mitigate the effects of castration fear and womb envy. Setting records and winning championships are akin to artistic or scientific achievements—substitutes for giving birth; narcissists can also parlay them into power over women. A narcissist always needs to have control over women, and they all share the common trait of feeling, consciously or unconsciously, inferior or superior to women.

Male narcissistic grandiosity—a compensation for womb envy— causes men to feel threatened by women's entry into the traditionally male workplace. Although women can do virtually anything men can do, men cannot do what women can do—give birth to and nourish new humans—and this threatens their male grandiosity. Although men can nurture babies after they have been born of women, they cannot suckle them with their breasts. To give birth to and nourish a human being is the prototype of creativity, and a primary means of obtaining immortality, to which all other forms of creativity—scientific, artistic, or athletic—are secondary. The fact that mothers tend both to exclude boys and men from the mothering process and to take a proprietary attitude toward childbearing and child rearing may also increase male resentment about women entering the workplace; they feel, perhaps unconsciously, that women are having it both ways. At the same time, on a deeper level, this animosity stems from a fear of re-engulfment and of disintegration (a return to infantile dependency), and it is acted out in the many ways in which men sexually degrade, ridicule, and "emasculate" women on the job.

All narcissists feel guilty about having penises, and they ward off this guilt in various ways. Fighting for women's causes is one of the most popular ways of assuaging phallic guilt. In general, deferring to women, putting them on a pedestal, and being chivalrous have the same effect. Other men feel resentment about having to feel guilty about their penises or their masculinity, and they express their resentment in counterphobic aggressiveness toward women, often laced with disguised or not-so-disguised sarcasm or contempt. Homosexual men are often of this variety.

Animosity may be expressed through condescension, physical or mental dominance, sadistic cruelty, psychopathic deceit, degradation, or suppression, and by making women the scapegoats of society's ills (the women-as-seductress syndrome). Men tend to laugh away, deride, and shout down that which they fear; fear of Woman may be their greatest fear of all.

4

Female Narcissism

PENIS ENVY

Male narcissism comes about as the result of the frustration of a boy's masculine strivings. Female narcissism springs from the frustration of a girl's feminine strivings. While each man's male narcissism hinges on the degree of unresolved womb envy, castration fear, and phallic guilt he carries, female narcissism turns on the degree to which a girl has been unable to resolve her separation anxiety (from mother), phallic remorse, and penis envy. Male narcissism reaches its apex in the Oedipus complex. Female narcissism takes its ultimate form as the result of the Electra complex.

Separation from mother is a crucial issue for females, as it is for males. Girls have the same underlying fear of Woman as little boys do, and if this fear is not resolved as the girl traverses the early stages of maturation, it will remain as bedrock for the formation of female narcissism. The less a girl is able to resolve her fear of Woman, the greater will be the separation anxiety with respect to developing her own identity, separate from her mother's, and a healthy sexuality leading to full merger with the male in sexual union. Mothers who frustrate their daughters' drive for independence during the symbiotic and early separation–individuation phases, and fathers who allow this to happen, set the stage for the development of narcissism. Mothers who frustrate their daughters' feminine strivings during the anal-rapprochement and oedipal phases, and fathers who likewise frustrate these earliest feminine strivings, will strengthen this narcissism.

Separation is more difficult for females than for males, since they and their mothers are alike. A girl's identification with her mother makes it more difficult to break from her, while the lack of identification spurs a son to separate from mother and identify with father. Gilligan (1982) makes the point that since males define their masculinity through their separation from mother, and females define their femininity through their attachment to mother, "male gender identity is threatened by intimacy while female gender identity is threatened by separation" (p. 8). This may be, in part, an explanation for the difference in the way in which men and women relate. Girls undoubtedly have the more laborious separation task.

The girl's feminine strivings become most manifest in the anal-rapprochement period, during which she becomes mobile—thus heightening her separation anxiety. At the same time, she is also required to control her anal and urethral functioning, discovers the pleasures of clitoral masturbation, and realizes that there is an anatomical difference between the sexes. The kinds of frustrations administered by mothers and fathers during this phase are numerous. A mother who tacitly, verbally, or physically expresses disapproval of masturbation, fecal play, or other forms of autoerotic activity will impede the normal blossoming of sexual and loving feelings. The little girl's feminine strivings will be frustrated when a mother refuses to answer questions about penises or vaginas, or answers such questions in a hostile way, or in any way that is not genuine; they will be frustrated when a mother refuses to give her daughter a name for her sexual organ or when she disparages her daughter's curiosity about her father, his penis, or her sexual feelings about the father.

The girl's feminine strivings will also be frustrated by a father who goes along with a frustrating mother, or by a father who responds inappropriately to the girl's erotic advances toward him. In fact the father's attitude toward his daughter is the deciding factor in the degree of female narcissism she develops. If, when the girl turns from the mother to the father as a sexual object, he acts out his male narcissism and animosity by taking advantage of her infantile-erotic advances, coldly rejecting these advances, or remaining passive and allowing the mother to intrude in his relationship with the daughter, the daughter will likely fail to separate from mother and to establish normal heterosexual relationships. A father's inappropriate response will leave the daughter with a wounded sense of feminine worth—that is, with low feminine self-esteem—and she will then remain to some degree or another bound to her mother. Roiphe and Galenson (1981) document a number of cases in which girls with hostile mothers and distant fathers clung even more tightly to their mothers. "In those girls with severe castration reactions," the authors assert, "the hostile ambivalence to the mother becomes very intense, the maternal attachment is heightened, and the turn to the father does not occur" (p. 275).

When this turn does not occur, the most severe degree of narcissism and animosity develops. Since the mother is more important as a source of love than the father is, the girl's aggression can be more safely expressed to the father than to the mother. Freud (1931) comments that little girls have "the dread of being killed by the mother—a dread which on its side justifies the death-wish against her, if this enters consciousness" (p. 237). McDougall (1984) observes that while punishment, or the threat of it, for sexual wishes and masturbation is fantasized by boys as castration, punishment or the threat of punishment for masturbation and sexual wishes is associated by girls, symbolically, with death. Thus the death wish against mother becomes a death wish toward father, who, by his own frustrating behavior, has delivered the decisive blow. He has been her last resort, and he has failed her as well. He has failed to give her a penis, failed to respond to her infantile erotic advances in an appropriate manner, and, worst of all, failed to rescue her from mother. The girl retreats to the mother with a deep contempt for father and for men in general. This contempt is often encouraged by the mother in families in which there is discord between the parents: Such mothers often sanction a girl's animosity toward the father, while punishing any anger or criticism directed toward herself.

Some analysts have misinterpreted Freud's writings about female psychology to mean that all women are destined, because of their anatomy (that is, their lack of a penis), to a status of inferiority. What he meant was that *some* women are destined to develop narcissism and feelings of inferiority with regard to their genitalia and to their femininity — namely, those who do not resolve their castration and Electra complexes.

This phenomenon may best be understood through an analogy to male development. Because of social values that extol the virtues of large over small, men with smaller penises (or who perceive their penises as small) often develop feelings of inferiority about themselves and their masculinity. They may compensate for these feelings by developing a narcissistic pride in their sexual technique, in an attempt to prove they can satisfy a woman as well as a man with a larger penis can. They may behave more aggressively toward men who they suspect of having larger penises, or to women who arouse their feelings of inadequacy. In general, their relationships with women will suffer because of this complex. Not all men with smaller penises will develop such a complex, however. The crucial variable is the way in which parents deal with a child's feelings. If they help him to understand that being small is not a form of inferiority, he will undergo healthy sexual development. Similarly, not all women develop feelings of inferiority about their anatomy or about being female. Even though boys have penises and grow larger and stronger (on the average), the initial feelings of shock and envy each girl feels can be assuaged by healthy parents, and the girl will eventually see the advantages of being female and realize that the sexes are truly equal and complementary.

A little girl's discovery of her lack of a penis can be a profound narcissistic blow, depending upon how emotionally healthy she is at the time of the discovery and also upon how her parents and siblings treat this discovery. Mahler and colleagues (1975) and Roiphe and Galenson (1981) note that this discovery is often followed by intense and sometimes violent masturbation and then by cessation of masturbation. Freud (1925) speculated that the little girl suddenly feels that her organ is inferior to the boy's and that the turning away from the clitoris represents, "in the narcissistic sense of humiliation which is bound up with penis envy, the girl's reflection that after all this is a point on which she cannot compete with boys and that it would therefore be best for her to give up the idea of doing so" (p. 256). My interpretation is that little girls give up masturbation out of a feeling of disgust at the unfairness of the world.

Following the giving up of masturbation, those girls who lack adequate parenting will begin acting out, sometimes for a period of weeks and in some cases for the rest of their lives. Typical behavior includes throwing tantrums, pulling the hair of other children and siblings, lifting the dresses of adult women, and generally being uncooperative. They will often become obsessed with penises, wanting to know who has them and who doesn't, and why they don't have one and when they will get one. At that point in a girl's existence, there is nothing more important than a penis.

The girl feels cheated of a most important organ—perhaps *the* most important a human can have. She sees little boys proudly playing with their penises, urinating while standing, enjoying the possession of this organ of pleasure and prestige, and her resentment mounts. Her own organ of pleasure is internal and almost invisible. As McDougall (1984) points out, the little girl neither can visually verify her genitals nor create anything other than a vague psychic representation of them; therefore, they do not even seem to exist. Further, the penis is associated with power, since boys usually grow stronger and bigger and usually win physical fights with girls. All this reinforces their envy and resentment of the penis. In adulthood, this envy and resentment can translate into a disgust with the male sexual organ and everything male, and a turning away—partially or fully— from heterosexuality.

The fantasy lives of little girls, once they have discovered the difference in the anatomy of the sexes, is filled with the longing for a penis. At first they hope to get a penis from mother, then from father. Such fantasies have been observed by numerous analysts, among them Klein (1932), Kestenberg (1968), Anna Freud (1965), Mahler and co-workers (1975), and Roiphe and Galenson (1981). To the extent that a girl has not been helped to resolve her phallic remorse (that is, her symbolic castration) and penis envy, she will be unwilling to give up her longing for a penis; women often retain this fantasy of getting a penis, or of actually having a penis somewhere inside them, long into adulthood. (This fantasy, naturally, is unconscious, but it comes to the surface during analytic treatment.) If they want to help their daughters develop normally, parents need to help them "mourn" their supposed castration, and to accept and value their femininity in its own right. They should be given the message at an early age that they have a sexual organ that is just as important as, and complementary to, the male's. A mother's narcissism and animosity toward men and toward her husband will have a frustrating impact on her daughter's feminine strivings. If the mother has not resolved her own penis envy and phallic remorse, she will not be empathic to her daughter's attempts to come to grips with hers. The mother's animosity and low feminine self-esteem will also be introjected by the daughter. Meanwhile, a father's male narcissism may cause the girl's mourning to turn into penis envy. He has the power to either "save" her or to let her sink into the abyss of narcissism (indeed, he may even give her a shove in that direction, due to his animosity). To repeat, it is the father's final betrayal during the oedipal phase which lies at the root of the bitterness toward men that many women feel.

As is the case with male narcissism, female narcissism is a character formation that evolves as a defense against the frustrations of a girl's normal feminine strivings. On its deepest level is rage at having been cheated of a penis and of the pleasure, prestige, and power associated with it. It is also a rage at the mother's frustration of the girl's feminine strivings and at the father's weakness, hostility, or exploitativeness. This rage against both mother and father for their attitude toward her genitalia and her femininity is later manifested as sexual animosity toward men. The girl defends against an inner core of rage and an outer core of separation anxiety, phallic remorse, and penis envy by withdrawing her libido from the father, the final betrayer, and later from men. The libidinal drive gets turned back on the self, with a resulting grandiosity to compensate for deeper feelings of low feminine self-esteem.

Female narcissists do not outgrow the unconscious (and sometimes conscious) feelings of inferiority to men, nor the resentment that results from such feelings. The sexual animosity stemming from this character formation is acted out in various ways: Female narcissists may control men, induce guilt feelings in them, hide from them, manipulate, defer, depreciate, suppress, exclude, or idealize them. They may be friends with them, become maternally interested in them, or seek revenge on the entire male gender. Like the male narcissist, the female narcissist largely withdraws into a shell, never to give her heart to a man again.

CHARACTER STRUCTURES

The forms of female narcissism generally correspond to those of male narcissism. All the forms attempt to defend against feelings of feminine inferiority as well as against envy of the male for his supposed superiority. Each female narcissist expresses animosity differently, based upon her character structure. Few are conscious of either their feelings of inferiority or their penis envy.

Masculine-Aggressive Narcissism

The masculine-aggressive is sometimes referred to as the "phallic woman," as she represents the girl who does not give up the fantasy of having a penis, even when she becomes an adult. Many masculine-aggressives take pride in their intelligence. It was this type that Reich called the "big brain hysteric" (Baker 1967). These women often say that men are afraid of them because of their intelligence, but it is actually they who are afraid of intelligent men; upon meeting a man who threatens them, they attempt to castrate him psychologically by conquering him with their brain/phallus; that is, they try to outsmart him. Many leading feminist writers are masculine-aggressives of the "big brain hysteric" variety. Other masculine-aggressives will try to outdo men at traditionally male occupations such as firefighting and construction work. They may have an abrasive, competitive attitude toward men and a desire to dominate or defeat them. If they marry, they tend to choose passive narcissists whom they can dominate and mold to their own image. In essence, they want to "feminize" their husbands and force them to play the female role in the relationship.

Masculine-aggressives are the female counterpart of the phallic narcissistic male. Like the phallic, they are open and direct in the expression of their aggression, which comes out as contempt for the men and for everything masculine. At the same time, there is a strong identification with the aggressor which causes them to have a masculine ego. They defend against separation anxiety by maintaining a somewhat symbiotic relationship with their mothers and by joining with other women to fight for feminist causes. They defend against phallic remorse and penis envy by striving to psychologically castrate men—on a social level through the vehicle of feminism, and on a personal level through direct intimidation and manipulation, using their intellect or their emotionality as a wedge. In their writings and personal manner there is a tone of contempt and sarcasm that serves to put others on the defensive and scare them into submission. They also have the ability to use their intellectual skills to manipulate situations, so that in a conflict with a man they can make it appear that they are being victimized, although in reality they are victimizers. They seek oedipal revenge. If they cannot have a penis, then no man is going to have one either.

Sexually, masculine-aggressives need to be the initiators and the aggressors, and to control every aspect of the sexual experience. They are seldom satisfied with the performance of their male partners. They often cannot achieve orgasm, not wanting to surrender to a male; or if they do, it will be through their own self-stimulation of the clitoris during intercourse. Because of their sexual demandingness, the effect of which is to make the man feel sexually incompetent, their partners generally lose interest in sex.

There is an attitude among masculine-aggressives, both in and out of bed, of wanting their way with a man—a compensation for their unconscious feelings of having been castrated. Their mothers are usually masculine-aggressives or hysterics, while their fathers are generally passives or absent. Upon discovering their "castration" as little girls, they act out their narcissistic rage in extreme ways, and they are often called "brats" by their parents. (As adults they tend to have a strong aversion to all labels, especially psychiatric labels.) Both parents are hostile and respond to the girl's acting out by ignoring or shaming her; such tactics serve only to reinforce the acting out. "You think I'm a brat?" the little girl seems to say, "I'll show you what a brat is!" The mother is generally intrusive, interfering with the little girl's turn to the father during the oedipal phase. The father is usually intimidated by the mother and full of unconscious animosity toward women, which he acts out by ignoring or rejecting the little girl, often ridiculing her efforts to get his attention and to get him to understand the pain she feels. Hence she grows up fixated at the anal- and phallic-sadistic stages, stuck in a mode of acting out castration rage. As an adult she tries to extract from her husband what she could not get from her father and is again destined to fail. (This character-type is dealt with at length in the case history in Part II, "Lizzie the Brat.")

Hysterical Narcissism

The hysterical narcissist generally harbors the notion that all men are predators, out to devour and destroy her with their phalluses. Her animosity toward men is denied and projected onto the man: It is men who are full of animosity. On the surface they feel anxiety, a result of the talion principle, fearing that men will do to them the very thing that, unconsciously, they wish to do to men: obtain sexual revenge. They defend against phallic remorse and penis envy through their hysterical maneuvers. Unlike the masculine-aggressive, the hysteric is unable to express aggression directly or even to acknowledge that she has any. Like the passive narcissist, she acts it out indirectly, usually through sexual teasing. Many hysterics are attractive and seductive, conveying a message that they are sexually available. Yet the hysteric will turn on the man who makes a sexual advance and sometimes ridicule him. The degree of animosity varies; some hysterics can be charming, competent women whose animosity is minimal and subtly expressed. Others can be lethal, driving men to an impotent, violent rage, or to abject apathy. Movies such as "The Blue Angel," in which a night-club dancer drives a middle-aged college professor to his ruin, provide graphic and moving illustrations of this theme. A typical maneuver of the angriest type of hysteric is to act seductively toward a male authority figure, such as a boss. When the boss makes an advance, she spurns him. The man, enraged, retaliates by firing her or with some other punitive action. She then sues him for sexual harassment. (Unfortunately, men are usually too embarrassed to sue women for sexual harassment, although, as in this instance, it does happen.)

The hysteric has a need to believe in her own innocence. In a relationship, she needs to be in the right. If her spouse criticizes her, she will play the martyr, accusing him of persecuting her. If all else fails, she will explode in a hysterical fit in order to get her "tormentor" to back down. She will surrender sexually, sometimes faking orgasm, to control him, but generally she can enjoy sex only when she feels "taken by force" and does not have to take any responsibility for the interaction (a defense against the unconscious guilt and shame associated with infantile eroticism). Scarlett O'Hara, in *Gone With the Wind,* is a typical hysteric. Only when Rhett Butler (a phallic) carries her up the stairs and "rapes" her does she respond sexually.

Usually the mothers of hysterics are hysterics, and the fathers are either phallics or passives. The hysteric is fixated primarily in the oedipal stage, during which time, after the turn to the father, she is sexually exploited or humiliated by him. The hysteric is usually very attractive and seductive as a little girl; indeed, oedipal-age girls can be bold and unabashed in their sexuality, since they have not yet learned that such behavior is frowned upon. When the father spurns her advances, it creates in the child a feeling of shame, guilt, and anger. Often both mother and father make the girl feel guilty about her sexuality, and the fact that she is such an attractive girl may make her even more of a target for parental rebuke, since the parents will find themselves even more conflicted about the feelings aroused in them by their daughter. The little girl will respond by acting even more seductively, while denying that she is doing so. It is as though she were saying to her father—and later to other men—"I'll behave as I want to and I'm not naughty! If you think I'm bad, you're imagining it. It's you who's the naughty one!" In essence, the hysteric wants to turn the tables on father.

Anal Narcissism

Female anal narcissists, like male anals, tend to have sadomasochistic relationships. They may be sadistic or masochistic, and they will have a strong obsessive-compulsive substructure to their character. The sadist views men as beasts who need to be tamed; their penises and everything else about them is seen as dirty, including their feces, urine, and sperm. She will attempt to dominate and "train" her spouse, nagging him about lifting the toilet lid before he urinates or insisting that he use condoms during sex. The more sadistic anals will often humiliate their spouses in front of their children, deriding their manhood in various ways. They are skilled at using their own perceived martyrdom as an excuse to abuse their mates and other men: "Men have always abused me, so now I'm going to keep them in their place."

The masochist will be drawn to sadistic men and will provoke them into being sadistic to her. Masochistic women may be overtly and consciously provocative or may provoke sadism subtly and be unaware of their behavior. The typical masochistic "battered woman" elicits violent behavior from her husband by behaving in a submissive way while casting accusatory glances that ask, "Why are you acting like a beast when I'm being so good to you!" Her denial of her aggression and her anxious overpermissiveness only serve to incite him; she is repeating the same behavior shown him by his mother, and perhaps modeled by her own. Like the sadist, the masochist thinks of herself as a victim of male abuse. Her chief defense is to play the martyr and induce guilt in her sadistic partner; in so doing, she can maintain the illusion of moral superiority. This becomes her source of secondary gratification.

Female anal narcissists defend against separation anxiety by remaining closely tied to their mothers and to other women while maintaining distance from men. They defend against phallic remorse and penis envy through their obsessive-compulsive character structure and through their sadomasochistic process. They are fixated primarily at the anal-rapprochement phase, when toilet training and anal eroticism was intermixed with the discoveries of masturbation and the difference in sexual anatomy. Their mothers are either sadistic, humiliating their daughters into masochistic submission, or masochistic, allowing the daughter to sadistically defy her out of a need to play the martyr. The fathers are likewise usually sadomasochistic, and often either actively take charge of the daughter's toilet training (if they are sadistic) or take a masochistically permissive attitude toward it. During the oedipal phase a sadistic father may reinforce the little girl's masochistic character structure by being sadistically brutal (perhaps by spanking her). He may reinforce her sadistic character structure by allowing her to have her way, but without expressing his real feelings.

Oral Narcissism

The female oral narcissist, like the male oral narcissist, is fixated primarily at the breast-feeding stage of development. She defends against separation anxiety by identifying with the role of the mother or of the infant in the symbiotic phase. If she identifies with her mother, she will take a maternal attitude toward the men in her life; she thus defends against phallic remorse and penis envy by infantilizing a man and regressing him to a state of passive dependency on her "breast-feeding" thereby psychologically castrating him. If her identification is with the bad breast and her fixation is oral-sadistic, the castrating behavior may be more pronounced. She may, for example, become the spouse of an alcoholic so that she can alternately build him up or tear him down (while keeping him dependent on her).

If she identifies with the infant, she will defend against phallic remorse and penis envy through merger with a man (devouring his penis). Such women have an infantile-submissive attitude toward men, wanting to be "fed" by them. Without a man in her life, an infantile oral will feel worthless. When she has a man in her life, she will tend to be unrelenting in her demand for narcissistic supplies (sex, for instance). When she does not get these supplies as often as needed, she will attempt to manipulate her provider by deriding his masculinity. If his penis does not satisfy her, it becomes a bad penis.

The female oral, like the male, tends to be an addictive personality. She is more likely than a man to be addicted to food, however. Perhaps through eating there is a symbolic re-creation of the infantile symbiosis with mother and a suppression of the sexuality and feminine strivings that might threaten mother's approval. (For a man, eating would threaten his masculinity; that is, it would threaten his separation from mother and arouse the fear of re-engulfment.) Orals are addictive—or phobic—about food as a way of controlling their narcissistic supplies. The same is true about their addictions, or phobias, connected with other substances, such as drugs. These addictive substances are transitional objects that help them control rage. By overeating, self-inducing vomiting, taking drugs, drinking, or smoking, they can dull the pain of their pent-up rage, the direct expression of which they fear would mean the loss of love, approval, admiration.

Oral narcissists generally feel abandoned by their parents during early childhood. Since the primary fixation is in the oral phase, all subsequent phases tend to reinforce the earlier fixation. The parents of orals tend to be oral. They relate to their daughters as narcissistic extensions (Miller 1981) rather than as individuals in their own right. Hence many orals are out of touch with their feelings and want to escape them, so they play the (often perfectionistic) roles assigned by their parents instead. During the oedipal phase, when an orally fixated girl turns to her father, it is not only for his "penis" but also to satisfy the narcissistic need for approval and love left unfulfilled by her mother. His rejection sends her back to mother. The turn to father often is not made, for mother has already "smothered" the girl and kept her at the breast. The passive father allows it.

Borderline Narcissism

Borderline narcissists can be cruel in their expression of animosity to men or to themselves, often burning themselves with cigarettes or mutilating themselves with razors. They may have a wide mood swing, from manic to depressive. Their superegos range from severe to barely adequate. Those with severe superegos tend to attack themselves, and those with inadequate superegos vent their rage on men without feeling much guilt.

A borderline may have a strong paranoid personality component, often harboring the fear that all men secretly want to rape her (a projection of her own hostility toward men). She may be a militant feminist and will be religiously wedded to the notion that all women are victims of male tyranny. Or, out of touch with her rage at men, she may compensate through a reaction formation: She will idealize men and allow them to abuse her in order to win their approval, and then sabotage the relationship. Her relationships with men tend to be extreme. She may be alternately abstinent, nymphomaniacal, submissive, or an ogre. She unconsciously, and sometimes consciously, feels that all men are basically "creeps" who deserve anything a woman does to them. She is the epitome of the saying "Hell hath no fury like a woman scorned": If she feels betrayed (which she often does) she will be relentless in her vengeance. There is no consistency to her behavior: She will have little compunction, at times, about lying, stealing, or otherwise acting out against men who she has decided are "the enemy"; at other times she will treat the men around her as though they were gods. Separation anxiety, phallic remorse, and penis envy are warded off by keeping men always confused, at a distance, under control; if control is threatened, she will destroy them (by rejecting, degrading, and emasculating them) or herself.

Just as mothers of male psychopaths are invariably unconscious seducers of their sons, female borderlines have often been seduced or sexually abused by their fathers or others. Their fathers are often psychopathic or perverse narcissists, and their mothers are often borderlines who are either masochistically submissive or anxiously overpermissive (compensating for disguised hostility to the daughter). In some cases the mothers are homosexuals who shape their daughters toward an aversion to men.

Homosexual Narcissism

In analyzing a case of female homosexuality, Freud (1920b) stressed two factors: an ambivalent relationship between the daughter and the mother, and paternal rejection. He notes that his patient "remained homosexual out of defiance against her father" (p. 159). Lesbians often have hostile, distant, or intrusive mothers; frequently the mother is insecure and competes with the daughter for the father's allegiance; at the same time, the father is invariably rejecting. Thus if the daughter makes the turn to the father at all, she makes it half-heartedly, fearing mother's disapproval. The father also fears the mother's disapproval, and sometimes such fathers, after having had a close, sexually charged relationship with the daughter up to the oedipal phase, now suddenly back away from the daughter as though she were diseased. The girl feels hatred for the father's hypocrisy and weakness, and guilty toward the mother; she later seeks a symbolic merger with other women to assuage the guilt toward mother. The homosexual act is both a merging with mother and a revenge against father, serving to ward off separation anxiety, phallic remorse, and penis envy.

Lesbians have a strong aversion to the penis and to men. Sexual intercourse with a woman constitutes a revenge against men and a "snub" of men's penises. Animosity is also acted out through the exclusion of men from their lives. In the writings and personal manners of lesbians there is a tone of contempt for men, accompanied by a narcissistic-grandiose attitude about their femininity and a chauvinistic braggadocio about womanhood.

Psychotic Narcissism

Psychotic narcissism represents the most extreme form of withdrawal from men; indeed, psychotics no longer have meaningful contact with either sex. Extreme frustration during the symbiotic phase leaves the psychotic in a state of infantile dependency on her mother (and sometimes on institutions) and defenseless against aggression (her own and that of others). The result is that the girl is rendered nonfunctional by the severity of her early childhood frustration. Animosity is vented on the self; aggression floods the system and jams it, producing hallucinations and other symptoms. Withdrawal from men is withdrawal from their poisonous penises—partly to reject them, partly to protect them from her rage, and partly to guard against the acknowledgment of this rage, which she fears will annihilate her. Separation anxiety is warded off through delusional merger with the symbolic, symbiotic mother of infancy; phallic remorse and penis envy are defended against through withdrawal.

MANIFESTATIONS

Female narcissists share certain attitudes that are an outgrowth of their unresolved masculinity and Electra complexes. They harbor feelings of inferiority about their femininity and defend against these introjected negative judgments about themselves by projecting them onto men and erecting an armor of female grandiosity. They make men the scapegoats for their inner conflicts about their femininity. It is men who judge them, and their femininity, as being inferior. They will therefore prove to men that they are not only their equals, but also superior. The need to constantly prove female superiority—moral, intellectual, and even physical—stems from this grandiosity that compensates for feelings of inferiority.

They also share an attitude of unwillingness to compromise that is related to unresolved penis envy and phallic remorse. Because they feel cheated and have never overcome the wound to their feminine self-esteem, their behavior toward men is demanding and selfish, as if to say, "You were given the penis, so I'm going to have my way!" There is a self-righteousness, an unwillingness to admit to wrongdoing, which would mean a loss of face. On an archaic level, being wrong means being reprimanded by mother for masturbating or for "talking dirty," or being sexually rejected by father. Such experiences represent a disintegration of the self and arouse fears of re-engulfment and death. They are shattering to the girl's sense of self, and to her sense of mastery of the external world. Therefore, as an adult, she is dedicated to ensuring that she does not allow herself to be hurt in this way again. She chooses a man whom she can control, often lambasts him for being too passive, and finds ways to make sure he does not enjoy his penis too much.

Female narcissists share an unwillingness to acknowledge or take responsibility for their sexual feelings. They will seldom admit that they have sexual feelings about a man, especially if he arouses strong feelings—that is, if he elicits transference feelings and becomes a father or brother figure to the woman. In such a case, sexual feelings would be taboo and she would anticipate oedipal rejection from the man. Projection and denial are major defenses used to ward off sexual feelings and sexual animosity, which are projected onto men and denied by the woman herself. She views men as potential sexual bandits, out to sexually conquer, humiliate, or ravish her. At the same time, she views herself as innocent, without sexual feelings (at least not toward the man in question) and certainly without sexual animosity. Female narcissists are convinced that men are sexists but that women are without sexual bias. They are convinced that men are misogynists but that women harbor no hatred of men that is not justified by male sexism. In short, while female narcissists will insist on their rights, they will at the same time absolve themselves of any responsibility for their "wrongs," particularly in the sexual arena.

As illustrated in Table 4–1, female narcissism (like male narcissism) ranges from moderate to severe. Masculine-aggressives and hysterics, who are fixated in the later oedipal period and act out animosity by attempting to control the object of their desire, generally have less pathology in their character structures than either the homosexual, who is fixated in the symbiotic and oral phases and withdraws completely from men in order to destroy them, or the psychotic, who is fixated in the symbiotic phase and withdraws

Table 4–1
Forms of Female Narcissism

	Defense against Penis Envy	Mode of Aggression	Fixation Point	Character of Mother	Character of Father
Masculine-Aggressive	Intellectual or "masculine" conquest	Control of object	Oedipal and anal phases	Masculine-aggressive or hysteric	Passive or absent
Hysteric	Seduction and abandonment	Control of object	Oedipal-phase	Hysteric	Phallic, passive, or absent
Anal	Sexual dominance and submission	Control of object	Anal phase	Anal or hysteric	Anal, psychopathic, or absent
Oral	Passive dependence or infantilizing behavior	Control of object	Oral phase	Oral	Oral, passive, or absent
Borderline	Sexual subterfuge	Destruction of object or self	Oral and anal phases	Borderline	Psychopathic, anal, or absent
Homosexual	Flight from (rejection of) man	Control or destruction of object	Symbiotic and oral phases	Homosexual, hysteric, or borderline	Perverse, passive, or absent
Psychotic	Total withdrawal	Destruction of self	Symbiotic phase	Psychotic or borderline	Psychotic, psychopathic, or absent

completely from men *and* women and tries to destroy herself. (There are also mixed types, such as a masculine-aggressive who is also a homosexual, in which case the fixation points and pathology would take a different form.) The more severe the pathology, the more pathogenic the character structures of the parents.

Related to the acting out of female animosity is female sexual magnetism. In nearly all species of animal, particularly mammals, the female has a way of attracting the male and letting him know that she is sexually available. Some female animals give off a scent or turn a certain color when they are in "heat," drawing males to them. Other animals attract males with a ritualistic, genetically determined mating "dance." Irenäus Eibl-Eibesfeldt (1970), an ethologist, believes that the mating behavior of the human female is also genetically determined. Human females have many ways of letting males know that they are sexually available. Their mating behavior may consist of a childlike or submissive attitude—perhaps a blushing response and down-cast eyes—toward the man of their desire. Alternatively, their demeanor might be provocative and goading, designed to incite in the man an urge to "take" them. The way in which a woman looks at a man—whether directly or with a certain shyness—can convey the message of sexual availability, as can body movements—touching the man on the arm, making an elaborate display of crossing one's legs, and so on. A healthy woman uses these mating rituals to seduce the man she desires into sexual action to which she will then be receptive. A narcissistic woman will often use signals to get a man to make a move in order to prove to herself that all men are "only interested in one thing." Or she may be entirely unconscious of her signals and feel threatened when a man makes an advance. Narcissistic wives will often give mixed signals to their husbands, as a result of their ambivalence about sex. On one hand, they may demand sex and complain about their husbands' indifference; on the other hand, their body language and their sexual performance reflects their own fears of and revulsion toward sexuality. Their husbands retreat into confused passivity and the wives, unconscious of their own behavior, do not understand why. Narcissistic career women often use their sexuality to climb the ladder of success; their sexual encounters are merely ways of conquering and using men. Sexual magnetism provides women with a major means of acting out sexual animosity without taking responsibility for it. A man cannot prove that woman gave him any signals, which is an advantage narcissistic women make full use of.

As male narcissists fear women, female narcissists fear men. Their fear of men is both rational—the fear of someone generally bigger than they—and irrational—the obsessive fear of being raped, humiliated, and obliterated. These latter fears are primarily an outcome of the projection of their animosity onto men. They want to castrate men, and they project that men have these same designs on them. These fears are also related to the dread of re-engulfment (from the symbiotic phase) and to infantile fears of being devoured by the bad breast or being penetrated by poisonous feces (from the oral- and anal-sadistic phases). The obsession with being raped is typified by Brownmiller's (1975) introduction to *Against Our Will*:

> Man's discovery that his genitalia would serve as a weapon to generate fear must rank as one of the most important discoveries of prehistoric times, along with the use of fire and the first crude stone axe. From prehistoric times to the present, I believe rape has played a critical function. It is nothing more or less than a conscious process of intimidation by which *all men* keep *all women* in a state of fear. [p. 5]

One can glean from this statement, first, an ontogenetic reference to the infantile discovery of the difference in sexual anatomy ("Man's discovery that his genitalia would serve as a weapon to generate fear . . ."). To a little girl who first discovers a penis, it probably is a frightening event, due to the talion principle. The immediate desire to pull it off, to dispossess the male and take it for herself, arouses the counterfear that the male will penetrate and destroy her with the penis. Second, one can also detect in Brownmiller's statement a hysterical obsession with rape, which is generalized and directed to *"all men"* (italics are Brownmiller's). Finally, there is an attempt to castigate men, to attribute to them all sexual animosity and to portray the penis as some vile weapon of fear, rather than as an instrument of pleasure and reproduction.

5

Sexual Animosity in Society

MASCULINISM AND FEMINISM

Male and female narcissism in society often takes a fanatical bent, evidenced by the masculinist and feminist movements. Masculinism and feminism are conduits through which men and women can act out collective rage toward the opposite sex. Masculinists and feminists are engaged in a war, and the objective is the same as that in any war: the control or destruction of the enemy. This war takes place in all aspects of society: within the halls of government, inside the offices and factories of corporations, among members of professional societies and labor unions, within institutions of learning; throughout the entertainment industry, and on construction sites where men sneer at women or in rap groups where women express contempt for men.

The forces that drive this war of the sexes are the same as those that drive individual conflicts: frustrated Eros and the aggression (Thanatos) associated with that frustration, springing from pent-up rage. Masculinism and feminism are an outgrowth of sexual narcissism and an expression of Thanatos. Narcissists generally seek control through dominance, and they attain dominance by emphasizing the virtues of their own sex while casting aspersions on the other sex. When they cannot obtain control through dominance, they try to destroy the other sex through scapegoating and degradation.

Baker (1967) points out that one's political views are related to one's upbringing. Active male narcissism, as expressed by the ideology and political activities of masculinism, usually stems from family constellations in which the father is narcissistically dominating; and active female narcissism, as expressed by the ideology and political activities of feminism, usually stems from family environments in which the mother is narcissistically dominating. The narcissistically dominating parent controls the family in a manipulative, pathogenic manner and models sexual chauvinism. The extent to which a parent is narcissistically dominating (and hence pathogenic) is directly proportional to the degree to which the child's political views will be extreme and to the degree of adult identification with masculinism or feminism.

The male narcissist identifies himself as a man first, then as a human being. He disowns the feminine part of himself, extols masculinity, and disparages femininity. His self becomes identified with maleness and with the ideology of masculinism. A female narcissist identifies herself as a woman first, then a human being. She disowns the masculine part of herself, extols femininity, and disparages masculinity. Her self becomes identified with femaleness and with the ideology of feminism.

The more sexual narcissism a group possesses, the more it will make a religion of masculinism or feminism, and the more biased it will be toward the other sex. Each side projects its feelings of low sexual self-esteem on the other sex and then believes it is the other sex which views it as inferior. Thus masculinists often think that women judge them inferior and then set out to prove that they are not, and feminists often think that men think them inferior and then set out to prove their worth. Through group consensus, each forges its own truth. Their ideologies serve to prove the superiority and goodness of their sex and the inferiority and badness of the other sex, while justifying the acting out of sexual animosity *en masse* toward the enemy. Collective animosity and a common enemy bonds them.

Hoffer (1951), writing about the psychology of mass movements, notes that passionate hatred can give an empty life some semblance of purpose; it is chiefly the "unreasonable hatreds" that drive people to merge with others who hate as they do, and that become the "kind of hatred that serves as one of the most effective cementing agents" (p. 98).

Kardiner (1954) examines the effects of mass movements on male–female relations and on society, and he takes a view similar to Hoffer's, asking whether the feminist movement, women's increasing aggressiveness, and men's increasing passivity are related to the enormous rise in homosexuality and mass movements. He wonders whether this increase in homosexuality will lead to a society in which homosexual values become the dominant force, in which the heterosexual life-style and the family gradually disappear. He wonders whether our society can survive such a trend, asserting that the separation of the sexes as typified by homosexuality leads to a decrease in the number of opportunities to be masculine and feminine, which in turn "depresses self-esteem and gives rise to aggression and hatred" (p. 188). This aggression and hatred can easily be directed against oneself, as it is in neurosis; however, it may also become displaced. "Rage requires only an avenue of discharge and a pretext to release it" (p. 180). He explains that mass movements serve to channel the collective rage, because the leaders of such movements invariably tell the individuals that they are suffering through no fault of their own; rather, they are being victimized by others. He notes:

> This elevates fallen pride and mobilizes aggression, which in itself brings relief, because it implies hope and action. Even without such public leadership the depressed individual will vent his rage on his favorite hated object. Hatred is a powerful solvent for conscience, and that is why, in an atmosphere of universal rage, acts of injustice are committed with more or less good conscience. Aggression is enlisted in the aid of justified self-defense. [pp. 180–181]

Kardiner adds that the "general contempt of male homosexuals for females is notorious" (p. 189). Likewise, female homosexuals are generally contemptuous of males.

By forming mass movements or clubs, male and female narcissists can use an ideology to justify and sometimes sanctify their rage, thereby avoiding their own individual psychological conflicts. Scape-goating is central to both masculinism and feminism—the enemy is branded in pejorative terms: Women who do not tow the masculinist line are "man-haters," and men who do not take the correct feminist position are "sexists." These "brands" are used to control the opposite sex, the message being "Either you behave as we want you to behave or you will be ostracized and stigmatized." Each side attempts to gain dominance through these and other tactics; it is a kind of psycholog-ical warfare in which unreasonable hatreds are made to seem reason-able by sheer force of numbers. "Sexual difference is an obvious difference, and obvious differences are especially convenient marks of derogation in any competitive situation in which one group aims to get power over the other" (Thompson 1964, p. 54).

THE MASCULINIST PHENOMENON

Although masculinism has been around since the beginning of hu-mankind, it has never been formally called masculinism. Instead it has been a tacit, nameless value system through which men have banded together to disparage and control women. Throughout history there have been political actions that can be defined as masculinistic, and the ideology of masculinism is a part of various religions and philosophies.

Clower (1979), recapitulating the history of misogyny, provides some highlights of masculinism. The Greek myth of Pandora's box makes women responsible for all the misery and hardships in the world; that is, all misery stems from the womb of Woman. The Bible also holds women responsible for all human misery, since it attributes the fall of humankind to Eve and her impulsive eating of the forbidden apple. The men who wrote the Old Testament condemned Eve, and the voice of God in the Book of Genesis proclaims, "In sorrow shall thou bring forth children and thy desire shall be to thy husband, and he shall rule over thee." Elsewhere in Genesis, womanhood is de-scribed as follows: "What else is woman but a foe to friendship, an unescapable punishment, a necessary evil, a natural temptation, a desirable calamity, a domestic danger, a delectable detriment, an evil of nature, painted with fair colors!"

In the Muslim religion, women are also degraded. Muhammad was said to have asserted, "When Eve was created, Satan rejoiced." The Persian prophet Zoroaster states that sex makes women diabolical. The Hindu Code of Manu declares, "In childhood, a woman must be subject to her father; in youth to her husband; when her husband is dead, to her sons. A woman must never be free of subjugation."

St. Jerome, a founder of the Catholic Church, observes that "Woman is the true Satan, the foe of peace, the subject of dissension." St. Paul, one of Christ's disciples, states, "Let the women learn in silence with all subjection," and "Wives, submit yourselves to your husbands." St. Augustine, who described woman as a temple built over a sewer, believed that virginity was better than marriage. Plato wondered whether women could be considered reasonable beings or if they ought to be categorized as animals, and Aristotle suggested that females might be produced because of a mishap during pregnancy.

There were debates during the Middle Ages about whether women had souls. In the 1480s the book *Malleus Maleficarum* (Kramer and Sprenger 1486) used religious doctrine for attacking women. They were said to be liars, to have inferior intelligence, and to be sexually lustful. Further, they were the source of witchcraft, which is rooted in carnal lust.

During the Reformation, Martin Luther expressed the belief that women were naturally inferior to men. John Calvin, who thought that women were useful *only* for bearing children, asserted that political equality for women would be a deviation from the "original and proper order of nature"; however, he made an exception of Elizabeth I, who was "raised by Divine Authority." The enlightenment of the eighteenth century, the scientific discoveries of the nineteenth century, and the democratic philosophy of the twentieth century failed to completely eradicate both the masculinist belief in the basic inferiority of women and its attempt to keep them in their place.

The masculinist wants to suppress the power of Woman, to assuage his castration fear, womb envy, and phallic guilt, and to compensate for his feelings of inferiority—all by controlling and destroying women through masculinist psychological warfare. Winnicott (1965) notes that the fear of Woman is "responsible for the immense amount of cruelty to women, which can be found in the customs that are accepted by almost all civilizations" (p. 164). This fear causes both men and women to seek male domination. "The dictator can be overthrown," Winnicott explains, "and must eventually die; but the woman figure of primitive unconscious fantasy has no limits to her existence or power" (p. 165). It is this primitive fantasy Woman which the dictator attempts to delimit, and which masculinists fear.

Adler (1929) observes that the worst insult that can be hurled at a boy is, "You're acting like a girl," or "You're a sissy." This points up the core of the masculinist ideology: It is a value system in which women are seen as inferior to men, as beings whose emotional excesses must be kept in check, lest the forces of depravity and evil be unleashed. The masculinist value system is deeply ingrained in our child-rearing practices and in our culture. Each male narcissist has been indoctrinated to see women as inferior—either because they are "sissies" or because they are powerful but immoral monsters waiting to castrate and corrupt men and divert them from the true path.

Zilboorg (1944) contends that the beginning of the family corresponded with the first sexual assault of a woman by a man, and that the assault had economic overtones. "There is ample evidence in all quarters of the globe and in all strata of savage culture to the effect that the idea of the family was originally born not out of love but out of the drive for economic exploitation" (p. 120). He adds that, throughout history, man had to maintain his mastery over woman in order to secure his investment. And in order to justify his enslavement and domination of his wife, he had to resolve "his rivalry with the primordial mother by way of projecting into her a good part of his own sadism" (p. 128). Zilboorg's repudiation of men, however, is extreme. Some men may use sex or marriage for economic gain, but to attribute this motive to all men, throughout history, is to be biased in the other direction.

Psychoanalytic knowledge, Zilboorg asserts, is hampered by an "androcentric bias" which overlooks the fundamental envy with which man treated women throughout history and his essential hostility toward her. He believes that "The whole question of so-called passivity and activity will have to be restudied, as well as the question of masculine and feminine narcissism" (p. 129).

MASCULINISM AND WAR

Freud (1933) wrote about war in a letter to Einstein. He believed that war would be prevented with certainty only if humankind united in setting up a central authority to which the right to judge all conflicts of interest would be handed over. He associated war with the psychical modifications that go along with the process of civilization, which involve a progressive displacement of instinctual aims and a restriction of instinctual impulses. Although he does not directly link the repression imposed by civilization with war, he does link it elsewhere (Freud 1930) with neurosis. What Freud implies, and what I am stating more directly, is that war is the result of the collective frustration of Eros in civilizations that have pathological (male and female narcissistic) child-rearing practices.

A society in which the needs of Eros are frustrated will be a society in which Thanatos (the collective aggression of society) will accumulate. Peace cannot be maintained for long in such a society. Sooner or later, the aggression that builds up as a result of the continued frustration of Eros is bound to explode. The greater the aggression in an individual or a society, the lower the individual's or society's self-esteem, and the greater the need to prove one's worth through aggressive action. The masculinist sees in war an opportunity to raise his lagging masculine self-esteem through acts of "heroism" — acts which are portrayed as courageous and noble in such transmitters of cultural values as movies, books, and television. Throughout history, wars have been documented, usually by male writers, in romantic and sometimes epic terms, and a masculinist, machismo lore has come to sanctify the mass killing of our own species.

From a psychoanalytic viewpoint, war is an oedipal phenomenon, a rivalry between fathers and sons and a competition among sons for the right of sexual possession of the mother and sisters (and all women). On an international scale, each nation represents a father or brother, while the instruments of war, from the smallest handgun to the most powerful bomb, are phallic symbols. The unconscious aim of war is to prove who has the biggest, most powerful phallus, and the victors often take literal possession of the women of conquered territories by raping them. The more narcissistic a nation is (that is, the more its collective Eros has been frustrated), the more viciously it will fight. Nazi Germany, which, having been humiliated in World War I and then having endured a severe depression in which social pathology was rampant, frantically slaughtered people in World War II.

In times of war, male dominance is at its zenith; as such, sentiments of masculinism generally emerge. This is not to say that women do not contribute to war or violence, for the existence of male narcissism depends upon female narcissism; each is an outgrowth of the other, and each is transmitted to children. A cursory review of "great quotations" (Seldes 1960) by men about war reveals the following masculinist statements:

"War is to man what maternity is to women," said Benito Mussolini. "From a philosophical and doctrinal viewpoint, I do not believe in perpetual peace." Also by Mussolini: "War alone brings up to its highest tension all human energy, and puts the stamp of nobility upon the peoples who have the courage to meet it."

Georgi Zhukov describes war in a purely abstract, unfeeling way, calling it "a science, a series of mathematical problems, to be solved through proper integration and coordination of men and weapons in time and space."

"Eternal peace is a dream," according to Helmuth von Moltke, "and not even a beautiful one, and war is a part of God's world order. In it are developed the noblest of virtues of man, courage and abnegation, dutifulness and self-sacrifice at the risk of life. Without war the world would sink into materialism."

And, finally, William McKinley justifies war in a typical manner. "You understand," he told his ambassadors, "when we go to war it will be for humanity's sake." Narcissists, male and female, always justify their cruelty behind the highest ideals.

While war represents a pathological attempt by men to raise their masculine self-esteem, athletics are a healthy effort to achieve the same goal. A television commentator once jokingly suggested that international conflicts should be settled through athletic competition. Because of their innate aggressiveness, stemming from male hormones, and also because of their need to compensate for their womb envy, men have a need to assert their masculinity and their identity as humans through heroic achievements. Simply watching athletics

helps to build masculine self-esteem: Spectators identify with participants and vicariously enjoy their victories. In addition, by rooting for
their team and against the opposition, they release aggression. Indirectly, athletics may indeed help to mitigate war.

In the past, wars were fought directly over women, as in the case
of Helen of Troy, who became the object of dispute in the Trojan War.
The oedipal symbols here are obvious, and masculinism is all the more
evident, whether it is manifested in the degradation of a woman, or in
her extolment (another way of compensating for the fear of Woman).

Ethologists have long debated the issue of whether war and
violence are innate drives in man or are brought about by the
environment. Humans, like other animals, have an innate aggressive
drive to assert dominance and defend territory. To some extent, wars
and acts of violence are a natural process, a striving for dominance and
an effort at establishing a "pecking order" among individuals and
nations.

Two ethologists, Ashley Montagu (1976) and Irenäus Eibl-
Eibesfeldt (1970), contend that, for the most part, the pathological
aggression of wars and violence stem from nurture. Among all verte-
brates who fight over dominance, only humans habitually kill other
members of their own species. Therefore, Montagu asserts that man's
violence is determined "not by his genes, although of course there is
some genetic contribution, but largely by the experience he has
undergone during his life in interaction with those genes" (p. 7). The
development of narcissistic rage causes man's innate aggression to
become a force of cruelty and violence. As previously noted, he cites
anthropological studies demonstrating that where aggressive behavior
is strongly discouraged—as among the Hutterites and the Amish, and
the Hopi and Zuni Indians—it is practically unknown. Malinowski
(1927) and Mead (1949) have described primitive cultures in which
children are allowed more sexual freedom than in American society.
The Trobriand Islanders, Malinowski observed, encouraged their
children to play genitally with one another and to practice free love
until such time as they themselves decided to have children. The
needs of Eros being amply gratified by both the children and the
adults of this tribe, they were a peaceful people. Neither masculinism
nor feminism, in any form, was in evidence.

War is not universal. As Montagu affirms, it is largely the result of one's experience. A culture that produces male and female narcissism will produce masculinism and war.

THE FEMINIST PHENOMENON

Waves of feminism have occurred throughout history. Feminism was evident during the waning years of both the Greek and the Roman empires (causing some to interpret that the rise of women's power corresponds to a decline in social cohesion). Traces of feminism were seen in various historical events, such as the Salem witchcraft trials. It became a formal doctrine during the Victorian era, perhaps as a by-product of the Protestant revolt against the autocracy of the Catholic Church that had begun in the previous century but had reached an apex during the Victorian period. It recently emerged again in America and Europe as an organized mass movement, as an outgrowth of the protest against America's involvement in the war in Vietnam, and as a by-product of the so-called sexual revolution. Betty Friedan's *The Feminine Mystique* (1963) sounded the keynote, launching a verbal attack on a society which she saw as dominated by men and by masculine values that assigned women to "inferior" roles such as housewife and mother. There followed a deluge of other books, articles, television programs, movies, and plays propagating the feminist position, which produced the feminist cultural revolution of the 1970s and 1980s.

The first stage of this revolution was a verbal assault on men and on the male establishment. Women banded together in "consciousness-raising groups" from which men were barred, and where women aired their many grievances about men and formulated strategies for dealing with "male oppression." A collection of writings from those early days of the movement (Tanner 1971) provides samples of feminist rage:

"We identify the agents of our oppression as men," stated the "Redstockings Manifesto," a feminist flyer handed out on May Day. "They have used their power to keep women in an inferior position . . . All men have oppressed women" (p. 109).

"Let it all hang out," Robin Morgan exhorted her "sisters." "Let it seem bitchy, catty, dykey, frustrated, crazy . . . nutty, frigid, ridiculous, low-down, stupid, petty, liberating. WE ARE THE WOMEN THAT MEN HAVE WARNED US ABOUT" (p. 271).

Anne Koedt depreciated heterosexual love as an aspect of male oppression and proclaimed that "It is the clitoris which is the center of sexual sensitivity and which is the female equivalent of the penis" (p. 158).

"I control my own body," Dana Densmore asserted, "and I don't need any insolent male with an overbearing presumptuous prick to clean out my pipes" (p. 266).

Detectable in these writings are the underpinnings of sexual animosity and female narcissism. The portrayal of men as oppressors is a way of destroying men through character assassination in order to justify women's animosity toward men. Statements such as "I don't need any insolent male with an overbearing presumptuous prick" and "It is the clitoris which is the center of sexual sensitivity and which is the female equivalent of the penis" harken to fixations in the anal-rapprochement stage and to unresolved castration complexes. In general, these statements reveal an aversion to the male and a desire to merge with other women (sisters) in a homosexual alliance (symbolic merger with the mother) against men (the father).

The first phase of the feminist cultural revolution, which served to intimidate opponents with its intensity and hysteria, was followed by a second stage, during which a subtle political transformation occurred. At the core of this stage was a kind of cultural revisionism and censorship, not unlike those that had accompanied previous cultural revolutions. For example, the late 1940s and early 1950s saw a right-wing cultural revolution, during which "McCarthyism," with its emphasis on patriotism and hatred of communism, became the prevailing value system. Books and papers propagated the new McCarthy "line," and a hearing was held to purge from the government all Communists and Communist party sumpathizers. If an individual even looked like a Communist, he might be fired, censored, snubbed by friends, and stripped of his basic rights as a citizen. Similarly, in the second stage of the feminist revolution, feminist values—with their emphasis on women's emancipation from "male oppression"—replaced earlier values. A new form of revisionism and censorship took hold in which "sexists" and "sexism" became the new scapegoats for women's (and society's) pent-up aggression. An individual who became known as a sexist might have his writing censored, might be denied promotion at his job or tenure at a university, and in general might find himself snubbed, ostracized, and stigmatized by colleagues and friends.

The feminist movement had a topcurrent and an undercurrent; that is, it had a conscious and an unconscious component. Consciously, feminists were fighting a cause for humanitarian aims centered on male–female equality and women's rights. Their unconscious aim was to control or destroy the enemy: men. McCarthy's scapegoating of Communists served as a vehicle for the acting out of collective rage; in the feminist revolution, scapegoating men served the same purpose. Men were blamed for everything from women's depression to their weight and addiction problems; castigated as rapists, molesters, and murderers; accused of being too aggressive and too passive; and portrayed as witting or unwitting participants in a sexist society. Feminist writings narcissistically glorified femininity with a universal theme of "women can do it better than men." Feminism thus provided an organized vehicle for the acting out of separation anxiety, phallic remorse, and penis envy in the social arena.

Bayley's (1986) review of the diaries of the writer Leo Tolstoy and of his wife, Sophia, which appeared in *The New York Times Book Review*, typifies the kind of feminist censorship that prevailed. In it Bayley implies that Tolstoy's many accomplishments were tainted by his male chauvinism. He writes: "Asked in later life about the problem of sexual equality, he [Tolstoy] replied that women were superior to men in so many ways that they had no need to compete with them. That, of course, is the oldest trick in the male chauvinist book, and it shows too that he, who came of a long line of diplomats, had a streak of natural cunning in him" (p. 14). Nearly all the male writers reviewed in the *Times Book Review* received a similar treatment: Their writing was always judged according to how they stood toward women or toward feminism.

Women were also censored if they went astray. In another issue of the same publication, Greenhouse (1986) reviewed a book by two women authors who followed the lives of the women who graduated from Harvard Law School in 1974. Greenhouse chides them for coming to "muddled" conclusions as to why most of these women fell short or dropped out of the partnership race in the world of corporate law. "This is too important a point to be left so muddled," she says, "especially given the provocative research now being published by scholars like Carol Gilligan on the different ways women and men view the world" (p. 12). The authors had not come to the "correct" conclusions—those that would reflect the feminist line.

We can discern how feminists used the crusade for women's rights as a means of acting out animosity toward men, as well as toward women who were seen as loyal to men. The movement's campaign of censoring and ridiculing authors allowed it not only to act out narcissistic rage, but also to manipulate American social values. During the McCarthy era, everything published was judged on the basis of its patriotism and anticommunism; during the feminist era, everything was judged according to its allegiance to feminism and its opposition to "sexism." The message of the two reviews just cited was that those who did not adhere to the feminist line were "bad" and would be publicly embarrassed. Many writings that were critical of feminism never reached print at all, and many formerly published writers found themselves unofficially blacklisted. This campaign of censorship also extended to other media—movies, television, and art. Such a campaign of censorship has an intimidating effect on society, inhibiting free expression.

THE ATTACK ON FREUD

The feminist perspective eventually began to influence psychoanalysis, as feminist revisionism and censorship crept into analytic theory. The most notable features were an attack on Freud—the man and the analyst—and on his theories of female development and sexuality. Feminists tried to dismiss Freud and his writings as antiquated Victorian, and sexist.

Kanefield's (1985) previously cited article debunked Freud's writings on female masochism and penis envy, asserting that "Freud's view of women as castrated men, reconciled to inferiority due to their biological lack, is misogynous." She went on to criticize what she saw as Freud's presumption that "women are lesser because they are different from men," calling it "deeply sexist and unfounded." Nowhere is there any proof in this or any other article by a feminist critic that sufficiently demonstrates that Freud actually believed that women were inferior because of their difference from men. Nor have I read anything written by Freud showing that he viewed women as "castrated men, reconciled to inferiority due to their biological lack." These are exaggerations of Freud's observations, which result from Freud's provocative language and from his readers' narcissism. Indeed, feminists' distortions of Freud's writings led Clower (1979) to comment that she could not always judge the accuracy of feminist references and that they revealed "an incomplete grasp of the original theories and an almost total ignorance and disinterest in what psychoanalysts are thinking and saying today" (p. 310). Freud did not feel that women were innately inferior due to the lack of a penis; he pointed out that only *some* women feel that way—narcissistic women who feel inferior about being women because they are fixated at a pregenital phase of development.

In the *Psychoanalytic Review*, Chasseguet-Smirgel (Honey and Broughton, 1985), interviewed on female sexuality, was asked about Freud's view of women. She differed with those who label his view as Victorian, suggesting instead that his works on female psychology were influenced by his having cancer. "I believe that he introduced this particular theory of the instincts [Eros and Thanatos] because of his cancer and that his theory about female sexuality is connected to his cancer and his concern about his own death." Asked by the interviewer to elaborate on this idea, she explained that Freud viewed female sexuality as something mysterious, something terrible, an enigma. "This could also be seen as a disguise, a reaction-formation against his fear of femaleness as something that is linked with death, for all of us" (pp. 534–535). This is one of the more subtle forms of character assassination. Freud was not described as sexist, but rather as diseased. His cancer brought out his fear of the female, and of the feminine part of himself, which in turn caused him to misinterpret female psychology: In order to stave off his cancer, he needed to denigrate women.

Another recent attack on Freud, spearheaded by Masson (1984), centered on Freud's abandonment of the seduction theory. The attack attempted to prove that sexual molestation by fathers lay at the root of female hysteria. Masson contended that Freud abandoned the seduction theory in order to protect fathers and himself (as a father) from blame, as well as to gain acceptance in the male-dominated scientific community of Victorian Europe. Freud never seemed to back away from a controversial theory at any other period in his life, however, and it is difficult to believe that he did so with the seduction theory. He came to believe that his patients had fantasized these seductions, based on his understanding of the hysterical process, in which denial and reversal loom large as defense mechanisms. Indeed, hysteria *is* associated with how a father handles his daughter's infantile erotic advances during the oedipal stage, and in some cases fathers *do* sexually molest their daughters; but not *all* fathers of hysterics are molesters, and mothers also contribute to a daughter's development of hysterical symptoms. At any rate, the percentage of fathers who molest their daughters is not nearly as high as Masson leads us to believe. In effect, he took a complex theory and simplified it in order to join the bandwagon of anti-Freudians. Once again feminists used this as proof of Freud's chauvinism and of the culpability of fathers and men.

The American Psychology Association *Monitor* (Turkington 1986) reported on another attack on Freud, this one less direct. Citing Freud's theories about primary female masochism, which they contended was sexist, a group of two hundred feminists, calling themselves The Feminist Therapy Institute, took exception to a new diagnostic category, "masochistic personality disorder." The diagnosis had been proposed by the American Psychiatric Association, which was in the process of revising the *DSM-III*. The feminists complained that this new category reflected Freud's Victorian notions of female development and was unfair to women. They lobbied against it for some time, finally succeeding in persuading the American Psychiatric Association to change the category to "self-defeating personality disorder." But this category also was not entirely satisfactory to them; they still insisted it was biased against women.

Another indirect attack on Freud and an excellent example of feminist censorship was contained in "Female Psychotherapists as Portrayed in Film, Fiction, and Nonfiction," by Samuels (1985). Samuels is concerned with how female therapists are portrayed by writers and directors. Tracing male bias toward female therapists back to Freud, she "studied" eighty-three titles offering depictions of female therapists. The author concludes that "with exceptions so rare as to be noteworthy, portrayals of female therapists are sexist, unprofessional, unethical, and unbelievable" (p. 367). Here the underlying aim was to restrict how women were written about or portrayed.

Not only Freud's theories on female psychology, but also his views on male psychology were attacked. A special issue of *Psychoan-alytic Review*, edited by Friedman and Lerner (1986), offered revised psychoanalytic concepts of masculine development. A preface by Lerner stated, "In the last twenty-five years the advent of feminism and the reworking of the psychoanalytic psychology of women have overshadowed a parallel development in the reassessment of the psychology of men" (p. v). There followed articles offering the sugges-tion that castration fear, like penis envy, be considered a metaphor, and presenting a new interpretation of homosexual development that dismissed Freud's concept and replaced it with a genetic model. A symposium of five papers, all written by women, described how womens' relationships with men have changed as a result of the feminist movement. In essence this issue was a work of feminist revisionism.

Why did the feminists attack Freud and his theories so vehe-mently? Although some aspects of his theories contain traces of male narcissism, his work as a whole is sound and he was just as unequiv-ocal in his analyses of male development as of female development; in addition, he was manifestly moral and progressive. Feminists attacked him because he was the father figure extraordinaire, the "Moses" of his day; hence he aroused their unresolved hatred of their own fathers; that is, he aroused a mass negative transference. In addition, his theories poked at their "sore spots"—their envy of the penis and of men, and their feelings of inferiority. In a sense, the very vehemence of their attack on the concepts of penis envy and the masculinity complex validates those concepts. In analysis, it is generally the case that the more a patient protests a particular interpretation, the more likely that the interpretation is valid. An old proverb puts it another way: The truth hurts.

Freud (1925) himself counseled against abandoning concepts about female psychological development that ruffle female feathers. "We must not allow ourselves to be deflected from such conclusions about the anatomical distinctions between the sexes and their psycho-logical outcomes by the denials of feminists," he asserts (p. 260), pointing to the feminist drive to force society to regard the two sexes as equal in every respect, despite anatomical differences which render such equality impossible. This is a reiteration of Freud's often-stated theme of not allowing the protests of the public to deter him from his search for the truth. Mead (1949) also warned against the "contemporary attempt to deny many of the differences that have been accepted historically" (p. 30). Unfortunately, during this second phase of the feminist cultural revolution, Freud's voice (and all other critical voices) were drowned out. Few dared to defend him.

As the attacks on Freud and on men continued, many analysts began to accept and then adopt the feminist perspective. Under the new feminist value system, women were innocent and men were guilty (a reversal of the Adam and Eve myth). Women's misery resulted from male oppression, from the imposition of corrupt male values on women (Gilligan 1982); hence, women generally were accorded more sympathy than men. Women's misery was men's fault, while men's misery was their own fault. I have noted elsewhere (Robertiello and Schoenewolf 1987) how cultural counterresistances—therapeutic biases—often get in the way of analytic neutrality, as happens when, for example, therapists unconsciously apply feminist values when working with patients of either sex.

By the time the third phase of the feminist cultural revolution set in during the 1980s, feminist values had pervaded not only psychoanalysis but also all other aspects of Western culture, from movies to television and newspapers to the scientific community. Feminists had succeeded in convincing many that feminist doctrine was a kind of morally unassailable gospel. They had also influenced the courts and the political machinery. A report on *60 Minutes* by Morley Safer (1987) described how a feminist-black coalition had taken charge of a public school system in England, with sweeping changes. These changes included the censorship of certain books, in an attempt to rid the system of sexism and racism; among the books banned were *Snow White and the Seven Dwarfs* and *Huckleberry Finn*. At the same time, included in the revised curriculum and required of all students, were courses in Marxism, women's studies, and black studies. The parents in this school system eventually began to take their children out of the schools and then staged a public demonstration, which was countered by a rally of gays and lesbians who supported the schools.

MASCULINISM AND FEMINISM IN CONFLICT

Baker (1967) notes that conservatives have their religions and liberals their ideologies. Both can become dogmas from which spring fanaticism and fascism. Conservatives tend to defend the topdog (that is, the government), to be blind to the faults of the establishment or of fellow conservatives, and to be acutely aware of the faults of liberals. Liberals tend to defend the underdog (that is, the "rebel"), to be blind to the faults of their fellow liberals, and to be acutely aware of the faults of conservatives. Baker suggests that, psychodynamically, the conservative is defending father and the liberal is siding with mother. Feminism and masculinism may be seen as outgrowths of liberalism and conservatism, representing the polarity of discord between men and women as well as the polarity that causes societies to disintegrate. Like an individual in whom id and superego are at odds, a society in which liberalism and conservatism are in conflict, and which does not have a strong center (ego), will not flourish.

Masculinism and feminism cannot resolve social problems. Both actually worsen them. Masculinists who castigate women as "witches" or "evil seductresses" who need to be suppressed are encouraging the very behavior they attack by laying the groundwork for defiance. Feminists who denounce men as rapists, child molesters, and oppressors are fanning the flames of discontent. By villainizing and dehumanizing those whom we see as a threat, we re-create the kind of treatment often accorded young children, who are treated as though they are "naughty" and less than human. Masculinists unconsciously want women to behave badly so that they can feel morally superior, and feminists want men to molest women in order to prove their view of men. And the cycle persists.

As noted earlier, Kardiner (1954) associates social problems with the rise of female aggression and male passivity. He believes that in times of social unrest, there is always an increase in neurosis, crime, and homosexuality. He cites as an example an Asian culture in which there was an abrupt change from one form of rice cultivation to another: In the old way, needs were satisfied because the entire community cultivated and distributed food; in the new way, everyone was responsible for his own subsistence. As a result, neurosis, crime, and homosexuality increased markedly. Kardiner suggests that during times of social unrest, male homosexuality represents a self-preservative device—a flight from masculinity and from the responsibility of masculinity—while female homosexuality represents a similar self-preservative device—a flight from femininity and from the responsibility of surrender to a weakened male.

He alludes to observations made by ethologists and others on primates. When male monkeys fight over food or over female monkeys, the defeated one indicates defeat by assuming the female sexual posture. "The remarkable feature of this behavior is that the passive sexual attitude of the defeated monkey halts the assault of the stronger one," Kardiner notes. "The feminine posture is a self-preservative device when aggression fails" (pp. 172–173). He interprets that the homosexual response to societal tension represents a similar preservative device. In the family milieu, it can be a reaction to a castrating mother, a terrifying father, or some other parenting combination that threatens a boy's masculinity. (The family itself may be responding to a larger social tension.) The boy reacts by taking the passive sexual attitude of the female, inviting the father, or father surrogate, to take him anally. (Or, if he plays the male role in the homosexual dyad, he plays the part of the father.)

This self-preservative device is also seen in females; the overpowering fear of the mother can compel the girl to abandon her heterosexual objectives and become homosexual. The fear of the male genital becomes the justification for the flight to the reassuring love of the mother. Here again, sexuality becomes inverted in the interest of self-preservation. "The female believes that she is running from the dangerous male to the protecting female, and the male organ has become the menace. The real danger was originally the mother; the abandonment of the father was only a way of settling the rivalry with the mother in order to be guaranteed her protection" (p. 174). Thus male homosexuality is viewed as a flight from mother and female homosexuality as a flight from father.

The rise in homosexuality (or narcissism in general) results in increasing masculinization of women and feminization of men. Women, disowning their femininity, become increasingly competitive with men and adopt an increasingly aggressive posture. Men, particularly those who are more vulnerable, retreat from masculinity and become increasingly passive. Both male and female homosexuals have underlying low self-esteem, and an "impoverishment of resources" which, according to Kardiner, causes them either to shrink from competition (if they are male) or to want to destroy the competition (if they are female). In a society of male and female homosexuals, the males will shrink from competition while the females will compete in order to psychologically castrate males. In either case, sexual separatism and animosity will prevail. Feminism, as an outgrowth of female narcissism and homosexuality, tends to rationalize this masculinization of women and feminization of men under the rubric of egalitarianism and liberation. However, the long-term result of this trend is the separation of the sexes and the extinction of humankind, for homosexuals do not tend to propagate the species. In addition, the imbalance of the sexes also leads to increasing sexual animosity, which translates to increasing collective rage.

It was humankind's narcissism which resisted the knowledge that the world was round, that humans were descended from apes, and that humans' motives were largely unconscious. Similarly, homosexuals (who represent the two poles of male and female narcissism) resist the knowledge that their sexual behavior is a deviation from the norm, and that such behavior on a wide scale may threaten the future of society. For homosexuality is more than an act between consenting adults. It is a long-term social movement which is destructive to male-female relations, the family, and child-rearing, since homosexuals are invariably carriers of sexual animosity and have problems with cross-sexual relationships.

Neither male nor female oppression are responsible for human misery—as masculinists and feminists would claim. Rather, misery would seem to be the result of humankind's increasing narcissism. It is narcissism that underlies nearly all social ills, from drug addiction to mental illness and criminality, and that as Spitz (1965) points out, spells the "rapid deterioration of those conditions which are indispensable for the normal development of our earliest object relations" (p. 299). It is arguable whether this increase in narcissism is related to a decline in our society's status in the world, to the loss of a war, or to a general increase in international tension and the cumulative threat to our existence by nuclear war and environmental pollution. Narcissism itself is an undeniable fact, however, and its rise has been attested to by clinicians around the world.

Neither masculinism and its aspect of misogyny nor feminism and its undertow of hysteria is a viable form of liberation. Liberation is related to mastery of the self, not of others. What sexual narcissists call liberation is actually a kind of narcissistic-sadomasochistic ritual— one that has recurred throughout history when one group wrests political or moral control from another, with the grandiose notion that its vision was superior to that of its predecessors. Political liberation, according to Lao Tzu, is a false liberation, dependent upon the illusion of right and the forcing of that illusion on others. Spiritual liberation—the only kind of liberation that can resolve individual and social conflicts—requires self-understanding of a type advocated by psychoanalysts and by sages from ancient times to the present. Liberation means the resolution of psychic conflicts that stand in the way of gratifying the needs of Eros. It entails neutralizing one's animosity and learning to live in harmony with oneself and others. It requires us to relinquish the notion that we are right and "the enemy" is wrong, for when one looks at life from an objective analytic perspective, there is no right or wrong. There are simply many variations of life, some adaptive, others not, all being a matter of luck. A Chinese proverb says, "To search for right and wrong is a sickness of the mind."

"Religious ideas are illusions," Freud said (1927b, p. 25), and this goes for the religious and ideological ideas of masculinism and feminism. They are illusions designed to serve the needs of narcissistic grandiosity and rage. Societal health comes from a collective ego that is strong enough to mediate between the forces of left and right, collective id and collective superego, male and female narcissism, and masculinism and feminism.

6

Sexual Animosity in Family Life

THE FAMILY AS A MICROCOSM OF
SEXUAL CONFLICT

A story appeared in the July 10, 1987, issue of *New York Newsday* describing the fatal beating of a child. Police reported that a 28-year-old woman and her 17-year-old boyfriend, living on welfare in a room at the Saratoga Inn in Queens, New York, became annoyed by their 3-year-old daughter, who they said was "crying and fussing." At 2:00 A.M., the girl's mother got out of bed and, using a medicine bottle as a weapon, struck the child on the head and body about ten times until the child quieted down. At about 4:00 A.M., the child awoke again. This time the boyfriend took the child to the bathroom and scolded her, then dragged her outside to a hallway, where he repeatedly punched her in the head and body. The child struck her head on the wall, police said, and began to have trouble standing up. The boyfriend carried the child to the bed she shared with her 7-year-old sister, opened a window, and threw water on her face in an attempt to revive her. At 6:30 A.M., the child's mother tried again to revive her but discovered that she was stiff and cold. She dialed the police emergency number. Upon arrival, the police pronounced the girl dead.

This incident is an example of animosity in family life. Although the story does not clarify what was going on between the man and woman at the time, it seems obvious that they were frustrated by, among other factors, their familial responsibility, and that they vented that frustration on their youngest child. Instead of nurturing the child and trying to find out what was bothering her, they apparently wanted to defeat her.

Adler (1927b) notes that when men and women feel inferior—as all narcissists do—they need to conquer each other (and their children) rather than relate in a way that facilitates closeness. Thus the family lives of male and female narcissists, if they have family lives at all, are full of tension. Neither the male nor the female narcissist ever entirely lets down his or her guard in a relationship, for each distrusts the other. Some couples manage the appearance of harmony because they have reached a détente in which the conflicts between them are denied or ignored. Other couples, such as the one just described, broadcast their problems to the world.

The driving forces of family animosity are frustrated Eros and the aggression (Thanatos) associated with that frustration, the aim of which is to control or destroy. Because these relationships cannot satisfy the libidinal needs of the partners—that is, because they do not, and in fact cannot, form a strong, nurturing bond of trust and love—they attempt to obtain the needed supplies through defensive maneuvers, each experiencing the other as frustrating and threatening. When defensive maneuvers do not succeed in controlling the object and gaining some kind of secondary gratification—such as extracting a response of obedience, guilt, or anger from the partner—then psychological or physical destruction, either for the self or for the other, becomes the goal.

Children are often the pawns in this family battle. Who will control their minds and hearts? Who will exert the most influence on their lives? Who will gain their allegiance and thereby "win"? Children also are often cast as judges and juries, their "votes" deciding who is right and who is wrong. To have to continually choose one parent over another only serves to exacerbate the child's fixations and complexes, particularly the Oedipus complex. Children sometimes become scapegoats for one or both parents, as in the news story just paraphrased. Inevitably they are the big losers, for their needs are neglected by parents caught in the throes of their defensive maneuvers.

Male and female narcissists have different ways of fighting, based on the differences in their genetics and in their psychological constitutions. Jung (1926) speculates that men tend toward thinking and sensation and repress feeling and intuition, while women tend toward intuition and feeling while repressing thinking and sensation. Male and female narcissists, because of their animosity, cannot satisfactorily incorporate their own masculine and feminine components. In other words, their left-and right-brain functions are not synchronized. They are one-sided creatures.

Balint (1948), writing about the concept of genitality, describes pathological male–female relationships according to psychosexual stage fixations. He infers that pathological relationships contain (1) oral features, such as greediness, insatiability, and the wish to devour the object and deny it independent existence; (2) sadistic features, such as the wish to hurt, humiliate, boss, and dominate the object; (3) anal traits, such as the wish to defile the object, or the tendency to despise the partner for his or her sexual desires or pleasures, or the habit of being disgusted by the object or of being attracted only by some unpleasant features; and (4) traces of the phallic phase or the castration complex, including a compulsion to boast about the possession of a penis, to fear the partner's sexual organs, to fear for one's own sexual organs, to envy the male or female genitalia, or to feel incomplete or faulty with regard to genitalia. His schema falls along essentially the same lines as I have outlined for narcissistic relationships.

Ambivalence seems to be a primary feature of all narcissistic relationships, and its denial, according to Dicks (1967), is the source of continued discord. The tendency to deny hate and anger and to project it onto the partner, or, alternatively, to exalt the partner as all good while taking on the guilt and badness, precludes either partner's relating in a gratifying way. "The less secure the relationship, the more does it have to rely on various defensive devices—e.g., the absence of aggression, or even sexuality from it!" (p. 43). By absence of aggression,

Dicks means *direct* aggression, the expression of which might lead to a resolution. Narcissistic couples seldom express their anger or hatred in a direct, constructive manner. Instead it is acted out in ways that serve to keep the flame of discord burning and to allow the partners to remain unconscious of their aggressive behavior. Unless we are conscious of our aggression, we cannot do anything about it.

NARCISSISTIC PARENTS AND THEIR CHILDREN

Miller (1981, 1983, 1984) describes how narcissistic parents are unable to relate to their children in a genuine way, causing the children to develop "false" selves in order to accommodate their parents. Some parents mold their children into narcissistic extensions of themselves; parents who urge their children to enter professions to achieve goals that they themselves were frustrated in achieving are a typical example ("My children are going to have everything I didn't have!"). These parents choose the child's path instead of allowing the child to choose. Other parents sexually or physically abuse their children, venting their narcissistic conflicts, sexual frustrations, or rage on them. Miller explains that "poisonous pedagogy"—value systems passed down from generation to generation—often provides a justification for such practices; for example, the saying "Spare the rod and spoil the child" long justified physical cruelty to children.

Freud (1921) and Laing (1971) point out that what we refer to as child rearing is actually a form of hypnotic induction. Each generation of parents rears its children to rear its children as the previous generation did. As Laing puts it, "the hypnotists (the parents) are already hypnotized (by their parents) and are carrying out their instructions, by bringing their children up to bring their children up . . . in such a way, which includes not realizing that one is carrying out instructions" (p. 71). Laing explains that this state is easily induced under hypnosis, when an individual is instructed, for example, to walk across the room and open the window upon waking from the trance. The hypnotist might also instruct the individual to remember nothing about the instructions but to think of a good reason for opening the window. The individual wakes up, opens the window, and exclaims "It's warm in here." A parent may induce a particular form of behavior by suggestion, such as by telling a child again and again that he is bad or that she will end up an old maid. The child grows up feeling that he is bad and acting that way, or becomes an old maid, and yet does not remember the suggestions; instead, he thinks of a reason that he is bad, and she rationalizes being single.

Adults hold power over children that is unmatched by any relationship that occurs in adult life, except for slavery. Miller observes that children have no rights and little power; hence their word, when in conflict with the word of an adult, is usually disregarded. The child is said to have a vivid imagination. This makes it easy for parents to act out with impunity their animosity toward children. The story of a patient with whom I worked illustrates this point.

Suffering from symptoms induced by childhood sexual abuse by her mother and physical abuse by her father and siblings, she related how she ran away from home when she was 8 years old, seeking refuge in a nearby church. She told the nuns in charge what had happened and described a recurrent dream in which a train ran over her mother. The nuns responded by chastizing her for having such a "naughty" dream and for disrespecting her parents. They took her home, against the little girl's pleas and cries that she would be harmed, and reported to her parents what she had told them. The parents accused the child of making up stories, and the nuns left feeling they had acted appropriately. The parents then beat the child and berated her for "betraying the family." This was, indeed, hypnotic induction. The girl grew up feeling like the family traitor; this suggestion had not only been implanted in her psyche by her parents, but had also been reinforced by the nuns' response. The patient did not remember this incident until it came up in the course of treatment.

Parents often act out the same defensive maneuvers with their children as they do with their spouses. A phallic narcissistic father will sexually tease and abandon his oedipal daughter, and a hysterical narcissist will tease and abandon her oedipal son. An anal narcissist will sadistically dominate or masochistically submit to the child, and an oral narcissist will infantilize or "cling" to the child. In these interactions, sexual animosity is unconsciously transmitted as the child's needs are frustrated and he is given no opportunity to redress this frustration or to vent rage—that is, to control or destroy the frustrating object. The rage is repressed, along with the memories associated with it. When the child becomes an adult, he passes this rage along to a new family.

Spitz (1965) relates the disintegration of the family in Western society to the progressive decay of healthy values, which in turn leads to a deterioration of the mother–child relation. "From a societal aspect," he writes, "disturbed object relations in the first year of life, be they deviant, improper, or insufficient, have consequences which imperil the very foundation of society" (p. 300). He speaks of the victims of disturbed object relations who lack the capacity to relate, who are not equipped for the advanced and complex forms of personal and social interchange without which the human species cannot survive. Although he refers to these people as "emotional cripples," it is clear that he is talking about narcissism when he says, "Even their capacity for transference is impaired, so that they are handicapped in profiting from therapy." He later adds, "Infants without love, they will end as adults full of hate" (p. 300).

Dicks (1967) writes about marital partners who have not adequately separated from their parents. He describes a wife with a hysterical dread of consummation and a "nice" young husband, both in their early 20s. The father of the wife was a stern, possessive man who picked a husband for his daughter who would not threaten the bond between the daughter and himself. The wife's condition for being aroused was male mastery, linked to her oedipal incest taboo. "Exciting libidinal objects were split off—rough boys furtively met or symbolized as gangsters, whereas the father's nominee conformed to the unexciting anti-libidinal object" (p. 153). Thus the lack of separation from parents causes a barrier between mates, since the partners are still so bonded to their parents (replete with the ambivalence of these relationships) that they cannot love each other.

Dicks also observes that bad relationships often contain dominance–submission conflicts and a competitiveness that centers around the children. He speaks of a marriage in which the woman identifies the children with herself, overvaluing and possessing them as "bearers of her frustrated hopes and aspirations" (p. 146), and also exacting from them loyal affection and respect for her long-suffering martyrdom. In competition, the husband frequently retaliates with even more impressive symptoms of breakdown in his health, by which he threatens the very economic subsistence of the family, as a manifestation of passive aggression. "Power needs can be expressed also in competition as to which is the sickest!" Dicks remarks. Indeed, the sexual war can take a myriad of forms.

Winnicott (1965) notes how depression, in which sexual animosity is acted out by withdrawing from other objects and withholding libido, leaves a parent with impoverished affect for relating to the children. In particular, it can be severely disturbing to an infant, who needs his mother to be preoccupied with his care, to find suddenly that the mother is preoccupied with something else. He cites the case of Tony, a 7-year-old boy who was obsessed with string (string being symbolic of joining things together). He was "on the point of turning into a pervert with dangerous skills and he had already played at strangling his sister" (p. 75). The obsession was relieved when the mother talked to Tony, on Winnicott's advice, about his feeling of losing her. This feeling had resulted from several early separations. The worst was the mother's depression when Tony was 2, the age at which the boy first discovers his sexuality. An acute phase in his mother's depressive illness cut her off from him, and any return of her depression in later years tended to renew Tony's obsession with string.

Vogel and Bell (1981) have written of the emotionally disturbed child as the family scapegoat. The scapegoat is often a child who reminds parents of a figure from the past; alternatively, the scapegoated child can be particularly gifted, particularly stupid, or handicapped. Such families are invariably at odds with their neighbors, their extended families, and the communities in which they live: They feel scapegoated by their environment, and they in turn scapegoat each other and their children. The most severely disturbed children are often the victims of this kind of scapegoating; everything that is disowned by the mother and father (their hatefulness, their social ineptitude, and so on) is projected onto the child, and all forms of punishment and abuse are heaped upon this "bad" child.

THE TRANSMISSION OF ANIMOSITY

Animosity is transmitted to children both through modeling behavior and through the way in which parents treat their children. Male narcissists demonstrate a particular way of relating to women. Since they often, covertly or overtly, view women as inferior, they generally take a cavalier, derogatory attitude toward wives and other women. The male narcissist defends against castration fear by keeping women "in their place," using whatever defense mechanism befits his character. He will be dishonest, subtly or blatantly, and often tends to favor the company of men, as did Henry Higgins in *Pygmalion*, who asked, "Why can't a woman be more like a man?"

Male narcissists treat sons differently than daughters. Because of their masculine grandiosity, they often favor and projectively identify with their sons. At the same time, they displace their repressed anger at their mothers onto their daughters. This displaced anger is not consciously experienced as such; rather, it is experienced as a judgment that the daughter is inferior, and as a feeling of contempt for her. Alternatively, they may reject their sons and favor their daughters, using a reaction formation to defend against animosity toward and fear of the daughter and her femininity, while projecting feelings of masculine inferiority onto the son. In either case, there is an aspect of compulsiveness and dishonesty in these relationships, and a theme of favoritism.

Female narcissists will take an attitude of moral superiority toward their husbands. They often use feminism as a vehicle for keeping men on the defensive. They will talk of equal opportunities for women and point to the inequalities of the system, using these issue to gain the upper hand in their relationships with their husbands and other men. The men in their lives, anxious to prove that they are good, liberal, or nonsexist, will strive to live up to the female narcissist's expectations. Thus, while female narcissists speak of egalitarianism, their actions reveal attempts to control or destroy men. Their manner tends to be contemptuous of men, morally superior, and self-righteous. Like male narcissists, female narcissists often favor the company of their own sex, and they relate to their husbands and to men in a dishonest way, as if they were predators to be appeased or subdued.

Female narcissists often emasculate their sons, bind their daughters to themselves, and intrude upon their children's relationship with their father. They often favor their daughters and make them narcissistic extensions of themselves. In some cases they favor their sons, living out vicariously their desires to be men. The needs of the children are neglected, and the impact of their mother's narcissistic manner of relating to them stunts their development. For example, a favored child will often expect such favoritism as an adult and will feel frustration and self-hatred when it is not forthcoming.

Both male and female narcissists foster sexual separatism and prejudice. The resulting value system brings about discord rather than togetherness between men and women. A marriage that functions according to the dictates of either a male or a female narcissistic mode will be a lopsided marriage. Both will insist that they know best and should have the final say in the raising of the children. When a conflict erupts, each partner will blame the other.

The male and female narcissistic value systems are also conveyed to children in cultural works such as fairy tales, which reinforce the one-sided view of male–female relationships. Male narcissistic tales are personified by witches and cruel queens. Typical is *Hansel and Gretel*, the story of a boy and girl who get lost in the woods and come upon a gingerbread house and a witch, who tries to shove them into her oven and eat them. In this tale, women are portrayed as menacing individuals who are prone to cannibalism (symbolic castration). The fear of Woman is the underpinning of this story, and the oven represents the devouring womb which prevails in the primitive unconscious fantasies of children of both sexes.

Little Red Riding Hood, on the other hand, is a female narcissistic tale. Fromm (1951) has interpreted this story as that of a coming-of-age ritual for adolescent girls. The red riding hood is a symbol of menstruation; the girl has just come of age and is now confronted with the problem of sexuality. The warning not to run off the path is an admonition against the danger of sex and the loss of virginity. Further, the male is portrayed as a ruthless and cunning animal (a wolf) and the sexual act as cannibalistic: The wolf eats the grandmother. The tale is an expression of antagonism against men and sex, Fromm notes. The prejudice against men is even more graphic at the end of the story, when the wolf appears quite ridiculous as he attempts to play the role of a pregnant woman, with living beings in his belly. Little Red Riding Hood puts stones, a symbol of sterility, into his belly, and the wolf collapses and dies. His deed, Fromm concludes, has been punished according to his crime. The death by stones is an ironic turnabout to his attempt to usurp the pregnant woman's role.

Fairy tales and other myths represent symbolic codifications of value systems, as do cartoons and television serials. Such stories become ingrained in the child's unconscious, and the value system is internalized into character structure and mode of operation. This, too, is part of the hypnotic process.

What effect does this induction have on future adults? It reinforces the male–female animosity resulting from their unresolved castration complexes and fosters a simplistic view of life. As adults, such inductees retain a childlike need to categorize phenomena into good and evil, right and wrong, innocence and guilt. Women will tend to develop a self-righteous attitude, perceiving themselves as innocent Little Red Riding Hoods and men as wolves. Men tend to view women as either innocent and righteous or as witches, while viewing themselves as princes in a world of evil. These cultural artifacts also reinforce unconscious feelings of badness and a continued disharmony between the sexes.

Animosity is also transmitted more subtly. The husband and wife who are both career-minded, for example, and who resent spending time with their children, often unwittingly act out animosity by leaving their children with uncaring baby-sitters or in child-care centers. Spitz (1965) asserts that even a parent of dubious competence is better than an institution. Parents who do not take the proper care in selecting a suitable baby-sitter, or who rationalize that they can have careers and still spend the necessary time with their children, are controlled by their narcissism.

The family appears to play a crucial social role. It is the breeding ground of society. Our schools, prisons, psychiatric hospitals, and therapy offices are filled with the casualties of family life. The family is the first and most important institution to impact on the development of character and it can induce profound changes in individuals and in society. Sexual animosity can be its undoing.

7

The Harmonic Couple

GENITALITY

The harmonic couple is, perhaps first and foremost, a genital couple. The term *genitality* has been variously defined, probably because, as Fenichel (1945) notes, the concept of the genital character is an ideal. No one gets through the developmental stages without fixations. To the degree that individuals are able to achieve genital primacy, they can be said to be healthy and uninhibited by oral, anal, or oedipal character traits.

Genital primacy, according to Fenichel, implies the capacity to meet and enjoy sexual needs. Frustration is therefore minimal, and dependence on pregenital defense mechanisms is minimized. Genital primacy, further, makes for the full development of love and the overcoming of ambivalence. The capacity of genitals to discharge excitement means that such individuals will have little pent-up rage and that they will not need to deny aggression or use reaction formation and other pregenital defense mechanisms; instead, they can sublimate. They do not ward off feelings, but use them constructively to understand and master the external environment.

Reich (1942, 1945) stressed genital potency both as an indication of emotional health and as the sole requirement for health. He writes:

> Psychic health depends upon orgastic potency, i.e., upon the degree to which one can surrender to and experience the climax of excitation in the natural sexual act. It is founded upon the healthy character attitude of the individual's capacity for love. Psychic illnesses are the result of a disturbance of the natural ability to love. In the case of orgastic impotence, from which the over-whelming majority of people suffer, damming-up of biological energy occurs and becomes the source of irrational actions. The essential requirement to cure psychic disturbances is the re-establishment of the natural capacity for love. [1942, p. 4]

Although most analysts would agree with Reich's general thesis, some might quibble with his emphasis on orgastic potency as the *sine qua non* of psychic health. There are individuals who are able to have "genital" orgasms but whose relationships are marred by low self-esteem and infantile dependency needs, and who would therefore not be described as genital characters. Healthy sexual functioning is an important aspect of genitality, however. Indeed it is, as Reich implies, the ultimate expression of love. To the extent that a man and woman can surrender to their sexual feelings (regress in the service of the ego), their emotional and physical health will improve. Along with surrendering to their sexual feelings, they must also surrender to their emotional feelings of love and need for another human. Perhaps this is what Reich meant by "the re-establishment of the natural capacity to love."

Abraham (1925) notes that the genital character achieves a steady conquest of his narcissism. "Observation has taught us," he explains, "that no developmental stage, each of which has an organic basis of its own, is ever entirely surmounted or completely obliterated." Each new product of development possesses characteristics derived from its earlier history, including the primitive signs of self-love. Nevertheless, even though the primitive signs of self-love are to some extent preserved in the genital character, "we may say that the definitive stage of character-formation is relatively unnarcissistic" (p. 416). He adds that the genital character also overcomes his attitude of ambivalence, which in turn brings about the possession of a sufficient quantity of affectionate and friendly feelings to enable him to be tolerant towards both himself and others.

Erikson (1950) echoes Reich's definition of genitality, asserting that it consists in "the unobstructed capacity to develop an orgastic potency so free of pregenital interferences that genital libido . . . is expressed in heterosexual mutuality, with full sensitivity of both penis and vagina, and with a convulsion-like discharge of tension from the whole body" (p. 265). He adds that the climactic turmoil of the orgasm "takes the edge off the hostilities and potential rages caused by the oppositeness of male and female, of fact and fancy, of love and hate." On a broader level, he defines genitality as (1) mutuality of orgasm (2) with a loved partner (3) of the opposite sex (4) with whom one is able and willing to share a mutual trust (5) and with whom one is able and willing to regulate the cycles of work, procreation, and recreation (6) so as to secure the satisfactory development of offspring.

Writing about feelings of disgust and displeasure with particular institutions and people, Jung (1951) referred to the disgust and displeasure men and women feel toward each other (as well as to the institutions symbolizing masculinity and femininity) when they are beset by anima and animus. From a Jungian perspective, genitality might be said to consist of acceptance of one's own bisexual constitution and therefore also of the opposite sex. Along with this acceptance of the opposite sex is respect for a fellow human who, despite a different anatomy, has identical needs and frustrations. While male and female narcissists tend to emphasize distinctions between the sexes, see the other sex as the enemy, compete with the other sex, and generally place barriers between the sexes, the genital character makes no distinction between the sexes, acknowledging the male and female inside of every person and the complementary relationship of the sexes.

The genital male and female are interested in finding ways in which to cooperate rather than compete, ways to make each other feel good rather than ways to control or destroy each other, and ways to unite with rather than separate from each other. Male and female narcissists tend to focus on themselves and their own narcissistic needs, viewing the other as a supplier or frustrator of those needs. The genital male and female see in the other opportunities to actualize their capacity to love. The genital person, to paraphrase John F. Kennedy, asks not what a spouse can do for him or her, but rather, what can he or she do for the spouse? The genital person is not concerned about equal rights so much as about shared experiences.

Genital individuals are able to take responsibility for their feelings—whether they be of anger, envy, lust, or love. They are able to form a bond of love and trust with their partners because they are relatively free of inhibitory defense mechanisms. Being more in touch with their unconscious, they have, in Erikson's words, a "basic trust" of both themselves and others. They make efforts to work through conflicts, and they often succeed because of this basic trust. They are able to gratify the needs of Eros because they do not have a great need to control or destroy. Sexual animosity is minimal, and what animosity does exist is mitigated through their sexual unions.

The genital couple will respond appropriately to their children, enabling them to traverse successfully the stages of development. They are neither too permissive nor too strict, but are flexible enough to respond to each situation according to its dictates. Being relatively content with themselves, they will be relatively content with their children. They will be able to love their children as individuals, rather than projecting their needs or venting their frustrations on them. Hence, their children have a better chance of becoming loving, responsible, genital individuals in their own right.

PATRIARCHY, MATRIARCHY, OR EGALITARIANISM

Who should be on top? This difficult question about male–female harmony must be addressed. Should the male be dominant? The female? Or should they be equal? Is equality possible, and is there a "natural" way for men and women to relate that, if violated, brings about disharmony and animosity?

Eibl-Eibesfeldt (1970) and Lorenz (1963) suggest from an ethological perspective that mating behavior in which the male is dominant and the female submissive is common throughout the animal world, particularly among "higher animals"; as such, it appears phylogeneti- cally ordained. Eibl-Eibesfeldt notes that male genital presentation is used as a ritualized show of force by various primates, explaining that this genital display is a symbolic threat to mount. "In very many mammals, mounting by males is a demonstation of dominance. . . . This can also be established as a tendency in man" (p. 29). Both Eibl-Eibesfeldt and Lorenz note that the female invitation to mount, by turning her backside to the male, is a message of appeasement and submission, which is also adopted by weaker males against stronger males; this behavior is also common among humans.

There is also a universal attitude of chivalry toward the female, according to Lorenz. Male dogs and wolves never bite females. "Sim- ilar absolute inhibitions against biting a female are found in hamsters, in certain finches, such as Goldfinches, and even in several reptiles, for example the South European Emerald Lizard" (p. 118). Even when it appears that the female of the species is dominant—in the mating of bullfinches, for example, during which the female continually pecks at the male—in reality the male remains dominant. "When a male bullfinch is pecked by his wife, he in no way assumes the submissive attitude, but, on the contrary, he shows sexual self-display and tenderness" (p. 120). The male is not pushed by the pecking of the female into a subordinate position—he does not turn his backside to her—but rather shows his superiority by accepting her pecking without becoming aggressive himself; nor does he let himself be put out of a sexual mood.

In the mating behavior of the human species the male has also generally been dominant. In the act of intercourse, the male is the aggressor. He is usually physically on top of the female and penetrates her, aggressively thrusting his penis again and again to produce orgasm in the female and in himself. When the female becomes the aggressor, the male often cannot perform adequately, a fact borne out by the observations of family therapists working with couples. In couples in which the female is aggressive and the male passive, the female increasingly demands sex and the male becomes more passive and disinterested. Women who are narcissistic often cannot tolerate the idea, much less the actuality, of being mounted in intercourse by a man, fearing that they will be destroyed; psychodynamically, this fear is associated with the unconscious prohibition about breaking the incest taboo with father and with losing the approval and love of mother, the deprivation of which would be tantamount to disintegration of the self. Narcissistic men fear losing their power (their semen) to a woman.

Mead (1949) is critical of the trend in modern civilization toward minimizing the differences between the sexes for the sake of obtaining a kind of misguided egalitarianism:

> But every adjustment that minimizes a difference, a vulnerability in one sex, a differential strength in the other, diminishes their possibility of complementing each other, and corresponds—symbolically—to sealing off the constructive receptivity of the female and the vigorous outgoing constructive activity of the male, muting them both in the end to a duller version of human life, in which each is denied the fullness of humanity that each might have had. [p. 371–372]

She points to the vicious circle in which overestimation by each sex of the other's role leads to confusion and causes each sex to arrogate, neglect, or even relinquish part of its own humanity and to lose sight of what is best for society. Woman's receptivity and man's activity, she believes, are essential to a healthy society.

Mead defines the central issues of every human society: what to do with the men. In Western society, the vast majority of all crimes are committed by men; criminality is an expression of male impotence. Men need to have roles, jobs, rituals, or heroic tasks in order to affirm their masculinity. Mead describes the elaborate initiation rites for adolescent boys in various primitive societies that suggest men's reverence toward women. In ceremonies shrouded in mystery, from which women are excluded, the men ritualistically reiterate the process of childbirth. The boys are brought into a great womblike structure; they are sometimes maimed in the genitals, as if to provide them with symbolic vaginas; they are ministered blood, as if menstruating; they are fed, as if from a mother's breast; and finally, they are admitted into the world of men. The purpose of these rituals is to give boys the message that even though it is the woman who performs the indispensable marvel of producing babies, only men can create men. In our culture, the rituals of the Freemasons bear a similarity to these primitive ceremonies, and exclusive men's clubs help to bolster masculinity in adult life. Yet these conduits of masculinity—along with the nuclear family and the role of motherhood—have come under increasing attack in modern civilization. In their attacks on exclusive male clubs, feminists may be destroying an essential element of societal health.

Kestenberg (1968) writing on male–female relations, asserts that "Women who are teachable, but who are unsuccessful in meeting and attracting men able to teach and assume domination in a relationship, frequently adapt to habits, neurotic attitudes, and unconscious fantasies of the men they do find" (p. 479). In other words, in order for a woman to achieve a successful feminine integration, she must be able to be receptive to the sexual "domination" of the man, either by attracting such a dominant man or by teaching her husband to be so, at least some of the time.

Kardiner (1945, 1954) also writes of the importance of male activity and female receptivity, and warns of the dangers posed to society by unbalanced sexual relations in which the female becomes overly aggressive. He cites the tribe of Alor as an example of the consequences of aggressive, absentee mothers and passive fathers. In this tribe, the females did the heavy work in the field, while the husbands went out borrowing money or pleading for the payment of debts. There was little affection between husband and wife, nor much affection for the children. The mother fed the children early in the morning and did not take them with her to the field, but let them fend for themselves or left them in the care of some reluctant older sibling who had no interest in them. Toddlers screaming for their mothers, begging to be taken along, were an everyday sight in the community, and every Alorese was said to complain that his mother had abandoned him in childhood. Kardiner describes the Alor as a suspicious, distrustful people who were guarded, timid, insecure, and paranoid. Their capacity for cooperation was poor, and the cooperation that did exist was unreliable and merely utilitarian. In the exchange of favors, everyone cheated everyone. There was no creativity; their art was crude and careless. They lived in dilapidated houses and only for the moment, with no capacity for planning. Their folklore was pervaded with the motif of deprivation by and hatred of parents.

Spitz (1965) links maternal absenteeism and the decay of patriarchal authority to the rapid disintegration of the traditional family in Western society. The consequences of this decline, he says, "are revealed in the increasingly serious problems of juvenile delinquency and in the growing number of neuroses and psychoses in Western adult society" (p. 299). These developments have in turn brought about the establishment of new cultural institutions that attempt to take the place of the family but do not ever entirely succeed: foster homes, adoption services, child-care centers, child-guidance clinics, social-service agencies, baby-sitting services, an increasing number of psychiatric hospitals, and the ubiquitous call for large numbers of psychotherapists to treat the disturbances caused by civilization. "This evil," Spitz concludes, "is the rapid deterioration of those conditions which are indispensable for the normal development of earliest object relations" (p. 299).

Goldberg (1973), a sociologist, studied cross-cultural research on and between 1,200 societies that were relatively isolated from other societies and have been studied by anthropologists, and 4,000 groups that are known to exist, or to have existed, but that have not been directly studied by anthropologists. He concludes that male dominance is universal among humans, and that a society has never been documented in which female dominance prevailed. Societies often held up as examples of matriarchy, such as the Amazons, are actually, according to Goldberg, mythological: They never existed.

To return to our original question, research seems to indicate that male dominance may be the natural order with regard to male–female relationships. The term *dominance* may be misleading, however. While it seems natural and essential for the male to be aggressive in his relationship with the female, and for the female to be receptive to the male, such aggressiveness on the part of the male does not necessarily mean total dominance, nor does the female's receptiveness indicate total submission. Indeed, it may be best to dispense with the use of the words *dominance* and *submission* in describing healthy mating behavior. Does the female not initiate sexual behavior through her seductiveness (or, in some animals, by giving off a scent or a sound or a body signal)? In that sense, could she not be said to "dominate" the mating ritual in a receptive-aggressive way? Clearly, dominance and submission may be in the eye of the beholder. In reality, both male and female may be dominant in the relationship in differing ways; he in an active, aggressive way and she in a passive, aggressive way.

The hallmark of a healthy male–female relationship is an egalitarianism of just this kind: Both the male and the female fully accept and play their roles, and in so doing, both assume their masculinity and femininity and neither is dominant or submissive in the sense that one controls the behavior of the other. Instead, both are engaged in a cooperative venture, he with his "vigorous outgoing constructive activity," as Mead puts it, and she with her "constructive receptivity." This kind of egalitarianism differs from the one advocated by so-called progressives, which would have the sexes play identical roles and behave in identical ways, despite biological differences.

The terms *dominance* and *submission* are, furthermore, not applicable to healthy male–female mating because males (human or otherwise) do not normally engage in fights with females over dominance; the establishment of a pecking order is usually limited to the world of males and generally exists in order to determine who gains access to females. Once the pecking order has been established, male finds female and female finds male, and the two do their phylogenetically determined mating dance.

Included in the mating dance may be some testing and counter-testing by the two participants to determine whether they are a match. Each participant has a unique way of relating, and each looks for responses from the other that will match his or her needs. The mating dance determines whether a particular male and female will be able to relinquish their defenses and surrender to each other sexually and emotionally. A healthy male and a healthy female will be able to do so, and once they have surrendered, the mating dance will end and they will relate on a deeper level, based on commitment and trust. The mating dance may appear to be a contest over who will dominate—the male aggressing toward the female, the female approaching and avoiding—but it is actually a testing of the other's responses. Once the correct responses have been obtained, the relationship becomes one of mutual respect and interdependence in which neither is dominant and each depends upon the other.

When the male, the female, or both are narcissistic, they may get stuck on the dance itself and not surrender to each other. They may have the compulsion to repeat the dance with a succession of partners. They may form relationships that are dominant-submissive or that bear the earmarks of other modes of narcissistic relating. When individuals have not experienced, in early childhood, the satisfaction of trusting another person, they will not be able to trust in adulthood. A narcissistic male will find it difficult to be successfully active with a female, and a narcissistic female will find it difficult to sexually accept a male.

Just as male activity does not necessarily indicate dominance, so also, on a societal level, patriarchy does not necessarily indicate male dominance or oppression of women. Patriarchy may also be a form of healthy "vigorous outgoing constructive activity," while female passive-receptivity might be seen as vigorous "constructive receptivity." That is, neither dominates the other in a healthy society, but rather there is an egalitarianism of mutual respect in which each contributes to the relationship.

Let us look, for example, at the hunter–gatherer societies of primitive tribes, in which the men hunt or gather food, while the women rear children and tend to family matters. The men in such societies are more active but are not necessarily dominant. Male and female roles are equally important. Moreover, unless the women have been forced to accept it, the fact that the men handle policing and governing duties does not indicate domination over the women. In a healthy society, the women allow the men to "run" things because that's what works best—because of the male biological need to be active, aggressive, and protective toward women and children. This is a cooperative venture.

Some take a moralistic view of patriarchy, associating it with male chauvinism or slavery. But to condemn men for their tendency to be active and aggressive with females is akin to condemning male baboons for their genital displays. It is true that patriarchy can at times be masculinistic. Both constructive and destructive patriarchies have existed throughout the history of humankind; at times men have behaved in a healthy, active way, and at times they have behaved sadistically. Patriarchies now exist in which women are treated with contempt, as they are, for example, in certain Saudi Arabian countries in which men are permitted to marry as many women as they like and to dismiss wives at will, without payment of alimony, while retaining custody of the children. There are societies such as that in the United States, in which men and women have equal rights under the law.

A constructive patriarchy would appear to be one in which men lead because it is helpful for society that they be given active, vigorous roles to play, and in which women are receptive to men and enjoy fulfilling their own roles. Neither men nor women dominate in the sadistic sense. Male dominance leads to physical abuse and intimidation of children and breeds conservative and reactionary syndromes and violence, while female dominance leads to hysterical "mental cruelty" and intimidation of children and breeds liberal and radical syndromes and perversion. Harmony between men and women seems to depend on the natural, phylogenetic egalitarianism of the sexes.

COMPLEMENTARY RELATIONSHIPS

Healthy relationships are complementary. They are characterized by a certain responsiveness of each partner to the other that is essential for ongoing stability. The ancients spoke of the complementary harmony of the yin and yang, and Freud wrote of how Eros and Thanatos balance each other and of the interplay of male aggression and female passivity. In order for a man and woman to be harmonic, there must be a give and take and a checking of each other's irrationalism.

Many studies have explored the differences between male and female sexuality. A cross-cultural study of 190 societies by the anthropologists Ford and Beach (1951) found that in a wide range of societies males show greater sexual aggressiveness, compulsiveness, and lack of selectivity, and in only a few primitive societies do women equal men in promiscuity. Over the range of human societies, men are overwhelmingly more prone to masturbation, homosexuality, voyeurism, and sexual molestation; in virtually every known society, sex is regarded either as a favor by the woman to the man, or as an object of male seizure (in most societies men have to pay for sex through a gift or service). And although women are physiologically capable of greater orgasmic pleasure than men, they are much better able to forgo sex without psychological strain.

The research of Masters and Johnson (1966) explored the physiological differences in the sexual responses of men and women. They demonstrated that male sexuality is in many ways inferior to female sexuality. A far smaller portion of the male body is directly erogenous, and men can have only one orgasm during a short period, while women can have multiple orgasms. Moreover, the male sexual repertoire is quite limited; men have only one sex organ and one sex act, erection and ejaculation, and they are exposed to conspicuous failure. Women are not exclusively dependent on copulation for sexual satisfaction; sexual intercourse is only one of many sexual experiences. A woman's sexuality is reaffirmed monthly in menstruation, and her breasts and uterus further symbolize a sexuality that extends, at least potentially, through pregnancy, childbirth, lactation, and suckling. With respect to orgasm itself, Masters and Johnson demonstrated the importance of male–female coordination for purposes of reproduction; for example, too much movement by the woman during the man's ejaculation may disturb the vaginal pool, where sperm collects before proceeding to the uterus.

Sexuality also has a different meaning for men and women. For men, sexual intercourse is used, in part, to bolster masculine self-esteem. For women, the act of sex is not necessary for affirming their femininity, since they have so many other sources of affirmation; rather, intercourse is a way to bind a man to them, a physical certification of the man's protection and allegiance to them and to their future offspring. Thus women were reported to put more emphasis on foreplay – hugging and physical affection – than on the act of intercourse itself (hugging being symbolic of protection).

What does this research tell us about the prerequisites of male–female harmony? First of all, the fact that men need intercourse more than women do sets up a situation in which men are the petitioners. This gives women an advantage. The balance between them depends on a certain give and take, and it is through greater aggressiveness that the man can overcome the woman's advantage, acquiring the sense that he is mastering her, when in reality she has allowed him to do so. Too much aggressiveness on the part of the woman can jeopardize the process, destroying the man's rhythm and arousing his insecurity. The woman has the power to grant to the man a sexual affirmation that he needs more than she does, while the man has the power to grant to the woman his protection and his faithfulness. George Gilder, a social critic, points out, "It is on these terms of exchange that marriage – and male socialization – are based" (1973, p. 25).

Clower (1979), citing her clinical experiences with children and adults during the 1960s and 1970s, when the sexual revolution took hold in America, found that the demands of "sexually liberated" women produced anxiety in men that often resulted in impotence and other sexual symptoms. Offit (1977) noted in her work with liberated women that they were too afraid of dependency on a man to allow themselves to fully experience their sexuality and that their aggressiveness became a barrier to forming relationships. Such women presented a tough facade, but "inside, if one listens carefully, they are crying perpetually the anguish of their deprivation" (p. 264). Any imbalance in the relations between the sexes that thwarts their biological needs precludes the give and take that is vital to a harmonic sexual interchange.

Research on the differences in male and female sexuality also underscores that each has his or her own particular sexual needs, and each reacts differently to the frustration of not having these needs met. Men tend toward promiscuity, homosexuality, voyeurism, sexual molestation, and criminality; women become increasingly demanding, competitive, and exhibitionistic, and also drift toward homosexuality. Thus we return again to the importance of both the male and female castration complexes, the overcoming of which is crucial for healthy male–female relations.

Thompson (1964) notes that "It seems clear that envy of the male exists in most women in this culture, that there is a warfare between the sexes" (p. 74). Referring to male hostility toward women, she asserts that male castration fears and the fact of penis envy provide the man "a justification for his aggression against her" (p. 75). Freud, as previously noted, states that ". . . upon this penis envy follows that hostile embitterment displayed by women against men, never entirely absent in the relations between the sexes . . ." (1918, p. 205).

If the overcoming of penis envy and castration fear are central to male–female harmony, how can the tasks be accomplished? The answer is that in addition to a give and take, there must also be a system of checks and balances between men and women. The man needs to be strong enough to check the woman's tendency toward the hysterical acting out of animosity stemming from penis envy, and the woman needs to be strong enough to check the man's tendency toward the aggressive or passive-aggressive acting out of animosity resulting from castration fear. Honest communication is the mode of operation.

The importance of dealing with penis envy cannot be emphasized enough. Just as the man's womb envy must be considered, and just as he must be allowed to be active and to feel a sense of mastery both in and outside the family, so also the woman's envy of the male, and of the penis, must be considered. Everything possible must be done to ensure that she feels that her role, whether it be that of mother or physician or police officer, is as important as a man's. Thompson and Freud stressed that penis envy was the leading source of friction between men and women, and I echo that contention. Whether one sees penis envy as a metaphor for female envy of the male role or as a form of destructive behavior resulting from a fixation at the anal-rapprochement stage, the phenomenon of penis envy must be dealt with if there is to be harmony between the sexes.

One can gain an understanding of the change in the relations of the sexes in modern society by studying one of our chief rituals: social dancing. In the early days of the United States, group dancing, such as square dancing, involved communal interaction. Couples made physical contact and eye contact, and they coordinated movements with their own partners and with others. This form of dancing symbolized the extended families of those days and reflected the intensity of human involvement. "Close dancing," or ballroom dancing, began during the early part of the twentieth century. Such dancing was limited to cooperation between a man and a woman, again with physical contact and eye contact. In the 1960s dancing changed again: Couples no longer made contact, either physically or visually. At present-day discos, individuals do not dance together at all, but rather are isolated, each doing his or her "own thing." This trend reflects the progressive separation of the sexes in our society. Such separatism does not bode well for the future.

The separatism on the dance floor is reflected in the separatism of our marriages, which often comprise two individuals with separate careers, living more like roommates than like husband and wife, with separate cars, bank accounts, friends, and bedrooms. When they attempt sexual union, it is often unsatisfactory for both. Such couples often rationalize their separatism as independence, but it is actually sexual narcissism. When children come—often planned according to the "biological clock"—they may be viewed as an interruption of the parent's coveted "independence."

The secret of harmony between the sexes lies in mutual understanding and respect, which arouses a responsiveness and attachment to life. Feeling and attachment bring love, and when love is present, life has meaning and purpose. Intimacy between men and women shapes society and determines the quality of our lives.

PART TWO

Case Studies

8

Lizzie the Brat

INTRODUCTION

The following case history illustrates the vicissitudes of early child-hood, particularly in terms of the formation of a female narcissistic character structure. It describes the first six years in a girl's life, portraying her relationships with her mother, father, baby-sitter, and younger brother, and delineates the gradual build-up of rage, grandi-osity, and sexual animosity. It also conveys, primarily from the child's viewpoint, the relationship between the parents and how that rela-tionship affects her. The case is based on information provided by a woman who was in treatment with me a few years ago. However, I have changed some details in order to preserve anonimity and better illustrate my thesis.

In writing this case study (as well as the one in Chapter 11) I have used the techniques of fiction. My aim is to go inside the mind of the young child in order to convey without psychoanalytic terminology the various developmental forces at play, while, at the same time, preserving the anonymity of the characters portrayed. I have attempted to depict a case history through sequential scenes—to show, rather than to tell, what happened. An analysis of this story comes at the end of the chapter.

In essence, this case and the ones that follow are not intended as scientific validations, but as psychoanalytic interpretations of actual or literary events based on the theories presented in Part I. Freud occasionally used literary devices, as did many of his followers; notable are Robert Lindner, who created the genre of the psychoanalytic short story (*The Fifty-Minute Hour*, 1954), and R. D. Laing, who devised, in *Knots* (1970), a sort of psychoanalytic haiku. An interpretative narrative has the additional advantage of allowing people other than mental health professionals to understand the sometimes complex psychodynamics of behavior.

The process of developing a narcissistic character stucture from the frustation of sexual strivings is practically the same in both sexes— one sex's process being a mirror reflection of the other's. Hence, to understand the plight of the girl in this case history is to understand the plight of all children during the critical early years when they are so vulnerable to environmental influences.

Herewith is the story of "Lizzie the Brat" as recreated from my case notes.

THE HISTORY

The mother held the baby stiffly in her arms.

"I can't believe it. I'm a mother," she said to the father." "I never thought I'd be a mother."

"I never thought I'd be a father," he said.

They sat in the living room on identical easychairs—his turquoise, hers magenta—sipping martinis as she breast-fed the baby girl. She was a rather plump infant with strands of curly hair protruding here and there from her scalp. Her parents watched as she sucked hard at the nipple, making loud slurping noises, letting droplets of milk fall from the sides of her mouth. The mother kept flinching as the baby sucked, looking down at the girl child as though she were some crab whose pincer had caught hold of her nipple and wouldn't let go.

"You look like you're being tortured," the father remarked.

"You should talk," she replied. "You ought to see your face when you're changing her diapers."

"Maybe you'd like me to take over the mothering completely," he said sarcastically.

The baby could not understand their words, but she could feel their feelings. Their feelings were her feelings; they pulsed unquestioningly inside of her. Yet there was nothing she could do about them, so she sucked away at the nipple, every now and then stopping to spit up a little milk onto the mother's chest.

"Yuck!" the mother said, grimacing as she quickly wiped it off with a tissue. "Elizabeth is barfing on me," she muttered to the father. The baby looked up and reached out for her mother's face. Mother and baby gazed at one another. "But Mommy loves her anyway," the mother said. "Sure she does." The mother was smiling with her mouth, but her eyes were cold.

"Mommy, where's my penis?"

"You don't have one."

"But I want one."

"I told you, little girls don't have penises."

"Yes they do."

"No they don't."

"I want your penis."

"I don't have a penis."

"But I want a penis."

"Lizzie, stop bothering me."

Lizzie was two-and-a-half when she had suddenly become interested in penises. She had noticed that her new baby brother had a penis between his legs and she had nothing between hers, or what looked like nothing. She followed her mother around the house, watching her attend the new baby boy, looking up at her mother from beneath her blond bangs. The mother hurried here and hurried there, stopping in the kitchen to prepare the baby's bottle, in the living room to make a telephone call, in the baby's room to check on the little boy.

Lizzie, never more than a step behind, had a way of walking belly first, as though she herself were pregnant the way her mother had recently been. As the mother changed the boy's diaper, Lizzie pointed at his penis, touching it with her finger.

"Penis," she said.

The mother pulled Lizzie's hand away.

"Mommy, does Daddy have a penis?"

"Yes."

"Does Uncle Mike have a penis?"

"Yes."

"Does Grandpa have a penis?"

"Yes."

"Mommy, where's my penis?" She raised her skirt and looked at herself, cluching her rear, as though the penis might be found back there.

"Girls don't have penises. Girls have vaginas."

"Girls don't have penis . . ."

"They have a vagina."

"A bagina?"

"That's right."

"I can't see it," she said, lifting her dress again.

"Don't do that," her mother said, without looking up from the baby.

"Why?"

"Just don't."

"But why?"

The mother hurried off, Lizzie at her heels. She was a woman who had long forgotten her own early childhood disappointment of not having a penis, and who had never resolved her envy of males: Even now, in her job as an assistant district attorney, she took particular pleasure whenever she defeated a male defense attorney. In addition, she was a mother who had decided in her late 30s to have children, not because she liked them but because, as she would tell her husband, her "biological clock was running out" and she wanted to experience motherhood. But now that she had children, she found them annoying, especially Lizzie, whose questions about penises made her feel uncomfortable, and who seemed to need unlimited attention. She approached being a mother in the same way she approached being an attorney: She tried to be quite calm and professional about it. Thus, she dutifully answered all her daughter's questions and made time for her; yet all the while she gave out the message with her tone and manner that Lizzie was annoying her, that it was bad to be curious about penises.

Lizzie got the message but continued questioning and observing her mother and brother. She saw how attentively her mother bathed him, carefully washing his penis each time. Despite what her mother had said, penises were important. It was one thing to find out that her friend, Ellen, had a Barbie doll and she didn't, but it was yet another to find out that her little brother had a part of the body she didn't have. "Mommy," she said, chasing after her, tugging at her skirt. "*When* can I have a penis?" She imagined that her mother had a number of penises, somewhere inside her body, probably in her breasts, small, cute, pink penises like the one she had given Jimmy. She imagined herself crawling inside her mother, crawling up her anus, sucking up the penises, swallowing them, and keeping them inside her own belly until she needed them. "Mommy, tell me when?" she persisted.

"Lizzie, not now. I have to start dinner."

That night Lizzie wouldn't go to the potty. Her mother tried to use reason with her, asking her in a calm, lawyerlike voice to go to the potty because "you'll feel better if you do, dear". But Lizzie kept giggling and running off.

"Lizzie, what's the matter with you?" Her mother stood over her. Lizzie sat in the corner of her room, clutching a little girl doll.

"Where's her penis?" she asked.

Later that evening, Lizzie sidled up to her father. She had recently taken more of an interest in him, and in his penis. The thing she liked most about her father, a short, balding man who, like her mother, was a bit on the chubby side, was that he would play with her. Lizzie's mother never played; she was always serious about everything. His playfulness, however, had a teasing quality to it that usually left Lizzie confused and angry without knowing if she had a reason for feeling that way.

"Daddy, Daddy," she said, plopping into his lap.

"Well, well, if it isn't Lizzie the lizard," he said in his teasing voice.

"I'm not a lizard." She blinked at him.

"Yes you are, yes you are." He squeezed her nose. "You're Daddy's little lizard. Yes you are!"

"Ouch, that hurts."

"Aw, Daddy's sorry. Here, I'll kiss it and make it better."

"Let me see your pen," she said, ignoring his kiss. She pulled his fountain pen out of his suit and put it in her mouth, as though it were a cigar, then grabbed his glasses and tried to put them on her face; they hung from one of her ears. She clasped the fountain pen in her teeth and rammed the other end into her father's cheek. "Pee-pee," she said, giggling.

"Lizzie," the father said. "Why are you such a brat? Answer me? Why? When the stork brought you, did he bring you from the brat farm?"

"Daddy," she ignored him again. "Daddy, let me see your penis."

The father looked up at the mother, who was seated across the room, and smiled knowingly. "You can't see my penis, Lizzie," he said teasingly. "How many times do I have to tell you that?"

"Why can't I see it?"

"Because you're a little girl."

"But I can see Jimmy's penis."

"Yes, but you can't see my penis."

"I want to see your penis." She jumped up and down on his lap. "Why can't I see your penis?"

"Because little girls can't see penises." He winked at his wife. "Only Mommies can see penises."

"I can be a Mommy."

"No you can't. You're still a little girl. Only grown-ups can be Mommies."

"I can see your penis," she said, pointing at his crotch. She started to put her hand on it.

"Lizzie, don't do that." He held her by the shoulders. "Come here. Listen to me, Lizzie. Tell me why? Seriously. Tell me why you always want to be a brat. Can you tell me that?" She shook her head. "Do you want to grow up to be like Lizzie Borden? Do you?"

"No. I want to see your penis."

"Listen to me, do you want to grow up and be a brat like Lizzie

Borden? Do you know who Lizzie Borden was, Lizzie? Lizzie Borden was the biggest brat who ever lived. Lizzie Borden was such a brat that she took an axe and chopped her father's head off."

"Bill," the mother interrupted. "Don't tell her things like that."

"I'm just kidding around. You know I'm just kidding around, don't you Lizzie?"

"No. Let me go."

He still had her by the shoulders. "If I let you go, will you be nice?"

"No."

"Will you stop trying to grab my penis?"

"No."

"Will you let me watch the news?"

"No."

She started to cry and he finally let her drop from his grasp, holding out his arms and laughing as if to say, "What did I do?" Lizzie went to her room and brought some toys out, humming to herself. She was no longer sad at all. She had a car, a jeep, a man and two women. While her father watched the news and her mother read a law journal, she put the man and woman in the jeep. As they rode along, she made the toy man kiss the toy woman as though he loved her. Then Lizzie put the other woman in the car and crashed it into the jeep, which turned over on top of the man and woman, killing them. Then she put the car, the jeep, and the man and woman on top of her father's right shoe.

"Lizzie," he said in his teasing voice. "Why can't you be nice like Ellen. Isn't Ellen nice?" Ellen was the girl who lived next door.

"No."

"Why can't you be nice like Ellen?"

She tried to cram the man and woman inside her father's shoe. He reached out, grabbed the toys, and tossed them aside. She fetched them and again crammed them into his shoe.

"Lizzie, be nice."

"No."

The father had given Lizzie her "quota" of attention for the night. Like his wife, he resented the presence of children, viewing them as obligations. He turned now to the television set. He liked to keep up with the news because it was his way of maintaining some connection with his previous life-style. Before they had had children, he and his wife had been politically active on behalf of civil rights and other causes, and had gone to many parties, marches, and assorted cultural affairs. Now they mainly stayed at home, and activism was limited to ironic comments about events reported in the news.

"Did you hear that?" he asked his wife. "Now they're thinking of shipping arms to Bolivia too."

His wife rolled back her eyes in disbelief.

"Daddy," Lizzie said. "Daddy, hold this." She put the male doll in his hand.

"Lizzie, I'm watching the news now, okay?" He dropped the doll onto the floor. "What next, Mexico?" he said to his wife, shaking his head. "Why don't they just bomb Mexico, too, while they're at it."

Lizzie continued to play at his feet.

As they undressed for bed, the father went up to the mother and kissed the back of her neck. She moved away.

"Honey," she said irritatedly, "I'm tired."

"So?"

"So, let's not start anything."

"Who was starting anything? I was just expressing a little affection. I can't even express a little affection without you thinking I'm going to want sex."

"Well, you usually do, don't you?"

"Not really."

"I'm not in the mood for this conversation. Can we just go to bed, please?"

"You're never in the mood."

"Whatever you say. God, just look at that," she said, staring at herself in the mirror.

"Fine, we'll go to bed then," he said, rolling back the covers.

"Just look at the lines on my face."

"Have you seen the newspaper? Oh, never mind. Here it is."

"I'm getting old. We're both getting old."

He propped himself on the pillow and sat up in bed reading the sports pages, while she stood hunched over the dresser mirror applying lotion to her face. Their life had become routine. Neither of them knew exactly how they had gotten into the routine, or how they could get out of it. Once they had been a handsome young professional couple, both graduates of top law schools, full of hope for the future. They had met at a party in a Soho loft, and each had instantly felt that the other represented everything they wanted in a mate. He was liberal, wore fashionably long hair (the bald spot in the back of his head not yet visible) and turtlenecks, and read Russian novels. She too was liberal, though a bit more on the radical side (she started a women's consciousness-raising group and quoted Susan B. Anthony before feminism was popular), had long, straight hair and was usually clad in faded blue jeans. They fell in love and got married in a special ceremony at a Unitarian Church. In establishing their careers, he chose the "safety" of corporate law—something she constantly reminded him of, emphasizing the word "safety"—while she began as an attorney for the Legal Aid Society and then worked her way up to Assistant District Attorney for the Borough of Manhattan. Somewhere along the way, as their careers fell into place, as their East Side condominium took shape, as their house in Connecticut was being built, as their bellies and hips began to bulge, as their hair became shorter and their martinis drier, and as their two children began to act like "children," they had lost their vitality.

"Are you about finished with the paper?" the wife asked, sliding into her side of the bed.

"No, I'm not about finished."

She turned away from him and from the glare of the lamp. He held the paper in one hand and rested his other on her hip. She shook his hand off. He pretended not to notice; their lack of a sex life was a deep source of constant irritation that was spoken of sarcastically but never really confronted directly.

"Would you try not to rattle the paper so," she said.

"The Celtics have a 17-game winning streak."

"Wonderful."

Monday morning. The baby-sitter came and Lizzie ran up behind her and lifted her skirt, peering underneath, giggling and squealing. Then she ran up behind her mother, who was about to leave for work, and lifted her skirt as well.

"Lizzie, what *are* you doing?" her mother asked.

"Nothing." She scurried off, giggling excitedly.

"Sometimes I can't figure her out," the mother said.

"Who knows what they're thinking about," the baby-sitter said. As soon as the mother left, Jimmy began to cry.

"Do you know if your mother changed him?" the baby-sitter asked Lizzie. She was a neighborhood girl who had recently graduated from high school and was trying to save money to go to college.

"No," Lizzie lied. She knew that her mother had changed Jimmy earlier that morning, but Lizzie wanted the baby-sitter to change him again. She wanted to see his penis. Every time her mother or the baby-sitter changed Jimmy, Lizzie stood as close as she could in order to get another look at the penis. The baby-sitter changed Jimmy's diaper even though it was not soiled, and Lizzie watched intently. Jimmy grabbed his penis with one hand.

"Look," Lizzie giggled. "He likes his penis."

"Of course he likes his penis. Wouldn't you like it?"

"I want a penis."

"Lizzie, Lizzie, Lizzie," the baby-sitter exclaimed, clicking her tongue. Like Lizzie's father, the baby-sitter had developed a teasing attitude toward her. "You're too much, Lizzie. You really are."

Lizzie wasn't listening. She was watching Jimmy's penis and thinking about her father's penis. She imagined he must have a wonderful, big penis, like a big pink nipple, like the nipples on her mother's breasts, only bigger. Daddies had the biggest nipples of all. She imagined sucking on her Daddy's nipple-penis; imagined milk coming out of it; and imagined having a baby like her mother, only the baby would come out of her "hiny." And then, inside of her belly, all kinds of penises would grow: big and little, black and white and red and yellow and blue, bad penises, good penises, penises of all varieties. The bad penises would all drop out when she went to the potty. The good penises would stay inside and they would make her feel good and strong, like Daddy.

After the baby-sitter had finished changing Jimmy, he began to cry again.

"I don't think he needed changing," she said. "I think he wants to be fed."

"You could feed him," Lizzie replied.

One day toward the end of summer, when Lizzie was 3, she walked into her mother's bedroom while she was using her vibrator to masturbate. The door of the room had been closed, but not locked. Lizzie pushed open the door and saw her mother with a long white object between her legs. Mommy has a white penis, she thought. The mother, startled, dropped her skirt and put the vibrator in a drawer of a bedside table.

"How did you get in here?" her mother asked.

"I don't know. What's that?" she asked pointing at the drawer.

"Nothing. Come help Mommy fix dinner."

Later, while her mother was cutting up vegetables for stew, Lizzie went into her room and got out the vibrator. She lifted her skirt and put the vibrator between her legs, as she had seen her mother do. It was cool and smooth. She pressed the button at the top and the vibrator began to hum. She rubbed it between her legs and it felt good. She imagined that the vibrator was Daddy's extra penis, an extra penis for Mommy to use. If Mommy could use it, then so could she.

Suddenly her mother entered the room, stopped, and gaped at Lizzie for a long moment.

"Lizzie . . . ?"

She giggled with delight. Her mother took the vibrator from her and put it back into the drawer. She took Lizzie's hand.

"Come help Mommy fix dinner."

"Okay."

They went hand-in-hand into the kitchen and her mother didn't say any more about the incident; instead, she let it pass as though it had been an unpleasant hallucination.

A few days later Lizzie went back to the drawer and took out the white penis again. Her mother was at work, and the baby-sitter was in another room with Jimmy. Lizzie lay on her mother's bed and pressed the white penis against herself, her legs dangling in the air. She imagined that her father was in bed with her, not the mean, teasing father who called her "Lizzie the lizard" and "Lizzie Borden" but another father who looked like her father, who smiled at her in a warm, silly way and loved her because she was a girl and was real and breathed and laughed and had hopes different from his hopes and knew things different from the way he knew them. The white penis felt very good. It was the best thing she had ever felt so far in her young life. She thought about heaven, like in the storybooks, and imagined herself floating there. "I'm not bad," she said out loud.

The baby-sitter opened the door and peered inside. Like Lizzie's mother, she appeared to be startled. Without saying a word, she took the vibrator away from Lizzie and put it underneath one of the pillows. She never mentioned the incident to Lizzie's mother.

On Sunday Lizzie sneaked into the bedroom while her mother was out in the backyard. She hid in the closet and turned on the white penis. When she used it, it made her feel as though she herself had a penis, and she imagined she was her little brother playing with his penis. The hum of the white penis echoed through the closet, and she couldn't hear her mother calling her name. When the closet door opened, it knocked against her knee and the vibrator flew from her hands. A ray of light momentarily blinded her, and she squinted up at the dark figure of her mother. "Don't you ever let me catch you using this again!" her mother said, pointing a finger at her. She looked like a tall, dark witch. "Do you hear me?" She yanked Lizzie up by the arm and spanked her with the flat of her hand. "Bad girl! Bad, bad, bad!" In the dark Lizzie could see the whites of her eyes glistening with hate, as though she wanted to kill Lizzie, as though Lizzie were everything that was bad in the world. She was shocked.

She ran out of the closet, crying angrily. She slammed the door of her room and fell on the bed. She rammed her fists into the pillow and cried with all her might, screaming toward the doorway, where she hoped her mother was standing. She didn't see why something that felt so good had to be so bad. She could do whatever she wanted with her own body. She wasn't bad. If she was bad, then so was her mother. It was her mother who was bad because she used the white penis before Lizzie did. She hated her mother for not having a real penis, and she hated her mother's vagina and she hated her own vagina. And she hated her father's penis. She was angry at both of them, at her mother for being bad and at her father for making them be bad because he didn't have penises for them and they couldn't use the white penis without being bad. And she hated them and she hated herself and her body and especially her vagina, which she thought was a stupid, smelly, bad nothing, and she cried out angrily toward the door, hating everything and wanting to die.

"Stop that crying," her mother said through the door. "I said, stop it right now."

Lizzie cried all the more loudly.

Her mother, meanwhile, was circling around the bedroom, looking for a place to hide the vibrator. Finally, she put it in a shelf at the top of the closet, presumably out of Lizzie's reach. She thought that would be the end of the matter.

Within a few days Lizzie found it again. Her mother spanked her and hid it in another place, in another room. A week later Lizzie discovered this place. Another spanking; another hiding place. Lizzie was not to be denied. For her it was a game, like an Easter-egg hunt. The game went on for several months, and the spankings got harder and the hiding places more ingenious, but Lizzie wouldn't give up.

One day Lizzie's grandparents visited them. As they were about to leave, Lizzie's mother brought out the vibrator.

"I'm going to give this to you to take to your house," she said to the grandmother in a curiously loud voice. Lizzie watched with great interest as the vibrator changed hands.

"Lizzie, I hear you've been bad," the grandmother said to her.

"I'm not bad. *She's* bad!" she replied, pointing to her mother.

Father, mother, grandfather, and grandmother laughed and laughed. They stumbled around the room laughing. They thought Lizzie was cute. Lizzie thought she was serious.

"Well, we'd better go," the grandmother said, and she held the vibrator out where Lizzie could see it. "I'm taking this home with me, Lizzie. I'm taking it home now. Do you see what grandmother is doing?"

Lizzie started to say something but thought better of it. Adults didn't listen to children anyway. She had found that out.

Grandmother walked out the door with the vibrator in her hand, and Lizzie followed close behind, her eye on the object of desire. Grandmother got into the car and placed the vibrator on the dashboard. Lizzie, whose eyes barely reached the window, didn't let the vibrator out of her sight. "What're you looking at?" Grandmother said. "She's incorrigible," she said to Lizzie's mother.

"What's in . . . incorble?" Lizzie asked.

"Good-bye everybody," Grandfather said. He started the engine and the car crunched gravel as it meandered down the road.

"What's incorble?" Lizzie asked her parents.

"Brat," her father said in his teasing tone of voice. "It means brat, Lizzie. Brat."

Lizzie wasn't fooled. She knew the white penis would be back because she knew her mother liked the white penis as much as she did. They both liked the white penis, and Lizzie knew her mother was wrong to stop her from using it, and her father knew she was wrong, too. Sometimes she heard him yelling at her in the night, saw him looking at her during the day, like he didn't love her, even though he said he did. Someday, she thought, Daddy will send her away, and when I grow up I'll marry him, and he'll be nice to me. In the meantime, she thought, I have the white penis. It would be back, she knew it would.

Every day she checked her mother's room, but the white penis was nowhere to be found. Finally, after a week of searching, she tried the drawer; it was the one place she hadn't bothered to look. There it was, lying amid crumpled, lipstick-stained tissues, all shiny and white, as though in a gift-box.

"My pee-pee," she said.

Minutes later, her mother was in the doorway. "Okay," she said very softly. "Okay, Lizzie. You win." She had a very bright smile on her face. "You win, dear. Come, come with me." She took Lizzie by the hand and led her into the kitchen, where she plucked a hammer out of the cabinet. She laid a butcher block on the corner of the floor and put the vibrator on top of it. "Watch," she said softly, smiling strangely. Lizzie stood back, her hands on her ears. Her mother brought the hammer down on the vibrator, sending pieces of plastic and metal flying into different parts of the room. Then she stood up. "Gone," she said, smiling.

"Gone?" Lizzie didn't know whether to smile or not.

"Gone."

The mother chuckled a bit, and then she slapped Lizzie hard across the right cheek. "That's for being a brat," she said. "Now, go to your room and wait there until your father comes home."

Lizzie cried out with all her might. Her mother had never called her that before. She was used to her father calling her that name, but not her mother. She ran to her room and slammed the door. "I hate you!" she cried out toward the door, and she stomped around the room. She imagined herself growing big, twice as big as her mother, and slapping her again and again and again until her mother cried. She imagined herself flying through the air, flapping her arms, resting right above her mother's head, dropping do-do on her face, and the do-do would seep into her eyes and make her go blind, so that Lizzie would have to show her around. "I hate you, I hate you, I hate you!" she cried, stomping around the room.

"That's right," her mother called. "Keep it up. You wouldn't listen to me, maybe you'll listen to your father. Keep it up."

"I will keep it up!" Lizzie yelled back.

"Do that!"

"I will!"

Lizzie picked up her toy jeep and smashed it against the wall, then picked up her toy car and smashed it against the wall, then jumped up and down on the toy man and woman. "I hate you!" she said again.

Her mother burst into the room and looked at the floor.

"Sometimes I don't know about you, Lizzie. Sometimes you act like you're not even my kid." The mother's voice was sad now and tired. She shook her head and walked slowly out of the room.

As soon as her mother left, Lizzie locked the door. Then she lay in bed under the covers, sucking her thumb. She hated her mother and she hated her father and she hated Jimmy and she hated her grandmother and she hated her grandfather and she hated everybody. She felt like banging her head against the brass railing of her bed. Maybe they'll feel sorry if I do, she thought. She imagined herself lying on the floor, and her parents standing around her, crying and moaning. Someday, when I grow up, I'm going to have my own white penis, she thought. I'm going to have my own white penis, and I'm going to use it all I want. She tossed this way and that way, sighing, sobbing, waiting for her father to come, waiting for it to be over with. She knew he would yell at her when he came home. That's all he ever did, tease her or yell at her. When he was in a relatively good mood he would tease her and when he was in a bad mood he would yell at her.

She didn't expect he would be in a good mood today.

Finally came the knock and her father's voice. "Lizzie, open the door."

"No."

"Lizzie, you want me to break it down?"

"Go away."

The father kicked open the door and strutted to the bed, the mother following: "What's the matter with you?" he yelled at her. "Answer me when I'm talking to you. I would just like to know what's the matter with you. Can't you hear? You don't hear so good, is that it? Lizzie, I'm talking to you!" Lizzie pulled the covers over her head. "Hey, do you hear me? Take those covers off your head. I *said* take them off." She didn't move. He leaned over her and jerked the covers back. She whirled away from him, burying her face in her pillow, rolling herself into a ball so that her legs were bent under her like a frog's. "We have to talk, Lizzie. We have to talk. Now." He turned her around so that she was facing him, but her eyes were shut tight. "Lizzie, look at me. Do you know what you're doing to us? Do you know you're driving your mother and me crazy? Did you ever think of us?"

"I hate you!" she yelled, twisting away from him.

"You don't hate me," he smiled, holding her by the arms.

"Yes I do."

"No you don't."

"I HATE YOU!"

"Don't be silly. You don't hate your father."

"I do, I do, I do!"

"She doesn't mean that," her mother said. "She's just upset."

"Go away!" she shrieked, thrashing around on the bed. Her eyes were shut tight and her hands were pressed against her ears to block her parents out. She was kicking down on the bed with her feet. She was writhing and screaming, "Go away, go away, go away! . . ."

"Lizzie, would you stop that?" the father said. He had gone from yelling to teasing. "Lizzie, I wish you could see yourself now. You look ridiculous."

"No!" She kept thrashing around and screaming.

"Lizzie," her mother said. "Stop it."

"No! No! No!"

"Lizzie," her father said, "do you want me to bring a mirror so you can see how ridiculous you look?"

"Go away! I hate you!"

"Don't talk to your father that way," her mother said.

"Go away!"

"Lizzie, do you want me to tickle you? If you don't stop, the tickle bug is coming." her father said.

"GO AWAY!"

He began tickling her and she flipped around onto her stomach again, screaming and ramming her fists into the pillow. "Lizzie Borden took an ax," the father said, "and gave her father forty whacks . . . Come on, Lizzie, you know you want to laugh." She didn't want to laugh at all. What she wanted to do, she couldn't do. What she wanted to do was too awful to even think. She began to cry, angrily, at the top of her voice, her hands still pressed against her ears. The father backed away in shock and looked at the mother. He held out his arms as if to ask, "What did I do?" The mother quietly motioned for him to follow her out of the room. "We'll talk later," the father said, "When you're ready to listen." Lizzie heard them whispering outside her room for a while, and then they were gone. She cried for another half hour, until her lungs and throat were burning, and then she cried some more, just to show them. When she finally stopped and lay exhaustedly sucking her thumb, she could hear them laughing. Their laughter made her furious. Why were they so happy, she wondered, when she was so miserable?

Three years passed. Jimmy began to walk and talk. He always had a bright look in his eyes and a smile on his face. Lizzie stayed in her room a lot and learned to use watercolors, but nobody noticed. She frowned a lot. The mother called Jimmy her "Little Prince." The father would playfully sock him on the chin and asked him if he was his pal. Whenever her parents spoke to her, it was to express annoyance for something she had done or not done. She became more secretive about her feelings, and more demanding.

That spring, Uncle Mike came to stay with them. Uncle Mike wasn't really an uncle—he was really her father's cousin—but they called him Uncle Mike anyway. He stayed up in the attic, where there was a spare cot and a ping-pong table. When they were kids, Lizzie's father and Uncle Mike never got along, and they didn't get along so well now either. Uncle Mike always resented Lizzie's father because he was more successful. He had been more successful in high school, where he made better grades and was more popular with girls; and he had also been more successful in adult life, becoming a professional, whereas Uncle Mike went from job to job and from career to career, never able to make up his mind.

Lizzie used to hang out with Uncle Mike in the attic. She liked Uncle Mike because he would play ping-pong with her and let her win, and he never teased her. And once, when her father had snapped at her, Uncle Mike had said to him, "Why do you talk to her that way?"

One day Uncle Mike was lying on his cot reading a paperback novel and Lizzie came to sit on his chest. Everybody else was in town. The house was empty and Lizzie was bored.

"Ouch," Uncle Mike said. "Hey, you're heavy. You're getting to be a big girl. How old are you now?"

"Six."

"You're real grown up for your age."

Lizzie smiled coyly and slid back a bit so that her rear end was resting on his lap.

"Did you ever ride a horse?" she asked.

"No, I never did."

"I did. Last summer at Hagman's Park. It was fun. I rode on my Dad's horse." She began bouncing up and down. She had become a chunky girl, with her mother's large, muscular thighs. Her hair was short and curly, and a few curls hung down the middle of her forehead. There was always a look of sadness on her face, even when she smiled. She smiled now while bouncing on Uncle Mike's lap, and her brown eyes and brows seemed to form a frown even as her mouth widened to smile.

"Take it easy," Uncle Mike said, putting down his Western novel. "What're you trying to do?"

"I'm riding a horse."

"No, you're riding me. And if you don't watch out, you're going to get me excited." He gave her a strange look.

"That's okay." She pretended not to understand the look, although she knew it was naughty. She kept bouncing, smiling at him.

"I'm telling you, you'd better stop or else."

"Or else what?"

"You know what."

"What?"

"You know."

He looked at her and she stopped bouncing. She sat frozen for a few seconds. Then she started again, giggling.

"I'm telling you," he said. "You'd better stop." He brought his arms up on each side of the cot. They were poised to grab her.

"Why?" she asked coyly. "Just tell me why?"

"Stop that or else."

She stopped again, staring at him, her lips pressed together to hold back a giggle. She looked at his arms, one at a time.

"Just one more move," he said.

"And then?"

"You'll see."

She moved slightly up and down and looked at him daringly. His arms went higher and he raised his brows, smiling like a fiend. She giggled and he cackled. They were frozen for a few moments like cat-and-mouse in the rays of the afternoon sun that fell on them from the window beside the cot. Then she made another move and he grabbed her and held her still by bearing down on her shoulders. She squealed with delight.

"I know," she said, leaning toward him. She whispered into his ear, "Let's take off all our clothes and run around the room naked."

"You naughty girl," he said, pretending to be shocked.

"I'm not naughty."

"What would your parents think?"

"They don't care."

He looked at her. "Actually, I think you're right. I've known your parents since before you were born. They don't care. That's the truth." Uncle Mike smiled at her and nodded knowingly. He was a handsome man with curly hair and green eyes who wore his shirt unbuttoned to the chest, where there were patches of dark, woolly hair. He lifted Lizzie off him and sat her down on the cot. "All right," he said, pulling off one of his well-shined boots and then another. "Let's get naked."

"Okay," she said. She suddenly felt scared.

"Promise you won't tell your parents?"

"I promise."

"Cross your heart?"

"Cross my heart." She did so gingerly, gawking at him as though he had become a stranger.

"Last one undressed is a poophead."

"What's a poophead?"

"I don't know. But you're going to be one if you don't hurry."

They got undressed and then sat facing one another on the cot. Lizzie smiled at him, giggling shyly with her mouth but still gazing sullenly with her eyes. "Come here," he said, and he took her into his arms and pressed her tightly against his woolly chest, more tightly than anybody had ever pressed her for a long, long time, and then it was all right. He likes me, she thought. He likes me and he's talking to me like I'm a person. A grown-up likes me and is paying attention to me. A grown-up thinks I'm worth being with and listening to. She knew it was wrong and that her mother and father would be upset if they ever found out, but she didn't care. It felt so good. A grown-up, she thought, and he likes me.

In the fall, Lizzie entered the first grade. School brought with it a different set of situations and a different set of problems, but at least there were other people to be with besides her family: the teachers with their funny ways, and the students who ate candy and pulled each other's hair at recess. Uncle Mike never visited again, and she soon forgot him and everything that happened in the attic. She never told her parents about the incident. The closest she ever came to mentioning it was a few days after it happened during a fight with her mother, when she blurted out that she had seen Uncle Mike's penis. Her mother shook her head and smiled at Lizzie as though she were, yes, incorrigible, and told her to stop making up stories about Uncle Mike. Lizzie never tried to tell anybody again, not even her new schoolmates, and then she stopped thinking about it at all. In fact, she never even thought about Uncle Mike until the day she bolted up from the couch in my office, some twenty years later, after about a year of therapy, and, wiping the blond bangs back from her forehead, exclaimed, "You know, my uncle raped me!"

DISCUSSION

Here is a case history in which sexual animosity is transmitted from mother to daughter, from father to daughter, and from mother and father to baby-sitter to daughter. The central theme is that of a little girl's feminine strivings being frustrated in just about every way possible, creating in her a defensive posture of precocious sexuality. Another aspect of the theme is her parents' "typecasting" Lizzie to play the role of brat. In essence, they hypnotized her to play that role, while appearing to want the opposite, which illustrates the duality between the conscious and unconscious.

Laing (1976) writes of how parents induce certain behaviors in their children through hypnotic suggestion, creating family scenarios. For example, parents may tell a boy he is naughty because he does not do what they tell him to do. "What they tell him he *is*, is *induction*, far more potent than what they tell him to do" (p. 72). Laing explains that by telling him he is naughty, they are telling him not to do what they appear to be telling him to do. Thus, while on the surface they appear to be concerned about the boy's goodness, unconsciously they want him to be bad, in order to utilize him as an object of scorn upon which to act out their animosity and toward which they can feel superior.

Although it was not mentioned in the story, Lizzie's grandmother treated Lizzie's mother in much the same way as Lizzie's mother treats Lizzie. Both mothers performed all the duties of motherhood, but without real caring or empathy. They both thwarted their daughter's feminine strivings and harbored unresolved penis envy. Lizzie's mother, therefore, cannot be empathic toward Lizzie's curiosity about penises. Indeed, she repressed everything to do with her childhood sexuality, and therefore she has little understanding for Lizzie's predicament. The mother, a hysteric, cannot admit to any wrongdoing or take responsibility for how her daughter is behaving. It is her daughter's fault; she is bad, she is a brat, she is a "bad seed." The mother simply throws up her hands in exasperation at Lizzie's "brattiness" without ever asking "What did I do?" She is not conscious of the fact that she acts out animosity through her tone of voice, her eyes, her body language, and the emotional content of her relationship with her daughter; she thinks that as long as she performs all the duties of motherhood, or assigns them to the baby-sitter, her daughter should be grateful and cooperative and not make any waves.

The mother's relationship with the father is also full of unconscious animosity. She rejects him sexually and ridicules him for his passivity. This pattern of adding insult to injury is typical of hysterics. Because she has not resolved her castration complex and her oral rage, she has an ambivalent, alternatingly idealizing and contemptuous attitude toward men. During the time span covered in the story she has contempt for her husband; he has come to represent all that she envies and despises about men, and all that she despises about her own femininity (they have what she lacks), about which she harbors unconscious inferior feelings. However, at the same time, she idealizes her son. She sees in him the possibility of molding a man in her own image. His penis becomes the penis she always wanted, and she will live through him, turning him against the father, turning his penis against the father's penis, shaping him into a womanly man, that is, into a homosexual. The daughter, meanwhile, represents all that she has contempt for, and has disowned, about her own femininity.

The father acts out his animosity toward the wife by paying little attention to her outside the bedroom. He is an aloof, passive narcissist, the son of a hysterical woman who treated him like a prince, but a sexless prince. He had a younger sister whom he teased as he now teases his daughter, Lizzie. His father and mother were divorced when he was 7 and his mother never remarried; he became the "man of the house," and he teamed with his mother against his younger sister. This triangle is repeated in the present relationship, with him and his wife teaming against Lizzie. There is very little genuine communication between the father and mother; for the most part they act out transferences and resist true intimacy and honest communication. Hence their life becomes a ritual. She represents to him the mother who put him on a pedestal while psychologically castrating him, and he represents to her the father who was sexually rejecting and "weak." Of course, conversely, she represents his father to him, and he represents her mother—transferences know no gender bounds. Unconsciously, both get revenge against the symbolized objects through their relationship with one another. He does so by remaining emotionally detached while demanding to have his manhood affirmed sexually; and she attempts to castrate him by rejecting him sexually and deriding his manhood in subtle ways. Their relationship is characterized by an ever-present, low-keyed hostility.

The father's relationship with Lizzie is, as previously noted, a re-creation of his relationship with his younger sister. He views Lizzie as a threat to his relationship with his wife, just as he viewed his younger sister as a threat to his relationship with his mother. Like the mother, the father gives Lizzie a double message. On the surface, he appears to express tenderness, calling her "Daddy's little lizard," and dutifully plays with her. To a little girl, this affection seems normal. The father's teasing, however, provides a way of unconsciously transmitting animosity to his daughter, and his increasing detachment from her further adds to this transmission. His allusions to Lizzie Borden and his casting her in the role of the bad child, "the brat," highlight this trend. Finally, he thoroughly frustrates Lizzie's feminine strivings toward hm, refusing her request to see his penis in a teasing and belittling manner ("Only Mommies can see penises"). This helps to set the stage for her future sexual molestation, since his frustrating response fixates her at the stage of oedipal curiosity. The father is uncomfortable with his sexual feelings toward his daughter, while at the same time unaware of his transferred anger toward her and how he expresses it. He needs to tease her and thereby demean her in order to defend against these feelings.

Both the mother and father have an influence on the baby-sitter as well, for the baby-sitter also treats Lizzie in a detached and sometimes teasing way. As in most groups, power is hierarchical. The mother wields the most power, but her energy is primarily of an aggressive-hostile sort; she distances, frustrates, and degrades the father, Lizzie, and to some extent the baby-sitter—this latter relationship being only implied in the story. (In actuality there was a succession of baby-sitters which caused additional complications). The father, second in power, teases, distances, and degrades Lizzie, the baby-sitter, and the mother. The baby-sitter, in turn, controls and teases Lizzie. And Lizzie, though it is not shown in the story, teases her little brother. Meanwhile, mother, father, and baby-sitter idealize Jimmy, which further ostracizes Lizzie. In a sense, Jimmy becomes the family ego-ideal, while Lizzie becomes the family "shadow." She represents everything that they attempt to disown about themselves.

In the story we see the progressive frustration of Lizzie's feminine strivings and the development of her castration and Electra complexes. Because her mother has a rejecting attitude toward her and subtly castrates the father, Lizzie does not really turn to the father. She is too concerned about the possible loss of love and approval from her mother to risk turning to the father in a genuine way. When she turns to the father he is not really an object of love so much as an object of sexual curiosity, and her half-hearted turn to him is met by his animosity toward women (who represent his mother and sister and archaic memories of the bad breast). Eventually she turns to a transitional object, the "white penis," for comfort. In her fantasies (which I reconstructed from the patient's free associations), she indicates that the vibrator is "Daddy's extra penis," thus serving as a fetishistic symbol of her relationship with her father (and a symbol of her "phallic" mother), but not a real relationship with him, which would be threatening. The vibrator is also a pawn in the war between the mother and daughter. Symbolically, it is a war for Daddy's penis and a war of Lizzie's assertion of her femininity. Losing this war with the mother has devastating effects on Lizzie's development. It lays the seeds for her later using Uncle Mike for soothing and for sexual affirmation.

From the beginning, not only are her sexual impulses frustrated, but so are her aggressive ones. At her birth, neither mother nor father really want her, and each resents the responsibility of feeding and changing her. While feeding her, the mother cannot give her adequate mirroring, and the child begins picking up her hostile energy without being able to dispose of it. Throughout her childhood, her feelings are questioned or ridiculed—that is, her "self" was found unacceptable by her parents. Nowhere is this more obvious than in the climactic scene when the father comes home and knocks open Lizzie's door to "talk" to her. She is not allowed to have either angry or sad feelings, not allowed to cry, not allowed to shut her eyes, and not allowed to have a tantrum, even though none of these reactions would be harmful. The parents cannot stand such outbursts from her because they arouse guilt feelings in them. The father's defense, once again, is to tease the child, demean her, and invalidate her feelings so as to protect himself. The mother, as usual, assumes an attitude of self-righteousness. "Don't talk that way to your father," she tells the girl. Neither is concerned about the child's feelings. It is only their own feelings they care about. So they model an egocentric, narcissistic way of relating, one which was previously modeled for them by *their* parents. Meanwhile, since Lizzie can never verbalize the rage inside her, it must be repressed and become part of her character, whereby it will affect all aspects of her behavior.

Out of her anger toward her mother and father, and out of a need to find mirroring for her narcissistic grandiosity ("I can be just as sexual as any grown-up!") in order to defend against her feelings of low self-esteem she throws herself at Uncle Mike. She is the initiator with Uncle Mike because she has become fixated at that point of her development, her original innocent sexual curiosity having been derided and frustrated by her parents. So she exposes herself to Uncle Mike, submits to his molestation, and plays out her Electra complex.

At the time she entered therapy at the age of 23, she was an angry, hysterical young woman, prone to paranoia (she believed people were out to control her), occasional bulimia, and impulsiveness. She skittered here and there, joining various movements, schools, theater groups, and religions, never stopping very long to figure out who she was or what she felt. She was in constant escape from her unconscious feelings of guilt, rage, and low self-esteem. Though she knew many people, she let nobody get close to her; intimacy was anathema to her.

She would probably not have entered therapy at all had she not been given a hard push in that direction. She was dropped from a local institution of learning, not because of her grades but because of her "personality problems"—as the school psychologist put it. He urged her to see a therapist, and made it a prerequisite for readmission to the school. This was a shattering blow to her, for she was a strong-willed, proud person whose attitude was that she would get whatever she wanted from life and nobody would stop her. At the school, that attitude had caused her to get into power struggles with nearly all her teachers, both male and female. In one instance, she caused a minor uproar by initiating an affair with a male teacher and then, when he gave her a B+, creating a scene with him during class (a replay of the scenes she used to have with her father).

Although she was quite seductive with men in general (including her therapist), in actuality she was having only one relationship—that with a married man twenty years older than she and living in another town. She spent most of her daily hours—indeed minutes—obsessing about him, but she only saw him every other month for a weekend. She also spent most of her sessions talking about him.

"What do you think I should do," she would ask. "Should I call him? Should I write him? Do you think he's having an affair with somebody else? Do you think his wife knows about me? I know you can't tell me what to do, but I wish you would. I wish somebody would." She sat opposite me, wearing the same frown that I imagined had covered her otherwise pretty face since early childhood, along with a constant tint of bitterness in her eyes. It was a frown that seemed to say, "Nothing has ever gone right for me, but it's going to go right for me now or else!" She sat on the edge of the couch, and would not lie down, as though she had to be ready to fight or flee. She always looked at me, probing me with her eyes. Would I try to control her? Would I try to defeat her? Would I try to make her feel guilty? For her, the prospects of intimacy were permeated with disastrous consequences. Despite her frown, her bitterness, and her defiant attitude I was drawn to her. There was a fierce determination and an alertness about her eyes that was appealing, and now and then a shy, radiant smile would slip out of the corners of her mouth, a portent perhaps of the aliveness that was primarily repressed. I was also touched by the memories she produced about her childhood. But these memories were produced only in the rare interludes between her obsessive discussions of her boyfriend. "What should I do?" she would ask again. "What?"

"What should you do about what?" I asked.

"You know what. About Ross. What should I do about him? Should I call him? But then his wife might answer the phone. I could call him at his office, but he doesn't like that. Maybe I should just break off with him. I don't know. I don't know. Help!"

"Suppose you broke up with him. How would that be?"

"I'd feel relieved, I think. I don't know. Somehow that doesn't feel satisfying. I'd still feel angry at him. Because I know he wouldn't care if I broke up with him. He wouldn't care at all."

"Just like your father didn't care."

"No, my father didn't care either. You're right. But you can't just keep blaming your parents. I don't want to blame my parents."

"It's not a matter of blame."

"I know what you're saying. But I understand all that already, and it doesn't help. It doesn't help me to make decisions about Ross. So my father didn't care either. So what?"

Her narcissism was such that she was unable to tolerate my rare interpretations, and her indoctrination was such that she could not allow herself to experience or verbalize her rage at her parents even after all these years. There were too many introjections to the effect that any angry or sad feelings cast in her parents' direction (whether her parents were present or not) was tantamount to a betrayal.

I could, therefore, only silently analyze her. I understood the connection between her teasing, unavailable father and the teasing, unavailable father-figure with which she was now involved. Her quest — the repeating pattern to which she was prey — was to try to find somebody like her father and change him into a loving, available father-figure, thereby assuaging her archaic feelings of frustration and resolving the fixation. I could not tell her these things. Nor could I tell her about her relationships with women, relationships that were permeated with competition and antagonism. For the most part, she struggled to maintain a sense of power and control with women. In some instances she was able to forge an alliance with them against mutual enemies. However, such friendships only lasted as long as the mutual alliance was needed; when the enemy disappeared, the alliance fell apart. These relationships were related to the ones she had had with her mother and with the many baby-sitters throughout her childhood. On one hand, the power struggle with her mother over matters such as the "white penis" was translated into the power struggles with girlfriends over men, or with women teachers over how she should conduct herself in their classes. On the other hand, having gotten attached to, and then been abandoned by, a succession of baby-sitters, she was afraid of becoming too dependent on anybody, even if she were not a competitor.

In her relationship with me, as well, she sought a teasing, unavailable father-figure that she could change into a loving and available one. In fact, I found in the beginning that if I were too gratifying, she would retreat in some way — by missing a session, coming late, or distancing me during the next few sessions. In a sense, through such behavior, she trained me to be unavailable, and she also aroused in me an impulse to tease her. It was something about her frown, her woebegone manner, and sulky speech that caused me to want to be sadistic to her, to make fun of her as her father had. (To the best of my knowledge, I restrained this impulse; yet I found myself often feeling angry at her, which no doubt was impeding my effectiveness — angry about her constant rejection of my attempts to reach out to her.) There was a streak of masochism in her, no doubt, related to the power struggles that she always lost during the anal-rapprochement phase.

On a sexual level, her transference and the countertransference she elicited were more complex. She seemed to want me to desire her and to demonstrate that desire by making a play for her. This had to do with the way her father had sexually frustrated and ridiculed her. My desire for her would be the antidote to her father's rejection. At the same time, however, her rage at her father and brother (and, through a generalized projection, at all men), combined with the guilt her mother had engendered in her about her sexuality, caused her to be revolted if and when anybody did make a play for her. To complicate matters further, she tended to deny her sexual impulses. She brought in numerous dreams about sexual encounters with strange men in offices similar to mine, and she refused to lie on the couch because she said she did not trust that I would not make an advance were she to do so. However, she reported having no sexual thoughts or feelings about me, and the very idea was repugnant to her. In addition to these sexual needs, she also seemed to want me to play the part of the Good Daddy of the pregenital phase who would rescue her from the Bad Mommy and provide her with a penis of her own. Indeed, penis envy loomed large in her character structure. One problem of working with her was that there was no way I could gratify these complicated, often contradictory needs and impulses, nor was there any way I could explain to her why I could not do so, for she was not aware of the existence of these needs and impulses.

What she was aware of, for the most part, was her anger toward men, and nothing made her angrier than the notion that this anger was connected to penis envy. "Yes, I'm angry at men," she told me one day. "But don't say it's penis envy. I know that's what you're thinking, but don't you dare say that. I don't believe in penis envy. That's all a bunch of psychoanalytic crap. It's a concept devised by men. It has nothing to do with how women really feel. I don't envy penises. I just resent men."

I had not interpreted her penis envy. It was she who brought up the notion. Like her mother before her, she too had repressed the feelings of disappointment about and envy of the phallus; thus this primary penis envy had become an unconscious fixation, giving way to the secondary penis envy that manifested itself in her envy of the male role in society. Even though she could readily remember the events of her early childhood, including the struggle over the "white penis," she no longer remembered the intense feelings associated with the memories.

She claimed she did not envy penises, but she disliked them because she thought men used penises to exploit and gain power over women. She utilized the woman-as-victim theme as a defense against the feelings of penis envy, low self-esteem, and rage. Of course, she *had* been victimized by men—her father and Uncle Mike for starters—so it was difficult to convince her that men could be otherwise. She was driven by her paranoia and longings for revenge, and did not want to know that there was any other point of view. The secondary benefits of frustrating men's sexual advances, controlling them, and feeling morally superior to them, were very great, while the risks she would have to take in order to put aside her defensive posture and relate honestly and openly to men—to me—did not seem worth taking. Even if it had seemed worth it to take the risks, she was still nowhere near ready to do so.

Toward the end of a long year of treatment, it became more and more obvious that her unconscious need was to defeat me—and to exact revenge on me, as her transferred father and mother, for what had been done to her previously. Her need to do this seemed inexorable, superseding all other needs. At any rate, as previously noted, she had only entered therapy because a school psychologist had demanded she do so. Once her anxiety over having been dropped by the school had been addressed, and she had made the decision not to return to the school, resistance to the process set in. More than once she expressed doubt about the professional competence of the school psychologist, implying that he was sexually biased. "You could see he enjoyed dumping me," she said. Then her doubts about professional competence started to become directed at me, again centered on the fact that I was a man.

"Maybe I should see a woman therapist," she would say time and time again.

"All right." I joined her resistance, feeling it was the only option I had.

"I know you think I need to work through my father transference, but can't I do that with a woman therapist?"

"You could."

"I mean, I just don't think you understand me. I don't want to hurt your feelings, but you're a man. All my friends think I'm foolish to be seeing a male therapist."

"You seem to want to try a woman therapist."

"I do. And I know women therapists can be biased too. In the other direction. But maybe that's what I need right now."

"Maybe so."

Eventually, I resigned myself to losing her. Perhaps due to my countertransference, I had not been able to establish a therapeutic alliance with her. I cannot say whether there was something I could have done and did not do, or whether her character was such that it precluded the establishment of such an alliance with a male. Perhaps I will never know. At any rate, we parted amiably and have kept in touch since then. She has not gone back into therapy.

This case, however, brings into focus one of the dilemmas facing today's psychoanalyst: whether or not to interpret penis envy. Of course, this dilemma has existed from Freud's day, when penis envy and the resentment of male authority was seen as a leading source of resistance to the analytic process. Female patients today are even more sensitive about this concept, and many analysts are reluctant to interpret it. Many others have decided the concept is no longer valid. Yet, if we do not interpret penis envy, then how can we resolve a patient's female narcissism? We cannot, any more than we can resolve a male patient's male narcissism without interpreting his womb envy, castration fear, and phallic guilt.

Unfortunately, I was unable to work with Elizabeth long enough to help her resolve her female narcissism, and so Lizzie the Brat, with her forlorn frown, her rage, and self-defeating attitude, remained alive inside of her.

9

The Loner

His name was Harold and his appearance was gentle and sweet. Behind that façade, however, was the temperament of a killer. I found that out one day as he sat in my office talking about an encounter with a clerk in a corner grocery store.

"I felt like blowing her away," he said without any feeling. "I dislike rude shopkeepers. I dislike them intensely. She was treating me as if I were less than human. As if I were some ant that one steps on and walks blissfully away from. Maybe the next time I go in there I *will* blow her away."

"How will you do that?" I asked.

"How? I'll shoot her, right between the eyes."

"Where will you get the gun?"

"I have one."

"I see."

He looked at me with his soft blue eyes and his innocent, cherubic face. "I shouldn't have told you that. Now you'll probably ask me to turn in my gun to you."

"Actually, that wouldn't be a bad idea."

Harold was one of those loners who drift from place to place, always remaining on the periphery of life. His connection with other people was minimal. He did not have friends, did not belong to any organizations, did not hold a job, and had cut himself off from his family. He had been in the army and collected a disability pension. During his stint in the army, it had been discovered that he had epilepsy. The army doctors mistakenly thought the malady was associated with his army service, but actually he had had his first episode before that. Now he lived on the pension. His relationships were with roominghouse landlords and tenants, shopkeepers, and frequenters of shabby bars, gay and straight. Perhaps once a year he had sex with somebody, sometimes a man, sometimes a woman. It was usually at the end of a drunken night. He reported feeling disgusted by women, angry at men.

Working with Harold got me thinking about loners. Loners have always found a special place in American society. We are and always have been a melting-pot for mavericks—for those who seek freedom from some kind of conformity. Our nation was founded on the principles of freedom of speech and religion; that is, on the principle of independence. Loners have been celebrated and romanticized in fictional and nonfictional portraits of the Old West (where the hero always rides off into the sunset, leaving the beautiful heroine behind), and more recently in portraits of individuals who take heroic stands against, say, a corrupt government or corporation.

However, there is another, less heralded kind of loner that has also gotten some public notice. This loner lives a life of quiet desperation. Sometimes he does nothing to gain public attention, simply living and dying in anonymity. Sometimes he commits serial murders, runs naked through the streets yelling obscenities, extorts a million dollars from his company, or perpetrates some other outrageous act. And people say, "He was such a quiet, withdrawn type. He's the last person I would have thought would do such a thing." Harold was this type.

Are the two types of loner related? Both are prone to withdrawal from society. Both harbor feelings of grandiosity. And both are full of narcissistic rage. However, the heroic type of loner finds a socially acceptable way to take out his rage, pitting himself David-and-Goliath style against an evil giant, and knocking the giant off. The unheroic loner acts out his rage in less glamorous ways. The heroic loner may have his grandiosity reinforced by society, while the unheroic loner, if he acts out the rage, will meet with repudiation. He usually withdraws into psychosis.

Harold had withdrawn to a fairly great extent by the time he was assigned to me at the clinic where I was working as a staff psychotherapist. He was almost completely out of touch with his feelings. He would sit in the office before me, a saintly smile on his face, seeming to be completely cooperative. If I asked him to talk about his mother, he would immediately launch into a history of his relationship with her. If I asked him to talk about his father, or about army life, or his relationship with his older sister, he would do likewise, always with that sweet smile on his lips and an earnest look in his eyes. Yet, at the same time, the posture of his body belied the tension he carried around with him. He sat very still in the chair, his shoulders held high and hunched, his hands folded. The very stillness of his posture indicated an attempt to hold the tension (the rage) inside of himself, and the chronic hunch of his shoulders and rigidity of his neck confirmed this holding pattern. Indeed, he rarely turned his head; he would just look at me with those pale blue eyes from which I could hardly discern a trace of real feeling. Real feelings had been squashed by his family environment at an early age. He had, in essence, been trained to be an automaton.

His mother was one of those strong-willed, dominating women whose word was law in the household. His father timidly stood behind whatever the mother wanted. He was probably much like Harold, a man cut off from his feelings, unable to assert himself in any way. His older sister, following his mother's example, was also a strong-willed, self-righteous person, who teased and taunted her younger brother, continually deriding his sexuality. She was backed by their mother. "You make too much of things, Harold," his mother would tell him if he complained about his sister.

His memories of his mother indicated that she had been sexually teasing and taunting, as well as binding him to her in a psychologically incestuous relationship, impeding his attempts to gain independence. At the same time, there was a complete absence of physical affection; he could never recall receiving a single hug from her. During his early childhood he remembered that she never wanted him to leave the house to play with other children. "They're dirty," she would say. "They're beneath us." He remembered her scolding him and spanking him severely because he forgot to lift the toilet seat when he urinated. "You got the seat dirty again with your pee. How many times do I have to tell you?" He remembered that the only time she touched him was when she bathed him, and she bathed him until he was eight years old. The only reason she stopped was because he told her the other boys had teased him when they found out his mother still bathed him. Each time she bathed him she would pay special attention to his penis, which was uncircumsized. She would carefully pull back the foreskin and wash beneath it again and again. "We don't want you to get an infection down there," she would say. After she stopped bathing him, she continually asked him if he had made sure to wash under his foreskin. He remembered when he was an adolescent and wanted to buy a jockstrap for his bathing suit she laughed at him, and touching his crotch, said, "What do you need a jockstrap for? You've got nothing down there to protect." Throughout his childhood she would tell him he was the only person who meant anything to her, and that if he ever left her she would wither away. "Promise me you'll never leave me like my father did," she said to him once. The summer after he graduated from high school he had his first epileptic seizure. He had wanted to go to college, but his mother was adamantly against it— unless he enrolled in the local college. At the last minute he had joined the army. His mother reacted with shock and indignation. A few days before he was to leave, as he was sitting at the breakfast table, his eyes rolled back in his head and he fell to the floor, where he thrashed around for a few minutes and then passed out. The doctors called it an anxiety attack, and in a day or two he was feeling well enough to leave for the army.

His memories of his father were more vague, probably because the father's presence in the family was vague. His father was an accountant who never made enough money to satisfy his wife, and who, in a passive-aggressive manner, continually sabotaged any chances he had to rise within his company. His relationship with his son was, in fact, a nonrelationship. Harold had no memories of ever spending any time alone with the father. (His mother would have considered that to be a betrayal of her.) He stayed away from his father and his father stayed away from him. What he remembered most about his father were expressions on his face. He remembered his father scowling at him. But on the surface, the father was always pleasant to the boy. This family environment created a typical oedipal situation. The boy, knowing on some level that his relationship with his mother was unnatural, and that he had been drafted into a conspiracy with his mother against his father, found himself deluged with a lot of feelings that he could never acknowledge to himself, much less verbalize. At those times when he attempted to verbalize the sexual feelings or anger that was being aroused by his mother, or the fear, anger, and the desire to submit, sexually, to his father, he was repudiated. "What are you talking about. Don't you ever say such a thing," his mother replied when he spoke about marrying her when he grew up. He was constantly given double messages. On a nonverbal level both parents, as well as his older sister, related to him in a sexualized, sadistic manner. But if he responded to the nonverbal behavior with what would have been an appropriate response to such behavior, he was punished. So he shut himself up. The feelings became repressed, the memories muted. And he developed his sweet, cooperative façade.

Since joining the army, he had not gone back home. His mother still called him once a week, and he would talk to her sweetly, but ignore her entreaties to come home. He had lived in San Francisco, Los Angeles, Chicago, Key West, Miami, and New York, always on the fringes of society. When he could get his hands on it, he smoked marijuana, sniffed cocaine, and injected a plethora of other substances, from methadrine to heroin. He drifted from one group to another. For a while he was interested in acting and became involved with a theater group in San Francisco. That lasted about a year. Then he was involved with a gay political group in New York; a drug-smuggling venture in Key West; an after-hours massage parlor and sadomasochism club in Miami. He never stayed longer than a year with any group. His relationships with these groups probably resembled his relationships with the members of his family; no genuine emotional ties were formed, and relationships with individual members of these groups were tinged with sexual animosity. He could only tolerate sex when he was drugged, and when he had sex with a woman it had to be anal sex. Afterwards he would never want to see the woman again, feeling disgusted by her, feeling that she would infect him. Sex with men, in which he was penetrated by them anally, left him feeling angry and humiliated. He had unconscious castration fear toward both men and women.

He was unable to form a bond of any kind with me, not even the most rudimentary therapeutic alliance. His initial compliance was merely an act. It was the act he had learned worked best with members of his family. After a while his desire to seduce me emerged. Indeed, he freely spoke of his desire to have me sodomize him.

"Why don't you and me go someplace else," he said one day. He sat quite motionless in the chair, as usual, his eyes gazing vacantly at my eyes, a slight smile on his lips, as though he knew a secret.

"Where would you like to go?" I asked.

"I don't know." He looked at me without blinking. "Someplace private, I guess."

"Aren't we private here?"

"Somebody might come in."

"I see. What would we do at this private place?"

"I guess we'd have sex."

"What kind of sex?"

"You'd take me from behind."

"What would that do for you?"

"I don't know. I think it would help me in some way. I feel afraid of you. Maybe afterwards I wouldn't feel afraid of you anymore. Maybe afterwards I'd feel more like a man."

This, of course, is a typical homosexual fantasy—being taken anally by an idealized father-figure, who through the act of anal intercourse assuages the recipient's oedipal guilt and initiates him into realm of manhood. His grandiosity would be reinforced through the realization of the power of seducing an admired and idealized figure, and his rage could be temporarily dissipated by provoking an act of violent sexual penetration against himself. Harold wanted me to join with him in his hatred of and disgust toward women. Through the enactment of this negative oedipal sexual joining, we would form an alliance against Woman, against her witch-like power, against her threat to infect us with her cursed femininity, emasculate us, infanta-lize us.

"There's this fat, disgusting woman who has unfortunately developed a crush on me," he would say occasionally. He might be referring to a woman who lived in his roominghouse, or a woman who frequented a bar where he spent his evenings, or somebody who worked in a neighborhood store. His response was always the same. "The minute she smiled at me I felt turned off by her."

"Why did her smile turn you off?"

"I don't know. I guess I don't like women smiling at me. They're all so conceited. They think they're just going to take me over. They think I'll be putty in their hands. They think they can just grab my cock and lead me anywhere."

"Can they?"

"They probably could, if I let them get their hands on it. But I don't let them."

"What about the women you've slept with?"

"Well, sometimes if I get stoned enough, I can overcome the feelings of disgust. But it's usually with somebody I don't care about."

"How come you don't care about them?"

"Oh, because they're usually so out of it themselves that they don't intimidate me. But the next morning I feel disgust for them just the same. I mean, anybody who lets me bugger them, well, you have to wonder about them. Maybe I hate myself. Maybe anybody who lets me get near them becomes contemptible to me because of my self-loathing. What do you think, Doc?" He did not let me answer. "Anyway, I'd rather masturbate, to tell you the truth."

"Why's that?"

"It's safer and its cleaner. But I don't enjoy it."

"You don't?"

"No, I feel guilty. I have all these weird fantasies when I masturbate."

"Tell me about them."

"Someday. Not now. I don't know you well enough. Maybe someday after we've had sex."

"But after you've had sex with people you never want to see them again."

"That's true. But you'd be an exception."

"Why's that?"

"Because you're my shrink."

He never did tell me his sexual fantasies. He was teasing me the same way his mother and sister and possibly his father had teased him. Teasing and being teased was the mode of communication he felt comfortable with, while honest communication was threatening. Honest communication in his family had laid him bare to ridicule. To say, "You're hurting me," would have been a mistake there. "You're making too much of things," would be the reply. To say, "I need a hug," would have gotten the reply, "You're a big boy. Big boys don't need hugs." All attempts to get at the truth of his relationships with members of his family were met by such responses. They were not interested in the truth, any more than most politicians are interested in the truth. They were interested in being on top, on maintaining appearances, creating illusions of love and peace and joy that were intended to cover up the acting out of their aggression. So Harold had in turn created his own counter-illusion; he felt secretly superior to all of them. They, and all people, were secretly beneath his contempt. Why did his mother attempt to hold on to him so much? Because he was a superior person. Why did his father resent him so much? Because he was superior. Why did women want to get at his penis? Because his penis was superior. Why was I afraid of going away with him to a private place? Why did I have to hide behind my psychotherapeutic neutrality? Because he was superior and would prove it if I went with him, by seducing me and abandoning me. He knew things that other people did not know, and there was no use even trying to explain it to them, so he simply kept his distance. So he thought on one level. But on a deeper level, he felt inferior to everybody, and wanted to kill them all for making him feel inferior.

Unfortunately, I was only able to work with Harold for about six months, at which time I had completed my internship at this clinic and he was transferred to another therapist. When I told him I was leaving and informed him of his transfer, he took the news in a typical fashion.

"That's too bad," he replied, gazing at me with his emotionless eyes, smiling sweetly. "I wish you luck."

"Do you have any feelings about my leaving?"

"Not really. You said the clinic will assign another therapist to me?"

"That's right."

"Then I won't miss a session."

"Probably not."

"That's nice."

I thought at the time that had I stayed I would be able to reach him after a while, but perhaps that was my own illusion. At any rate, I later found out he terminated with his new therapist after a few months and moved back to Key West. Did he feel abandoned by me? Did he resent his new therapist? We'll never know. However, he seemed to have been pretty stuck into the loner style of life. For him, staying in a relationship, whether therapeutic or otherwise, represented a form of entrapment. Perhaps, in his own way, he felt as though he were riding off into the sunset. And like all the loners of old, his ride was not only toward the sunset, but away from involvement with Woman.

The tragedy as far as Harold was concerned was that instead of a loner of quiet desperation, he might have been one of the heroic kind. He obviously had a great deal of intelligence, sensitivity, and insight, plus the loner's originality of mind. The difference between Harold and a heroic loner was that the heroic type has a stronger ego, and his narcissism and rage is at the service of his ego, while Harold's ego was at the service of his narcissism and rage. He was paralyzed by ambivalence, by an eternal battle between id and superego.

Incidentally, he did turn in his gun to me, and I then handed it over to the local police precinct. I have not read any newspaper accounts of him "blowing away" any shopkeeper/mothers. I hope I never do.

10

Animosity in Africa: The Martyrdom of Dian Fossey

Two mornings after Christmas, according to an article in *Vanity Fair* (Shoumatoff 1986), Dian Fossey, the noted primatologist and feminist icon, was found assassinated in her cabin. The cabin was located in the Karisoke Research Centre in Rwanda, Africa—the station for the study of mountain gorillas that she had founded and run for nearly two decades. Someone had snipped out her bedroom window and broken in during the night, tearing apart her living room and ransacking her bedroom. Fossey was found lying on the floor with her head and shoulder slumped over the bed. She had been hit twice with a blunt instrument, once in the face, exposing her skull, and once on the back of the head. A pistol was on the floor by her side, as well as a cartridge clip, but the clip was still full; Shoumatoff speculates that in trying to load her gun, she had picked up the wrong clip. In interviewing a friend who had discovered her body, the author was told that Fossey had been having bouts of insomnia for two weeks and had been also drinking heavily for some time and possibly taking sleeping pills. Police reportedly came to believe that she might have been in a deep, drug-induced sleep when she was awakened by the intruder, and that she was attacked before she knew what was happening.

She was buried just above her cabin, under a circle of stones, in a pine coffin provided by the American Consulate. Buried around her, with plaques bearing their names, were the bodies of the gorillas she had studied and fought for: Digit, Uncle Bert, Macho, Mwelu, Kweli, Wageni, Marchessa, Frito, Leo, Quince, Nunkie, Kazi, Kurudi, and others who were unnamed. According to those who knew her, she cared more about the gorillas than about any human, including her family and friends. She was to the mountain gorillas of Rwanda, Shoumatoff notes, what Jane Goodall was to the chimpanzees of Tanzania. The people called her Nyramacibili, "Woman Who Lives Alone in the Forest." Through her book, three articles, and film documentary, she and her gorillas had become famous. She was concerned not only with studying gorillas, but also with dispelling the myth that gorillas were vicious and dangerous—she proved that they are among the gentlest of primates—and with bringing to the public's attention the fact that large numbers of gorillas were being killed by poachers.

Indeed, it was her war against the poachers that apparently did her in, according to Shoumatoff. During her eighteen years as director of the Karisoke Research Centre, she is reported to have fired shots over the heads of Dutch tourists who had hiked up uninvited, to have put a noose around the captured pygmy and threatened to hang him from a rafter if he did not talk, to have injected one poacher with gorilla dung to give him septicemia, and to have hired a sorcerer to poison another particularly incorrigible poacher. Kelly Stewart, wife of zoologist Sandy Harcourt, both of whom spent years on the mountain with Dian in the mid-1970s, describes even more bizarre treatment of poachers: "She would whip their balls with stinging nettles, spit on them, stuff sleeping pills down their throats . . . She reduced them to quivering, quaking packages of fear, little guys in rags rolling on the ground and foaming at the mouth" (p. 134). Further on, Stewart explains: "She always fantasied about a final confrontation. She viewed herself as a warrior fighting this enemy who was out to get her. It was a perfect ending. She got what she wanted" (p. 135).

During her last years she is said to have become increasingly reclusive and to have behaved more and more strangely, alienating even those closest to her. Shoumatoff quotes Bill Weber, an American who worked on the Mountain Gorilla Project, who gives a description of paranoi and fear: "She was riding on some kind of dedication she had once had. Why did she hardly ever go out to the gorillas if they were her life-motivating forces? . . . She kept threatening to burn the station down and all the long-term records. She was willing to take down everything with her—Karisoke, the gorillas" (p. 136). He adds that when he did a census that indicated a growing gorilla population, she tried to cut off his funding. She apparently wanted the public to believe that they were dying. In talking about her increasing isolation, cruelty, and madness, he says, "No one wanted to take over the place. She invented so many plots and enemies. She kept talking about how nobody could take it up there, how they all got 'bushy,' but in the end she was the one who went bonkers. She didn't get killed because she was saving the gorillas. She got killed because she was behaving like Dian Fossey" (p. 136). There were also reports that she was prone to frequent fits of temper, which were directed at whoever was around, particularly the native men who served as her helpers and guides. She would yell at them unmercifully, and when she left they would speak of a cloud having dissipated. Because she had so many enemies at the time of her death, the identity of her murderer was never determined.

The article offers little information about Fossey's childhood. She was an only child, and her parents divorced when she was still quite young. At the age of 6, she had to adjust to a new father when her mother remarried. According to the article, she also started taking lessons at the St. Francis Riding Academy at the age of 6, and she remained horse-crazy throughout adolescence, winning a letter on the riding team at Lowell High School. There was friction between Fossey and her stepfather, however; until she was 10, she reportedly dined in the kitchen with the housekeeper while her parents dined in the dining room. When she became an adult, she was supposedly estranged from both her mother and stepfather.

We are given only the foregoing facts of her early childhood. It is possible to read between the lines, however, and make some analytic speculations. First, she lost her father through divorce when she was quite young, some time before the age of 6. Such a loss is usually devastating to a child and usually leads to some degree of depression. She apparently then developed a negative relationship with both her stepfather and her mother (she ate in the kitchen with the housekeeper). The nature of this relationship indicates that the mother did not give her daughter the empathy, understanding, and soothing she needed in order to mourn her father's departure and accept a new father as his substitute. It also shows the development of the habit of estranging herself from people, her parents being the first of many from whom she would distance herself.

In another part of this article, the author remarks that Fossey had a particular antipathy towards couples. She could stand to be only with single people, usually single women and occasionally a single man if she was in complete control of the situation. For example, Wayne McGuire, the last man to live with her, claimed that Fossey had kept a lock of his hair and used it to control him through some kind of voodoo. her antipathy toward couples may also have begun with her atnipathy toward her mother and stepfather. Although we do not have much to go on, it is quite possible that Fossey's real father had been close to her before his departure, and that she felt abandoned after he left, It is also possible that her stepfather and mother somehow reinforced her feelings of abandonment. Her hatred of people, and particularly her hatred of men, had to have come from somewhere; this seems the most likely source.

And what of Fossey's attraction to gorillas? Shoumatoff suggests that Fossey was a Thoreauvian who, because of her lonely childhood, loved animals but hated people. He compares with her Joy Adamson, who fought for lions in Africa but was killed by one of her African workers, whom she had supposedly abused terribly, in a crime that closely resembled Fossey's murder.

I would speculate that Fossey chose gorillas because they represented her archaic father — an all-powerful yet gentle beast. Childhood dreams abound with such beasts, and they generally symbolize the father. Her love and mastery of gorillas may have also afforded her a way of acting out an apparent masculinity complex. She obviously strongly identified with her father, and gorillas, being fearsome aggressive animals (in the popular mind, at least), provided her with a substitute, identification-with-the-aggressor situation in which to play out her unresolved feelings about her father.

If the gorillas stood for Fossey's father, then all those whom she saw as antagonistic to the gorillas represented her mother and stepfather. What then emerges, psychodynamically, during her life in Africa was an attempt to protect and sanctify her relationship with her father and to keep anyone from separating them again. It appears that she had already begun to direct her libidinal energy toward animals by the age of 6, when she began to take an interest in horses. Animals, unlike humans, cannot betray, desert, reject, or humiliate. One can love them without much threat of being hurt. The problem in loving lower animals is that they cannot fully satisfy the needs of Eros. Therefore, her primal frustration in this area could never be assuaged by the gorillas, and they could not forestall her gradual descent into destruction and madness.

According to the article, her interest in gorillas began in 1963, when she was 31. At that time she took out a bank loan and went to Africa to see the animals and to look up Louis Leakey, the eminent anthropologist. Some time later, when Leakey was searching for a "gorilla girl" to go out and study apes, he decided that Fossey had the kind of character the job required. She returned to Africa at the end of 1966, stopping to visit Jane Goodall for a few days to see how she had set up her camp and to learn what she could from Goodall's methods. Eventually, the article relates, she ended up in Rwanda, in the Virgunga mountains, where gorillas were said to live. An incident then occurred that provides another important clue to Fossey's eventual breakdown. While on her way to find a camp, she got caught up in the Congolese civil war. She was taken captive by the rebels and held in a place called Rumangabo, where, according to Shomatoff, who quotes a former colleague of Fossey's, she was "sexually molested." Later she reportedly tricked the soldiers into taking her to Uganda, leading them to believe that they would be getting her vehicle and some money when they got there. Instead, she managed to have them arrested by Ugandan authorities.

In trying to understand Fossey's impact on Africans—be they rebels or police officers—one must consider that she would have been an imposing, perhaps even intimidating, figure to most of them. She was, after all, an attractive, strong-willed, 6-foot-tall white woman, with long brown hair usually worn in a braid. She seems to have been frightening to them, so that they needed to either come to her aid or mitigate the castration fear she evoked by "raping" her.

This sexual molestation by the rebels, according to Shoumatoff, haunted her for the remainder of her life. Although she is said to have sometimes alluded to the incident, she would never really talk about it; it left her feeling bitter and stated her off on a particular footing in Africa. In addition, it reinforced her already immense rage.

When Digit, her favorite gorilla, was brutally murdered in 1977, probably by poachers in retaliation for her persecution of them, her bitterness became blatant. The proverb "violence breeds violence" was certainly borne out by subsequent events. The more she waged war against the poachers, the more violence was direction back at her. One by one her favorite gorillas were killed off, and sometimes mutilated, by poachers, leading Bill Weber to draft a letter to the National Geographic Society, Fossey's main backer. He described what was happening and observed that there seemed to be a link between her persecution of the poachers and the fact that only her gorillas were being killed. Fossey reportedly got hold of this draft. She then took to sneaking up to various researchers' cabins at night, listening to their conversations, and opening their mail.

Fossey's war against the poachers points up her narcissistic ambivalence, a kind of splitting that harkens back to earliest infancy, when a child first develops a polarized perspective of the mother, splitting her into good and bad mother. The infant feels justified in biting kicking, devouring or killing the bad mother with his feces, urine, or any other available self-protective means. As Fossey withdrew further into what Klein called the paranoid-schizoid position (where Fossey apparently was fixated), she lost sight of reality. She had become transported by her own rage, and this rage colored her world, which she saw through the lens of her own delusional system.

Moreover, the methods that Fossey supposedly used to wage war against the poachers also hearken back to the primitive thinking of infancy. If it is true that she injected a poacher with gorilla dung engaged a sorcerer to poison another, and whipped the testicles of still others, such incidents would seem to be actualizations of childhood fantasies of revenge. Klein (1932) has detailed the various fantasies that infants and toddlers have toward parents and siblings. Such fantasies are attempts to compensate for feelings of powerlessness and to express the rage associated with frustrating relationships. The fantasies involve infants' belief that their feces and urine are poisonous and can therefore be used to destroy "the enemey," the belief in magical powers, and the belief that their parents are going to castrate them (stemming from their own unconscious desire to castrate their parents). In taking revenge on the poachers, Fossey was acting out pregenital rage, penis envy, and phallic remorse, displacing onto the poachers her anger at her mother, her stepfather, and the Congolese rebels who had molested her. In addition, there was an aspect of avenging her "good father," as each poacher who attacked one of her gorillas was assaulting her father surrogates.

The fact that Fossey never married may also be seen as part of her narcissistic withdrawal. Because of her purported fierce independence and her need for control, she could not maintain a romantic relationship with a man. It may be that no man could live up to the idealized father of her imagination. Moreover, her animosity toward men was apparently too great to allow her to be receptive to male sexual penetration except under controlled circumstances. Perhaps she had to defend against her deep longings for merger and for reunion with the father who had abandoned her, as well as against the fear that any new man might abandon her.

In her book *Gorillas in the Mist*, Fossey wrote that after Digit was murdered, she began to "live in an insulated part" of herself. This signified the beginning of her paranoid retreat, at the end of which she would have distanced herself from the poachers, the Rwandan authorities (whom she openly despised and defied), tourist agencies, the primatological community, colleagues who were carrying out similar research, and American authorities. Nearly everyone, Shoumatoff notes, wanted her out of Africa. They succeeded for a short time, when she left her research center for three years to be a visiting lecturer at Cornell and to write her book. Then she returned to the center, resuming her position as director. When she returned, in 1983, she reportedly told an American official that she had come home to die – an indication that she had become irrevocably stuck in a destructive mode. For Fossey, in 1983, there was no turning back.

Dian Fossey's life, and her tragic death, is a study of disharmony and destruction, of the victory of nurture over nature. She was undoubtedly blessed with many gifts – intelligence, grace, sensitivity – but these gifts were undermined by the vicissitudes of her upbringing and her life. One can only imagine that she must have been a bright, engaging child, possibly the apple of her father's eye' then, suddenly, he was gone, chased away (so it might have seemed to her) by her mother. In addition to the feelings of abandonment, she may have also been left with feelings of guilt, as it is common for children of divorced parents to feel responsible for their parents' break-up. Such feelings are usually related to their forbidden oedipal urges to take the parent of the opposite sex away from the parent of the same sex. Fossey might have seen her father's desertion and her mother's remarriage as punishment for her incenstuous wishes. When she became involved in a power struggle with her mother and stepfather and estranged herself from them, her repetition-compulsion was set. All her intelligence and sensitivity would then be enlisted in the service of this compulsive pattern of estranging herself from people and acting out her rage at the unfairness of humanity.

From early on she began viewing herself as a victim; fixated in the paranoid-schizoid position, she would therefore see the world in terms of good and evil, with no middle ground. Because she was stuck in that mode, she would look for evidence to reinforce her paranoia. To be sure, she *was* victimized – by her parents, by the Congolese rebels, and by others – and so she found plenty of fuel for her fire. A masculine-aggressive narcissist, she needed to prove that she was superior to any man; her determination to tame and befriend the gorilla was a testament to this superiority. No man had ever done it. Her determination to tame the gorillas was, I believe, also related to her fixation in the paranoid-schizoid position: If she could tame the gorillas, then she could control the menacing and potentially persecutory forces of life.

That she had a death wish (and was, in fact, carrying out the unconscious dictates of Thanatos) was evident not only in her statement that she had come home to die, but also in the sentiments she expressed from time to time that she would rather die than let anyone take her research center from her or interfere with her work with the gorillas. It was also evidenced by her isolationism, remaining alone in her cabin, turning to drink and then to pills. And, of course, an unconscious aspect of her persecution of poachers was a desire to have them kill her, to die a martyr's death. By the time she returned from Cornell, she had developed a full-scale delusional system comprising a grandiose view of herself as the only person who truly understood or cared about the plight of the gorillas, and a corresponding view that all others were enemies, out to ruin her and despoil her work. In her eyes she was a martyr on a mission to save gorillas from human corruption; she was not the troublemaker others saw in her.

Martyrdom has been a pervasive theme throughout history. In both the East and the West, victims are seen as martyrs and victimizers as devils. Thus the good/bad breast of earliest infancy and the long-suffering masochist of the anal stage become the martyr of society, and the myth of the martyr permeates history The Hindus martyr themselves by practicing self-torture and self-mutilation in the most imaginative and bizarre ways—walking on sharp nails or burning coals, plunging 9-inch-long pins through their arms or breasts, half starving themselves—all in an attempt to prove their courage in the face of pain (that is, in the face of self-victimization). In the West we have figures such as Jesus Christ, who was glorified because he was crucified for claiming to be the son of God, and Socrates, who was sentenced to poisoning by the Greeks for corrupting the morals of youth. Both of these men could have saved themselves: Jesus could have saved himself by compromising with religious leaders, but instead he defied them and treated them with contempt, thereby increasing the likelihood that they would request his execution; Socrates could have saved himself, both during his trial and afterward in his jail cell, from which he was offered a chance to escape, but he took the poison, clearly wanting to die a martyr.

The Catholic church is a haven for martyrs. Most Catholic saints were canonized because of their martyrdom. The Church itself was founded on the martyrdom of Jesus Christ. The Protestant church is no different: From Martin Luther on, they, too, have a history of martyrdom and are contributors to the cult of the victim.

Those who glorify martyrs claim that they sacrifice themselves, often by giving their lives, in order to make the world a better place. But have they really accomplished that goal? Christ's death resulted in the formation of the Christian church and eventually in the Holy Roman Empire, which in turn led to the Crusades—during which millions of Christians were exhorted by mercenary popes to slaughter, rape, and plunder as many non-Christians as they could in order to make the world a better place. This in turn led to more Crusades (spurred by a succession of power-hungry popes), culminating in the tragic Children's Crusade, during which hordes of young boys were sent out to fight, only to be butchered or captured for the slave trade.

Finally, Christ's martyrdom led to the Inquisitions, during which hundreds of thousands were beheaded in the name of Christianity. Did Christ's martyrdom make the world a better place?

Nor has any other martyr made the world a better place. Society takes note of their death for a time and pays lips service to the principles for which they died, but then society reverts to its old ways. In fact, martyrdom often worsens matters, as was the case with Christianity.

Martyrdom, or the glorification of victims, has from time immemorial been used to justify the acting out of unresolved narcissistic aggression. If one can prove that one has been victimized, that one has consequently suffered and become emotionally purified, and that one has therefore attained a superior moral status, one can then use that claim of superiority to justify the persecution of certain others whom one identifies as victimizers.

Most mass movements, whether political, religious, or philosophical, incorporate this theme. The Christians felt victimized by the Jews and then by the Romans, and their consequent feeling of moral superiority led them to assassinate non-Christians (heretics) via the Crusades and the Inquisition. After World War I, the Nazis felt victimized by the French and British, who they decided were influenced by the Jews; they responded by assuming a higher morality on the basis of their Aryan blood and by exterminating the Jews, who they determined were of the lowest morality. The Jews, in their turn, assumed a superior moral perch on the basis of their suffering during the Holocaust and proceeded to use this victimization to justify taking over Israel and becoming one of the most militant countries in the world, "victimizing" their neighbors. The Russian Bolsheviks felt victimized by the czar and took over the country through a bloody revolution; they then felt morally superior and justified, during the reign of Stalin, in executing millions of "traitors."

In the United States, blacks have developed a feeling of moral superiority over whites due to their history of enslavement and segregation, and they use this victimization to justify a reverse racism against whites that is just as poisonous as the racism of whites toward blacks. Feminists claim a higher moral status on the basis of what they perceive as men's oppression of them throughout history, and they use this suffering to justify a militant, depreicatory, and reverse-sexist attitude toward men. Thus, each new wave of victimization fosters yet another wave.

The glorification of victims is a narcissistic and sadomasochistic phenomenon. Individually or collectively, those who glorify victims are acting out a repetition compulsion stemming from the values inculcated in them in early childhood. If a young child is emotionally injured by narcissistic, sadomasochistic parents, the child can do nothing about it; thus the process of compulsive repetition is set in motion. The basis of this martyrdom is the inferiority complex that develops when one's primary needs are frustrated during the oral stage. A component of this inferiority complex is a need to prove one's superiority. Since a child—such as Dian Fossey, say— is too small and powerless to prove her superiority in any tangible way (particularly in a pathogenic environment that thwarts any such attempts), she must either assert that superiority in her own mind or put it off until the future. A sadistically dominating parent will reinforce this inferiority complex during the anal-rapprochement phase and the martyr syndrome will then make its appearance; thus the secondary basis for characterological martyrdom lies in the sadomasochism of the anal-rapprochement phase. The child finds a way to be superior without having to prove anything or to do anything: She can be superior morally. It is, in a sense, her only way out.

The child grows up to become masochistically narcissistic. She feels victimized by almost everyone and justifies this victimhood with the thought "They're just jealous of me" or some similar notion. She attempts to undo what was done in childhood or to defend against its happening again. She quarrels with the world and projects her own paranoia onto it—and then, of course, finds that she can never find peace or contentment. She becomes involved with men who are like her stepfather, for example, so that she can again feel unjustly victimized and displace her animosity onto this stepfather surrogate; or she becomes involved with a man who reminds her of her real father and then finds reasons to abandon him before he can abandon her. Or she becomes involved in a movement that serves to justify her martyrdom.

Movements—whether crusades to save gorillas or associations to save the world from sin—serve to institutionalize martyrdom and to validate narcissism, sadomasochism, and paranoia. The Christian church provided a framework in which members could feel morally superior to "heathens." The Nazis provided the higher authority that made it possible for Germans to feel victimized by Europe and hence morally superior to everyone. Fossey's crusade to save the gorillas served as a means by which she could institutionalize her own narcissism, sadomasochism, and paranoia. It kept her in a state of childlike innocence, in which she could maintain her delusion that she was a "good" person in a corrupt world.

In the end, Fossey was a victim not of the Rwandan poachers or the various others she designated as enemies, but of the circumstances of her early childhood. She was not just an only child, prone to the loneliness of all only children, but she was also an only child whose parental environment was unstable and toxic. Even in this light, however, she was not a victim in the sense that she was good and her parents evil. They too were acting out unconscious conflicts induced in their own childhoods, as we all do. There are no pure victims or victimizers; we are all victims *and* victimizers, unless we somehow awaken from our "trances" and overcome the human condition, and even then there is no such thing as perfection. Had Fossey given birth to children, it seems quite likely that she too would have transmitted her unresolved narcissism and animosity to her children. She too would have become, irrevocably, a transmitter of sexual animosity. Unfortunately, she could not transcend her fixations, and so the forces of loneliness and destruction caught up with her.

11

An Analysis of *A Streetcar Named Desire*

A Streetcar Named Desire, hailed by many critics as a masterpiece of American theater and cinema, is a classical duel between a phallic narcissist and a hysterical narcissist. The confrontation between them results in each succeeding, to some extent, in destroying the other. Blanche enters the drama as a borderline hysteric with a history of acting out; during the course of the play, due to her interactions with Stanley, she withdraws more and more into a schizophrenic mode, which eventually leads to a psychotic breakdown. Stanley also has a history of acting out (getting into brawls, beating up his wife), and during the course of his interactions with Blanche he ends up behaving in a psychopathic manner. Each brings out the worst in the other.

Indeed, the history of literature and drama is replete with confrontations between phallics and hysterics; they are the essence of melodrama as commonly encountered in, say, television soap operas, and many of the great works of fiction contain, as their centerpieces, the animositous relationships between these two character types.

Examples abound, from Shakespeare's *Antony and Cleopatra* to
Brontë's *Wuthering Heights*, from Austen's *Pride and Prejudice* to
Mitchell's *Gone with the Wind*, and from Lawrence's *Lady Chatterley's
Lover* to Williams's *Orpheus Descending*. Theatrics are unavoidable
when a phallic and hysteric confront each other, both being oedipal
characters with a compulsive sexual orientation. Each puts stock in
sexual conquests. The phallic uses his penis to conquer and then
abandon women, while the hysteric uses her seductiveness to entrap
and then abandon men. Their relationships are probably the most
dramatic of all unions between men and women because they are
always highly visible wars, each partner openly expressing contempt
for the other (unlike the relationship between two orals, for example,
whose animosity will be expressed subtly, such as through withholding). Their interactions are a series of defensive maneuvers—hysterical
outbursts, verbal derogation, and the like—leading to conquest and
submission, often in a period of romantic, sexualized intimacy (but
without genuine tenderness). The relationship between Stanley and
Blanche typifies this kind of relationship and takes it to an ultimate,
and tragic, conclusion.

Williams's description of Blanche, at the beginning of the play,
underscores her hysteria. He has her dressed "daintily" in white: white
suit (with a "fluffy bodice"), white necklace and pearl earrings, white
gloves, and white hat. "There is something about her uncertain
manner, as well as her white clothes, that suggests a moth." Words like
dainty, fluffy, and *delicate* suggest a hysterical defense against aggression. Her fragile persona seems to say, "Be nice to me, don't be
aggressive, because I'm delicate and dainty and soft and feminine."
Williams compares her to a moth, a moth in a white cocoon. When
moths come out of their cocoons, they can become quite aggressive
and destructive to the vegetation around them. She fears others'
aggression because, unconsciously, she is afraid that they will perceive
her own hidden aggression, her desire to destroy. Her display of
fragility is a manipulation to defend against the possibility of being
destroyed by aggression, hers or theirs, and to get people such as her
sister to take care of her.

Her delicate beauty must avoid a strong light, Williams notes.
This description, when applied to the moth metaphor, adds a new
meaning: Moths are attracted to light and, in fact, they are known to

destroy themselves by fluttering around light bulbs for hours. The phrase suggests the denial of reality that is typical of hysterics. In the play, Stanley is her symbolic light bulb, to whom she is compulsively attracted and from whom she cannot escape. He represents the brutal, yet unacceptable, truth. Stanley never accepts the fragile facade but rather responds directly to her sexual-aggressive undertone; thus his response to her is a brutal reflection of the aggression and seductiveness that she wishes to deny.

Williams uses the metaphor of the light bulb throughout the play. In the first scene, for example, a moment after Blanche has been reunited with her sister, Stella, she tells her, "And turn that over-light off! Turn that off! I won't be looked at in this merciless glare!" Later in the play she puts a Chinese lantern over the light to dim it. She is preoccupied with her appearance, and continually requests compliments. Stella not only complies, but insists that others do likewise. It is evident that Stella has played this overprotective role with her older sister since they were children, and although Stella no doubt feels that she is being kind by treating her sister "with kid gloves," she is actually being destructive. She is colluding in her sister's denial of reality, which serves only to reinforce it. The picture that Blanche presents—her fragility, her sensitivity to light, her need for compliments and protection—reflects the self-hatred and sexual animosity that she wishes to deny, as well as the oedipal guilt associated with those feelings, centered in the play around the screen memory of her husband's suicide.

Her recurring memory of her husband's death is no doubt a screen memory that covers an earlier memory, perhaps of the loss of her father or younger brother, literally or figuratively. (In a later scene she talks about the endless deaths that permeated her childhood.) This memory is central to the play. When, in Scene Six, Blanche relates the whole story to Mitch, we come to understand both the memory and her fear of light. She tells how, when she was a young girl, she met a boy and discovered love, suddenly and overwhelmingly: "It was like you suddenly turned a blinding light on something that had always been half in shadow." She describes the boy as different, nervous, soft, and tender, and expresses regret that she did not realize until after their marriage that he had come to her for help; she now feels that she failed him "in some mysterious way." She was simply not able to give him the help he needed but could not request, and this inability to respond to her husband's needs still haunts her.

It turned out that her young husband was having a homosexual relationship with an older man. When Blanche found out about it, she told the young man that he was disgusting, and he ran off and shot himself through the mouth. After that, Blanche's life had gone downhill, apparently becoming increasingly self-indulgent and culti- minating in the loss of the family mansion, Belle Reve. She suffered from guilt not only about this incident, but also about what it aroused from her early childhood, and the guilt caused an unconscious need to degrade herself and to sacrifice the family mansion, as well as the family name.

Her guilt appears to have been evoked by her inability to be empathic toward her husband's needs for sexual affirmation. Instead she added to his dilemma, as her unconscious animosity erupted and became directed at him. She says, "I made the discovery—love. All at once and much, much too completely. It was like you suddenly turned a blinding light on something that had always been half in shadow . . ." Her discovery of love had been wrought with the discovery of her ambivalence. Intimacy forces us to see things closely that we need not see as long as we maintain a distance from others. It forces us to see things about ourselves, our jealousy, our pettiness, our anger, and our fear. It seems that, just once, Blanche had allowed herself to come out of her narcissistic shell and care about another person, and it had turned sour. Hysterics such as Blanche are generally frightened of men who are aggressively virile and will often choose as mates more passive, sensitive, easily controlled types. At the same time, however, they then harbor contempt toward their mates for being weak. This seemed to be the case with her husband. She had contempt for his weakness, for his sexual problems with her, and for his homosexuality. She had a need, as hysterics often do, to see herself as good and right and loving and gentle; but when the light was turned on, she discovered that she was a "killer." This was too much for her: It threatened her ideal image of herself.

Stanley is exactly the type of man Blanche fears most and, therefore, toward which she has the most animosity. His confidence in his sexuality, his crude masculinity, and the fact that he has her sister's allegiance arouses in her the desire to castrate him and to separate him from her sister. She begins to act in a seductive, coy way almost from the moment she meets him, in an effort to keep the "beast" in abeyance; at the same time, she makes offhand remarks that aim at castration. In Scene Two, for example, she tries to be coy and flirtatious, but he won't buy it. "I'm going to ask a favor of you in a moment," she says, slipping into a dress. Stanley wonders what that would be. "Some buttons in back! You may enter!" He cannot do the buttons and is openly hostile toward her. She ignores the hostility and says something about men and clumsy fingers. Then she wants a drag from his "cig." She is being condescending and coy, using words like "cig" and making a gesture—asking to drag on his cigarette—that has sexual connotations. Again he does not buy it, offering her another cigarette instead. Later she playfully sprays him with an atomizer, causing him to remark, "If I didn't know you was my wife's sister I'd get ideas about you!" And still later, when he insists on seeing the papers on Belle Reve, she wonders what in the name of heaven he is thinking of. What's in back of that little boy's mind of his? Her strategy in dealing with Stanley, in order to defend against what she perceives as his threat to conquer her, is to sexually tease him and psychologically castrate him by belittling his intelligence and his very humanity.

Blanche sees Stanley as a predator, a destructive male force that she must control; yet her way of controlling him merely provokes the very response she fears. This is true of most narcissistic defenses. The more she teases and denigrates him, the more she is provoking him into aggressive action. She relates to him in a sexual and aggressive manner without being entirely conscious of doing so. At the deepest level of her unconscious, she wants to provoke him into sexual violence—and she succeeds toward the end of the play. She has been on a self-destructive bent for many years, since the death of her husband, and she wants to induce Stanley into serving up the coup de grace; this will not only help to assuage her tremendous guilt but will also allow her to go out with honor, the victim of male aggression. She will then be able to retain her grandiose self-image as a refined, fragile beauty trying to survive in a rotten world. More important, she also wants to destroy Stanley. By getting him to act the beast, she will be able to obtain a masochistic victory through defeat, turn public opinion against him, and prove that she is right.

Blanche despises Stanley because his crude, simple masculinity arouses her penis envy. She resents everything about his sexuality and about his liaison with her sister. When she discovers that Stella is pregnant, she responds in a dreamy voice, perhaps dissociating herself from the feelings that the news evokes. She seems to resent everything about her sister's actualization of her femininity. She does not want Stanley to have access to her sister, does not want him to use his penis in any way, does not want Stella to accept it. She has disowned her own femininity and all else connected with heterosexual love. She is basically a latent lesbian. She can deal only with men who are submissive, like Mitch, Stanley's sensitive poker-playing friend who lives with his mother. To be sexually receptive to a man, except in a compulsive way, is impossible for Blanche because of her deep aversion to everything masculine, particularly the penis.

In a telling scene, Blanche attempts to turn Stella against her husband after Stanley, in a drunken brawl, slaps Stella. Blanche tells Stella that Stanley is an animal, that he is subhuman, something out of the cave-man era. Thousands of years have passed him by, she says, and there he is, bearing the raw meat home from the kill. She is appalled that Stella puts up with him, waits for him, forgives him. She speaks of the progress that humankind has made, of art and poetry and music and the kinds of "new light" that have come into the world since the Stone Age. She speaks of the "tenderer feelings" that must be clung to and displayed as a flag.

Here again Blanche portrays herself as a progressive person, holding the flag of human decency and sensitivity and tenderness, while Stanley is everything that is vulgar, beastly, and bad. She tries to persuade Stella to leave him, but Stella is bemused, sensing her older sister's irrational fear of men. Blanche needs to "cling" to the notion of her moral superiority and "tenderer feelings," despite the fact that she was unable to treat her young husband with tenderness when he needed it. She has no tender feelings; they have been long subsumed by her narcissistic rage, which she must always deny.

Indeed, she denigrates Stanley for causing a ruckus the night before, but it was her provocative behavior that set Stanley off. Feeling excluded from the poker game (she had made a coy remark to Stanley earlier about how the women were "cordially not invited"), she retaliates by acting out in such a way as to eventually break up the game. During the course of the evening, she stands in her slip in the doorway so that the men can see her; she plays jazz music on the radio despite Stanley's protests (thus getting Stella to team up with her against Stanley); and then she manages to seduce Mitch away from the game, which finally succeeds in pushing Stanley to the limit. He blows up at his friends, throws the radio out the window, and then, because of her defense of Blanche, ends up hitting Stella. Blanche succeeds admirably in her unconscious effort to break up the poker game, which undoubtedly aroused her envy of males, and to induce Stanley to act like a beast, all the while maintaining her pose of innocence.

It is this tendency of both female and male narcissists to act out rage in devious ways, to refuse to take responsibility for their aggression, and to attribute aggression to their adversaries that leads to conflict, destructiveness, and violence. However, this is probably the kind of behavior Blanche's parents modelled. In fact, it would seem likely that her childhood feminine strivings had been severely frustrated, perhaps by an overprotective mother whose treatment of Blanche was similar to Stella's. Her father, if he were present, would have added to her frustration. The severity of her splitting—her tendency to view the world in terms of good and evil (she being good and Stanley evil)—reveals a kind of paranoia that harkens back to the early oral stage of development.

And what of Stanley? He also has his share of animosity, and just as Blanche's unconscious aim is to destroy Stanley, so also his unconscious aim is to destroy her. He is described as a man who, from earliest adolescence on, had enjoyed giving and taking pleasure from women, not dependently, but with power and pride, like a rooster among hens. He sizes up women in terms of sexual classifications. When he meets Blanche, it is clear that he has sized her up as a thief and a tart. In Scene Two he indirectly proclaims his disgust for her by remarking on female vanity. (He is just as bothered by female narcissism as Blanche is bothered by male narcissism.) He does not go in for "that stuff," he tells Blanche when she fishes for a compliment about her looks, explaining that he has never met a woman who did not know whether she was attractive or not. Some women, he complains, fancy that they are more attractive than they really are. He once went out with a woman who said to him, "I am the glamorous type"—to which he responded, "So what?" He makes it clear to Blanche that he is not impressed by female beauty.

Blanche then challenges him with, "I cannot imagine any witch of a woman casting a spell on you."

To which he replies, somewhat hesitantly, "That's—right."

Thus the duel is set in motion. He then proceeds, against the "jabs" and "punches" of Blanche's teasing, to try to pin her down about how she managed to lose Belle Reve. "Where's the papers? In the trunk?" he barks at her. He opens her trunk and roughly begins looking through it, remarking accusatorily that he has a lawyer acquaintance who will study the legal papers. While going through the trunk he picks up Blanche's love letters from her young husband and starts to read them, crudely disregarding her protests. Then he asserts his proprietary masculinity, saying, "You see, under the Napoleonic code—a man has to take an interest in his wife's affairs—especially now that she's going to have a baby." This is an attempt to assert his male dominance.

The increasingly vicious jousting continues throughout the play, she attempting to prove that he is an "animal," and he trying to prove she is a "slut," each trying to villify the other and claim victory (destruction of the threatening object and "ownership" of Stella's allegiance). On Stanley's part, his quest to destroy Blanche centers on an attempt to ruin her reputation and credibility. He eventually discovers the "evidence" he needs to condemn her. A traveling salesman who had stayed at a hotel in which Blanche had lived tells Stanley that she was thrown out of the Flamingo, presumably because of promiscuous behavior. In fact, she had been thrown out of a series of hotels and towns, and had established a reputation as a town character, as being "loco-nuts." Stanley, triumphantly telling Stella about all this as though he were a district attorney delivering the final argument, revealing the indisputably incriminating evidence that will lead to conviction, finally asks if she knew that there was an army camp near Laurel and her sister's was one of the places called "Out-of-Bounds"? Apparently Blanche's reputation had become so bad that even soldiers were warned to stay away from her.

He tells not only Stella, but also Mitch, about Blanche's past. He claims that he is looking out for his friend's best interest; but his main motivation is undoubtedly to further ruin Blanche by destroying her chances with Mitch. He has to know that Mitch is Blanche's last hope for salvaging her flagging sense of self, and he wants to separate Mitch and Blanche just as Blanche wants to separate Stanley and Stella. He wants to tear away every prop—Mitch, Stella, her love letters from her late husband, her "fine feathers," her idealized image of herself as a person of integrity and refinement—and leave her naked, flat on her face, absolutely defeated. In short, he wants nothing less than to psychologically murder her, mercilessly, and then go on his merry way.

Why does Stanley hate Blanche so intensely? Why does he so urgently want to destroy her? His animosity, like hers, stems not only from his immediate response to the hostility she directs toward him in the present, but also from the transference onto her of the frustrating female (and perhaps male) objects from his past. The play provides no background information about Stanley's childhood. However, if we assume that Williams projected parts of himself onto the character of Stanley, we may gain some understanding from Williams's own childhood. According to Rader (1985), Williams's father was a womanizing shoe salesman, mostly absent, who terrified Williams. His mother was of the smothering variety, squashing his masculine strivings. Once, at the age of five, she had the boy sleep in her bed while he was overcoming an illness. Williams later became homosexual. Stanley may be seen as a literary extension of Williams, a depiction of his male narcissism—the rage at his controlling mother, the identification with the womanizing father, and the male grandiosity to compensate for feelings of inferiority. (Incidentally, Williams probably also projected parts of himself onto Blanche, as he himself had several mental breakdowns; indeed, the conflict between Blanche and Stanley might be seen to represent the conflict between Williams's internalized male and female psychic representations.)

Stanley is a man whose castration fear is immense, and who therefore feels threatened by nearly all women, particularly women such as Blanche, who are attractive and intellectually threatening. If a woman threatens him, he reflexively attempts to conquer her as quickly as possible, preferably with his penis. But, like Blanche, he is not particular about his method of destruction: Whatever works will do.

Blanche and Stanley are also alike in that, while both are threatened by each other and by all members of the opposite sex who reflect their own narcissistic orientation and who have the same need to control and the same destructive urges, they also both chose as mates people who could be dominated. In choosing Stella, Stanley has gotten himself a mother surrogate—a protective, maternal woman who bears him a child, proving his manhood—not a "slut" like Blanche or, perhaps, his mother or sister. Yet, although he dominates her through his physicality and aggressiveness, he is at the same time dependent on her, as illustrated in Williams's brilliant ending of the third scene. "STELL-LAHHHH!" he bellows like a baby after she runs upstairs to spend the night at a neighbor's following the post-poker game uproar. She descends the stairs like some nurturing angel from heaven, and he falls to his knees before her and buries his face in her breasts. The next morning, he embraces Stella in front of Blanche, flashing a triumphant grin. On one level he has manipulated Stella into taking him back, knowing that Stella has a need to mother people; by crying like a baby, he has played into that need. At the same time, however, he genuinely is dependent on her, as dependent as an infant fixated in the "practicing" phase (Mahler et al. 1975). This combination of events leaves Blanche feeling hopelessly out-maneuvered.

Her only hope now is to achieve a moral victory, by inducing Stanley into behaving more and more boorishly toward her while she herself retreats further into psychosis as a way of protecting herself from the intensity of her rage toward him and toward men and people in general. She tells Stella early on that Stanley is "my executioner," thus prophesying her downfall at his hands. Viewed analytically, such prophesies are unconscious provocations aimed at obtaining exactly what is prophesied; hence those who prophesy doom ("Repent, all you sinners, the end is near!") actually want the end to come. Blanche wants the end; she is a suicidal terrorist, ready to sacrifice herself in order to destroy her hated rival, and with an additional motive to return to the womb, away from the strife of reality. It is her own self-destructive drive that does her in, and Stanley is merely an instrument of that drive, a convenient hammer to put the final nail in her coffin. To be sure, he wants to destroy her and would try to do so no matter what, but he could not succeed in her destruction without her help, without her own masochistic aggressive drive in complicity with his sadistic aggressive drive. His own rage and insecurity provide the edge he needs.

And so their sexual war reaches its denouement in their final confrontation, when Stella is no longer around to act as mediator. Stanley comes home from the hospital, where Stella's baby has just been delivered, and Stanley's virility has been confirmed. He smiles like a peacock and struts around the house with a cigar in his mouth. After some small talk, he stalks Blanche into a corner and tears away the veil of lies that she has invented to hide her past; then he does what both she and he want him to do.

In this climactic scene, she tells him to stay away from her because "some awful thing" is going to happen: "I warn you, don't, I'm in danger!" She is trying to convey to him the state of desperation she feels. To emphasize the point, she breaks a bottle on the table and wields it like a weapon. Stanley is amused, asking why she has broken the bottle. She tells him that she plans to twist it in his face. He makes a remark about her wanting some "rough-house" and proceeds to spring toward her. Before raping her, he proclaims that they have had this "date" from the beginning.

This scene is both a climax and a recapitulation of their ongoing conflict. Each wants to destroy the other, he with his phallus, she with her bottle-phallus. Again, in this short scene, Blanche seems to push him away but only succeeds in goading him into violent action. When she warns him not to take another step or "some awful thing will happen," her words are both admonition and a dare that would stimulate his curiosity and his stubborn defiance. A line later, she warns him that *she* is in danger. It is not he who is in danger, but she; by this time she realizes that her destruction is at hand, but the implication is also that if she is in danger, so is he. Yet telling him that *she* is in danger merely induces his sadism. There is nothing he would want more than that which signals her demise, her conquest. Their fates are intertwined, however, as is the case with all couples.

The tragedy of *A Streetcar Named Desire* is that, as is true of all wars, neither of the participants emerges victorious. Although Blanche succeeds in her aim of getting Stanley to act like a beast and of turning Stella against him, the price she pays is the final destruction of her flimsy hold on reality; she descends into madness, dependent upon, as she says, "the kindness of strangers." Yes, probably all she has ever known is the kindness of strangers. Such is the narcissistic predicament: Its essence is the inability to be genuinely intimate with another human, and hence to feel that others are always strangers. As for Stanley, although he succeeds in ruining Blanche's reputation and in sexually conquering and destroying her, he also destroys his own reputation in the process. One doubts that his relationship with Stella will ever be the same, even though the play ends with him again calling out to her — and she takes him back, allowing him to bury his face in her breasts once more. It would seem unlikely that she could ever trust him again, and, stigmatized by the event, he would be viewed with suspicion by his friends and neighbors. His violence against Blanche would be bound to come back and haunt him, whether through guilt feelings or in some other way. Thus, although life seems to go on just as before, all is not always what it appears.

Both Stanley and Blanche are sympathetic characters, and both in their ways are powerful beings — he a man's man, and she a femme fatale. At the same time, both have a fatal flaw: their narcissism. They are ruled not by their superior qualities, but by the unconscious, compulsive forces of unresolved penis envy and castration fear. Her response to him, and his to her, is completely involuntary, a conditioned reflex. The sight of his grandiose grin induces in her a destructive rage that goes back to her past. The sight of her coyness induces in him a similar destructive rage. They are but the hapless soldiers of Thanatos, going through their compulsive rituals in a place called New Orleans but which could be anywhere.

Tennessee Williams proved, in this play, that he was both an artist and a psychoanalyst. He possessed neither a degree nor a certificate from a psychoanalytic institute, but his work stands as an enduring monument to his deep understanding of the human predicament. He managed to convey in one play what a multitude of scholarly treatises could not.

12

On a Rooftop in New York

BACKGROUND

On December 2, 1984, at about 1:30 A.M., Caroline Isenberg was stabbed to death by Emmanuel Torres on the rooftop of a Manhattan apartment building. She died five hours later on an operating table at St. Luke's Hospital.

Such an event usually would not be of much significance in New York City, where an average of five homicides are committed daily. Yet Caroline Isenberg's story captured the hearts of Americans across the nation. The details of her fatal stabbing and the subsequent apprehension of Emmanuel Torres headlined the news for several weeks. Even *The New York Times*, in which city crime stories usually appear in the second section, ran the Isenberg murder on the front page.

Not only the media and the public, but also the police, took this event to heart. On the day after the murder, Assistant Chief Richard P. Dillon, who was in charge of detectives in Manhattan, announced at a special news conference that forty detectives were being dispatched on the case—the largest force to be used for one case in several years. Within six days, after an intensive manhunt, the police had found Torres, who confessed to the killing. A few days later he was indicted by a grand jury.

The question is, why did Caroline Isenberg's death create such an uproar? Anne Burton, a spokesperson for St. Luke's Hospital, was quoted in *Newsweek* as having provided the somewhat cynical explanation, "Because she was pretty and young and talented and white and from Harvard." Yes, all of those things were true. She was a very pretty 23-year-old promising actress who had recently graduated from Harvard. But was that all there was to it? Would the murder of *any* pretty, young, talented, white Harvard graduate have caused the same uproar? Suppose it had been a handsome, young, talented, white, *male* Harvard graduate? Suppose it had been a pretty, young, talented, white, *Russian* Harvard graduate? Or suppose it had been a pretty, young, talented, white, *vulgar* Harvard graduate?

Caroline Isenberg was more than a set of labels. As a report in *Newsweek* put it, "the unusually complete record of Isenberg's dying actions—and her own elequent words during her last hours—provided a dramatic glimpse into the horror of urban violence." In other words, because of a certain mixture of sweetness, determination, and eloquence, and due to the stubbornness with which she resisted her attacker, she became a symbol, a fulcrum around which a frightened and polarized society quickly gathered.

After her death, newspapers were filled with information about her background, her achievements, her dreams. Columnists across the nation lamented her death. Editorials discussed the pros and cons of resisting rape. Poems were written and read on street corners in her memory. Perhaps most important, her picture appeared everywhere—always the same one—showing a stunningly beautiful young woman with shoulder-length red hair smiling directly out at the viewer as though to say, "I like myself, I like you, and I like being alive!"

The vigil that was held on her block a week after her death attracted more than 200 people, many of whom had heard her cries on the night of the murder. A memorial scholarship fund was started in her name at the Williamstown Theater, at which she had served as an apprentice actress and appeared in several plays. At her funeral in Massachusetts, where a crowd of 1,000 gathered, she was all but canonized. Those who eulogized her spoke of her sweetness, goodness, love of life, self-sacrifice, courage, and religiousness. Her roommate quoted from Caroline's diary, in which she had pondered about heaven. Rabbi Leonard Behrman lauded Caroline's brave resistance of her attacker stating that (according to the *New York Post*), "We either collaborate with the enemy or we join the resistance; we insist upon being with those who strive to diminish the storm of violence."

The question remains, why did she resist? Why did she allow herself to be stabbed twenty-one times rather than submit to her attacker's demands for money (she had only $12 in her purse) and for sex? After the first stab wound—in her arm—why did she not see that her attacker was serious? Even after the attack, as she was bleeding to death on the way to the hospital and during the long ordeal that followed, she continued to pay little heed to her suffering; instead she "bubbled with all this information," as one witness put it, about the attack and the attacker. Only at the very end, when she finally became aware that death was at hand, did she question her act of resistance: "All this for $12," she told physicians and nurses. "I should have given him the money. I should have let him do it."

And what about Emmanuel Torres? While Caroline Isenberg became a symbol of virtue and a kind of martyr, Torres was castigated as an incarnation of evil. In the aftermath of the event there was almost as much attention on him as on her. He too became larger than life. His pictures appeared in all the newspapers and in several magazines. He was rather good looking and young, two years younger than Caroline, but his picture showed an unhappy young man who did not appear to care whether he lived or died. Not only his picture but also his writings and art work, published in the daily newspapers, demonstrated his unhappiness, loneliness, anger; yet his aspiration was to be an artist. In the days following his arrest (at which time he was quoted by the three New York daily newspapers and the television as exclaiming, "It was her fault! She deserved it! She was a slut!"), an outraged public heaped verbal abuse on him. New York Mayor Ed Koch was quoted in the *New York Post* as lamenting the fact that "the person who butchered her and murdered her . . . is not subject to the

death penalty!" In the same story, Prosecutor Patrick Dugan described
Emmanuel as an "aimless, irresponsible" youth whose life-style con-
sisted of "smoking dope and drinking beer."

From a psychoanalytic standpoint, it would seem that Caroline's
resistance was an expression of some mixture of hysterical denial,
magical thinking, and female narcissism, with its undertow of rage and
sexual animosity. If so, she would have been willing to die for, or
because of, a belief—the hysterical belief that she could somehow
triumph over an angry man with a knife or that neighbors would risk
their lives to save hers. At the same time, Emmanuel's attack on her
might be seen as an expression of male narcissistic rage and a kind of
oedipal revenge. At the moment of their confrontation, he developed
a narcissistic transference towards her, and she developed an hysterical transference towards him. This murder provides a definitive basis
for the study of sexual animosity and violence.

I have used as my sources for this study stories from three New
York daily newspapers (the *Times*, *Post*, and *Daily News*); a short,
unsigned report in *Newsweek*; and various reports aired by the local
television affiliates of NBC, CBS, and ABC. All appeared in the
aftermath of the murder, from December 3, 1984, through January
and February of 1985. Since there were more than 100 stories on this
murder in the newspapers alone, appearing in numerous issues, I have
decided for the sake of simplicity to list only the periodicals from
which direct quotations were taken, without giving more specific
information.

CAROLINE ISENBERG BEFORE THE
MURDER

Caroline Isenberg was born on October 27, 1961, and grew up in
Brookline, Massachusetts, a wealthy and primarily white suburb of
Boston. She had an older sister, Emily, and a younger brother,
Marcus. Her father, Phillip L. Isenberg, was a psychiatrist on the staff
of the Harvard Medical School and trained resident physicians at
McLean's Hospital in Belmont, another Boston suburb. Caroline's
mother, Ellin, was a housewife. They seemed to be the epitome of an
all-American family: A picture taken at Caroline's funeral showed a

tall, elegant-looking father with light, wavy hair; a youthful, thin mother, a pretty older sister; and a tall, handsome son.

The news accounts provided a little information about her early childhood. First, we know that she was the second daughter. The second-born often needs to try harder to prove herself, to prove that she can do as well as an older sibling. Perhaps this was the case with Caroline, for she was later described by several people as "determined." Second, and perhaps most important, we know that she was a beautiful child. Third, we know that she was intelligent and talented. The second and third factors are important because one's physical features, intelligence, and talents have a bearing on how one is treated by the world. Beautiful children are usually valued over plain ones, and children who demonstrate early talents or intelligence are often encouraged and accorded special attention.

The fact that Caroline was a red-haired child probably also gave her a sense of being special. Red hair is by far the rarest of any hair color, and their hair combined with their pale skin causes redheads to stand out all the more. Indeed, there is a lore with respect to redheads; for instance, they are said to have fiery temperaments and to be headstrong. In addition, children with red hair and freckles are viewed as the epitome of American wholesomeness. (Huckleberry Finn was a redhead, and Raggedy Ann, the classic, best-selling doll of all time, has red hair and freckles.) Caroline also had blue eyes. All these attributes — the red hair, the pale skin, the freckles, the blue eyes — would very likely elicit special treatment from her family.

Add to that the fact that she was also intelligent and talented, and that she no doubt displayed those assets at an early age, and the full picture begins to emerge. Here was a rare, unique, adorable child with perhaps a "second-born" determination to prove herself, growing up in a family that could afford to provide her with all the comforts and appreciate her many gifts. In fact, it may be that, because of her special qualities, her family overprotected her.

Two anecdotes about her childhood were reported. One, in the *Post*, was provided by her sister, Emily. She maintained that Caroline had wanted to be an actress since she was 7 years old, when she wrote plays and acted them out for her parents, brother, and sister. "She came alive on the stage," said her sister. "There was a transformation that I just can't explain. It was like it was my sister up there but it was more than that. She was just an incredible actress."

The other anecdote, reported in the *Daily News*, was offered by Rabbi Bernard Mehlman at Caroline's funeral. Speaking of her kindness, he told how, even at 8 years old, "she gave up the lead role in the school play. She told her parents she wanted another girl to get the part." He added that Caroline felt the other girl "needed bringing out."

From these anecdotes we discern not only Caroline's early interest in acting but also a sense of her precociousness, of a kind of noblesse oblige: She would sacrifice herself for the more reticent girl. It is also apparent that her parents must have modeled this kind of behavior and that they probably rewarded it in their children. We can therefore assume that one of Caroline's character traits was an awareness of her more fortunate status in society and an empathic (perhaps condescending) attitude toward those less fortunate than herself. In addition, these anecdotes reveal a person who was accustomed to being the center of attention and had a sense of her own value and importance.

After grammar school, Caroline entered the Brimmer and May School in Chestnut Hill, Massachusetts, an exclusive girls' school, from which she graduated in 1980. Perhaps it was here that she picked up the nickname "Icky," by which most of her friends came to know her. The name's meaning can only be a matter of speculation, although the term usually connotes something dirty, messy, or sticky. It is therefore an ironic nickname for someone so clean-cut and wholesome. However, she apparently did not mind this nickname, for her roommate referred to her by that name at her funeral. (In contrast, the nickname of Emmanual Torres—"Peanut"—was said to be quite bothersome to him.)

Upon her graduation from high school, Caroline entered Harvard University. Her drama career began to take off. She joined several drama groups at Harvard as well as taking dance, writing, and directing courses. She was a member of the Harvard-Radcliffe Dramatic Club, the Harvard Independent Theater, and the Lowell House Dramatic Society. She starred in student productions of *Who's Afraid of Virginia Woolf*, *Twelfth Night*, and *The Glass Menagerie*. During the summers she served as an apprentice at the Williamstown Theatre in Williamstown, Massachusetts, one of the more prestigious summer-stock companies in the East. During the summer following her junior year she studied acting at the Royal Academy of Dramatic Arts in London. She also appeared in an American Repertory Theater production of *Measure for Measure*. Both the Royal Academy of Dramatic Arts and the American Repertory Theater are steeped in the tradition of classical theater, and Caroline's involvement with them is further evidence of her seriousness and determination as an actress.

Then, in October 1984, she came to New York to enroll in the famous Neighborhood Playhouse School. "She wanted to be in the theater in many ways—acting, directing, any way she could," her mother told reporters of the *Times*. "She felt so good about going to that school." Although she did not get a chance to appear in any major productions at the Neighborhood Playhouse, she did manage to fit in a movie role along the way: She had a small speaking part in a CBS television production starring Loretta Swit.

Of her acting career at Harvard, Jonathan Marks, literary director of the American Repertory Theater, commented to the *Times*, "She was very promising." He spoke of the "sweet shyness" of her performance as Laura in *The Glass Menagerie*. "She was determined to be an actress," he added.

Of her acting achievements at the Williamstown Theater, we have the testimony of Susan Glassman, who was also an aspiring actress. Susan was not only Caroline's roommate when she moved to New York; she was also her close friend and companion for several years. At Caroline's funeral (according to a report in the *Post*) Susan revealed how Caroline had struggled to understand a role in *Spring's Awakening* during her last year at Williamstown—that of a 13-year-old girl who was confronted with her own death. In order to better understand this character, Caroline kept a diary, which Susan quoted:

> Dear, Dear Diary,
> The strangest thoughts have been coming to me. Where is this heaven that everyone talks about? Is it in the sky? What secrets might be up there?

Of her brief tenure at the Neighborhood Playhouse School, Kathleen Gibbons, a fellow student, said to the *Daily News*, "She would have been anything she wanted to be. Everybody loved her. You had to. She was the sweetest kid you ever met."

It is interesting to note the types of roles Caroline played during her stints at Harvard and Williamstown: The naive young coed in *Who's Afraid of Virginia Woolf*; the shy, socially backward girl in *The Glass Menagerie*; and the religious 13-year-old about to die. The kinds of roles an actress identifies with and accepts often say something about the nature of her own personality; and in each of the aforementioned instances she played something of a sweet, young child-woman.

The role of Laura in *The Glass Menagerie* is particularly intriguing. Here is a play about an overprotective mother and a reclusive daughter who prefers relating to her menagerie of glass animals than to relating to humans. Throughout the play the mother expresses her concern about her daughter's shyness and her marriage prospects; she fears that the daughter will become a spinster. She even enlists the aid of her son, asking him to bring home a "gentleman caller" to meet the daughter. On the surface it appears that the mother is behaving in a loving, caring way; but on a deeper level it is evident that she is actually maintaining the daughter's dependence. The mother's constant remarks about Laura's social inadequacies and her attempts to help her serve only to make the girl more self-conscious, for she has never been allowed to learn to do things for herself and develop her own confidence. On a conscious level the mother seems to want her daughter to achieve independence; but on an unconscious level – perhaps due to her own unfulfilled needs for intimacy – she is stunting Laura's growth. The play is a succinct portrait of this kind of symbiotic mother–daughter relationship.

Whether Caroline, like Laura, had such a relationship with her mother, father, or entire family we cannot know for sure. Indications are that she was very outgoing in many ways, yet at the same time also very childlike and perhaps socially backward in female–male relationships.

For example, Noreen Williams, who lived in the same building as Caroline, remarked to the *Times* on the night of the murder, "I only met her a couple of days ago. We met downstairs as we were both coming in and we introduced ourselves. She was a happy child, so very happy and smiling. She was so happy that she was meeting the other tenants. She felt good about being here." This woman saw Caroline as both outgoing and childlike.

Another testimony of this kind was given to the *Daily News* by Harold Baldridge, director of the Neighborhood Playhouse School:

"She was a bouncy kind of kid, always smiling, always happy," he said. "Some of the other kids I worried about; her I didn't." He apparently saw her as childlike (a "kid"), but one who could take care of herself.

Esther Mandell, another tenant in the building where Caroline died, also expressed (in the *Times*) feelings about her childlike appearance, recalling how she had tried to warn her about the neighborhood: "This neighborhood is a jungle and it's unsafe to go out at night." (Caroline reportedly replied that she thought it was a very convenient neighborhood to live in, and that New York was no worse than any other city!)

Eleanor Rosenbaum, whose son was a close friend of Caroline's, told the *Times*, "it kills me that *this kid* had to come from Massachusetts to get murdered in New York. So ambitious, so intelligent . . . as sweet as sugar" (italics added).

Finally, even Caroline's father gave witness to her paradoxical nature. Asked by reporters of the *Daily News* whether his daughter ever expressed fears of living in New York, he replied, "Caroline wasn't afraid of anything." After police arrested Emmanuel Torres, however, he exclaimed to the *Post*: "Are you joking, My God, he lived in the building? He was there all the time when *my little girl* was there?" (italics added).

We do not know much about Caroline's personal life. Fellow students at Harvard and fellow actors and actresses at Williamstown described her as someone who did not go in for a great deal of socializing. At Williamstown, where it is said that almost everyone sleeps with everyone over the course of the summer season, Caroline apparently remained aloof. It seemed that acting was her first love, and everything else was a distant second, including men.

When she moved to New York on October 10, 1984, her life again seemed to revolve around her theater training and career. She reportedly split her time between going to school and going to auditions, often accompanied by her roommate, Susan. She helped support herself by waiting tables (as many actors and actresses do) in a coffee shop a few blocks from where she lived. She had a date with a man named Steven Rosenbaum on the night of the murder (which he canceled due to illness), but he was said to be more a close friend than a romantic interest. Clearly theater came first with her and all else came second.

More than anything else, she was an actress. To be an actress is to be someone who has a need to express parts of her personality that she cannot express in her daily life. Nearly all performers have this in common; they seem to come to life on the stage or in film, to take on dimensions they never display in real life. Like an alcoholic who needs a drink in order to let go of inhibitions, so an actress needs to play a role in order to release the repressed forces within her.

Along with this need to express is a need for approval of this expression—the approval of an applauding audience. Beneath the persona of sweetness and bounciness there was, locked within Caroline, a core of pride and passion, a yearning to be seen and heard and felt, a desire for recognition. Where did it come from? Perhaps it had to do with being overprotected and not allowed to display the full range of normal feelings (because it would have been unladylike). Perhaps it was due to the fact that she was the second-born—as well as the middle child, sandwiched in between two others—and thus had to try harder to gain attention. At any rate, the passion for acting that began when she was 7 would not be stopped. Although her family, according to a report in the *Post*, had wanted her to enter a more secure profession, they had come to accept her decision to become an actress because it became apparent to them how much it meant to her. "Everybody thought she'd be famous, but that wasn't important to her," stated her sister. "I do believe some day she would have been famous."

Such, then, was Caroline Isenberg, who came to New York to pursue her dreams as so many young people do. Yes, she was "pretty and young and talented and white and from Harvard"; characterologically, however, what comes across most about her is her determination to do what she wanted to do, despite her family's objections, despite anyone's objections, and to resist (as she resisted her attacker on the night of the murder) any attempt to deter her from her goals.

EMMANUEL TORRES BEFORE THE MURDER

"Man is not born wicked," Voltaire once said. "He becomes so as he becomes sick."

There is no question that Emmanuel Torres was behaving wickedly when he murdered Caroline Isenberg on the roof of her building in the early hours of that December morning. But how did he become so? I agree with Voltaire, and I would say it a bit differently: People are not born psychopathic; they become so as their primary needs are frustrated.

The environment to which Emmanuel was born was a stark contrast to the one in which Caroline grew up. He was raised in a ghetto in the Bronx (not the clean, white houses of Brookline). He was trapped in a broken home, his parents having been divorced only a year after his birth (not at all like the stable, pristine family life in the Isenberg home); his skin was dark (not pale and freckled and "all-American"). His father, a man with a violent temper, was a sometimes building superintendent (not a Harvard professor) who tended to move from job to job. And his mother was a small, religiously zealous Hispanic woman (no genteel Boston lady) who had to struggle to raise four sons.

According to the facts presented in news reports, Emmanuel was only 21 years old at the time of his arrest. He had grown up in a part of the Bronx called Marble Hill, the youngest of four children. He was a rather smallish man, about 5 feet, 8 inches tall and 140 pounds. His father, Alex Torres, was the superintendent of the building in which Caroline had lived until she was murdered. His mother, Neida Bonilla, lived in a small apartment on West 225th Street in the Bronx. She told reporters of the *Post* that she had divorced Alex Torres 20 years earlier and reared her four sons alone. "I raised all my children with God," she said. Emmanuel's oldest brother, Alfredo, was 31 years old at the time of Emmanuel's arrest and in his third year of residency at Rochester General Hospital. His brothers Edward, 28, and Angel, 26, were unemployed. (Angel had once been, according to his mother, a medical technician at St. Clare's Hospital.)

As a child, Emmanuel was reportedly a church-going boy in a deeply religious home, according to the Reverend Angel Santos, a Pentecostal minister. "I gave him his religious training and I can tell you he is a good kid," Santos said to the *Daily News*. He recalled that at the age of 10, along with his three older brothers, Emmanuel had helped to build a Pentecostal church in the Bronx. Emmanuel had not only grown up in a "deeply religious home," he had also apparently grown up in a "meticulous" home under the shadow of his distinguished older brother, Alfredo; it was noted in the same article that "Nearly every corner of [the mother's] meticulously kept apartment in the Marble Hill housing project was adorned with framed photographs of her sons. The largest number of photos are those of Alfredo Torres." The mother seemed anxious to prove, in this interview, that Emmanuel was just as talented as Alfredo, showing reporters samples of her youngest son's short stories and illustrations.

"I have never had a problem with him," she added.

One of the stories, titled, "The Origin of the Black Shadow," was partially published in the *Daily News;* it reveals a lonely, bitter, paranoid individual. The story is about a young man named Roberto Negrone, a high school student in a Bronx neighborhood similar to the one Emmanuel grew up in. He makes good grades (all As) but he is also a daydreamer, always dreaming about visiting other worlds. He wants to "seek out new civilizations, to explore strange new worlds, to boldly go where no man has gone before." However, his classmates tease him because "they were jealous of him." He tries to ignore them, but they pick on him and call him names and destroy most of his school projects. "Pretty childish for so-called high school students, isn't it?" the author asks, then adding, "He used to hate most of his classmates because of this."

In another section of the same story, Emmanuel has his protagonist allude to problems he was having not only with schoolmates but also with his parents:

> Sometimes he got his butt kicked around the school but he never gave up without a fight. A rebel with a cause you might say.
>
> Life was not easy for him always, he had to deal with his mother and father fighting all the time until it ended in the divorce court. His father was killed in a plane crash said to be caused by a U.F.O. . . . .

In addition to these samples of his writing, the *Daily News* also published several of his illustrations. From a psychological standpoint, these illustrations, with their heavy black lines and depictions of violent scenes, reveal Emmanuel's depression and rage.

As was the case with Caroline, we have little information about Emmanuel's early childhood other than a few basic facts and whatever clues we can gather from his writings and illustrations. Indeed, his mother and the Reverend Santos seemed to conspire to paint only the most positive portrait of Emmanuel and cover up any calamities that might have occurred in his early years. If we want to understand him, we must probe more deeply.

Let us start with what we know. First, we know that Emmanuel's parents separated about a year after his birth. And it is evident from Emmanuel's short story that the divorce and his parents' fighting were painful for him. We know, too, that his father tended to be belligerent. (One of the tenants of the building for which Alex Torres worked, Joel Schwartz, told the *Post* that Alex had once thrown him against the wall when he complained about conditions in his apartment.) We can also discern that Emmanuel's mother was morally self-righteous, based on her comment, "I raised all my sons with God." The first year of Emmanuel's life was apparently spent in an atmosphere of fighting, perhaps violent fighting, between his parents, each of whom took a rigid position on matters of right and wrong.

First impressions are always the strongest, and this holds true for human development: The first year of life is the most important in terms of emotional health. The most severe emotional disturbances have their roots in the first year, when an infant is helpless and dependent and vulnerable to his environment; every event leaves a deep and lasting impression. In Emmanuel's case, therefore, it is probable that his mother was not happy during his first year of life, and that when she held him, her own misery, her anger at his father, her anxiety, even her need for vengeance, were conveyed to the child. It might have been conveyed in a certain roughness with which she handled him, or in a lack of response to his cries, or in an angry glint in her eyes when she looked at him. In addition, Emmanuel may have heard or witnessed violence between his parents—a terrifying experience for an infant.

Imagine being an infant and looking up into a contorted face and angry eyes. If this is your first impression, you will most likely conclude that you are not loved, wanted, or valued. Therefore, you do not think highly of yourself. You do not think of the world as a safe place, nor do you feel optimistic about your prospects. You do not like yourself very much, nor do you like anyone else.

Then there is the feeling of abandonment when a parent leaves.

Emmanuel must have felt that he was somehow the cause of the trouble between his parents, and that his father left because of him. Feelings of abandonment in early childhood (as in adulthood) always result in feelings of depression, as Bowlby (1979) documented, but even more so if there is no opportunity for mourning. Was he given the opportunity to mourn his father's departure by an understanding mother, or was such mourning blocked by a mother who refused to discuss the father in a positive way? When the normal course of mourning is blocked, one loses the capacity for empathy; instead one remains weighed down by repressed hurt, anger, even rage.

Finally, we should mention two other factors that may have had an impact on Emmanuel's emotional development in early childhood. The first is that he was the youngest son and that his mother obviously favored the oldest son. The youngest child often becomes the family scapegoat; the older children can tease him, trick him, and out-achieve him. In addition, the youngest son is often "babied" longer than his siblings, and his efforts at independence are thwarted. Add to this the fact that Emmanuel's mother favored the oldest son, Alfredo, and we begin to see why Emmanuel might feel angry and inferior.

It is interesting to note, in this connection, that Emmanuel was called "Peanut," a nickname he probably did not appreciate, and one which symbolized his position as family scapegoat. The fact that he was a scapegoat is borne out in his story, when he refers to classmates who tease him and pick on him and call him names—Peanut perhaps? It is likely that such was the case in real life, and that it happened not only at school but also at home.

The second factor concerns the nature of Emmanuel's relationship with his parents. Emmanuel apparently had a very close relationship with his mother. In fact, it must have seemed to him that his mother chose him over his father; after his father left, he became, as a baby, the focus of her life. Since she never remarried, she may in fact have made him a substitute for the physical relationship she was not having with an adult male. Hence their relationship may even have been a quasi-incestuous one.

I am reminded of a patient with whom I once worked. He had raped several women. An analysis of his early childhood revealed just such a quasi-incestuous relationship with his mother and a distant relationship with his father. This mother was also very religious and would constantly give her son double messages. On the one hand, she would be physically affectionate and flirtatious with him, fondling his genitals in the guise of bathing him or adjusting his clothing; she would call him her "one and only" and make him promise never to leave her. In general, she fostered an expectation that she would some day be sexually available to him. On the other hand, if she caught him masturbating or if he mentioned anything about sex, she would ridicule him and tell him, "Don't talk like that," and give him a religious sermon on the sinfulness of the male sex. This teasing, castrating relationship with his mother, combined with his distant, rejecting relationship with his father, left the patient in an unfocused rage, which he later directed toward women in general. His masculine strivings had been severely frustrated and his sense of his masculinity impaired, and the rapes were a perverse attempt to assert his masculinity. Groth (1979) has documented similar cases.

Whether or not Emmanuel's relationship with his mother was precisely of this nature we cannot say for sure; however, it must be assumed that something of this kind happened in order to engender the sexual animosity that was so evident on the night of the murder. In addition, there is also the anger at his father, borne out of his short story, in which the father is killed. He was angry at his father not only for fighting with his mother, but also for leaving him. Instead of having a father who helped him to establish a firm masculine identity, he had a father who was purportedly antagonistic toward him. Hence he would have to seek other ways of proving his manhood. Moreover, when a son has won his mother away from his father (which is how it may have appeared to Emmanuel), he is terrified of that father's jealousy and fears retaliation.

Admittedly, these are all speculations, and we have no way of confirming them based solely on the clues at hand. When combined with existing knowledge about the developmental factors that shape psychopathic personalities, however, these speculations seem to have some validity. At the least, they serve to illustrate forces that might potentially have come into play.

This brings us to the next piece of information provided by the newspapers. It was reported that Emmanuel, at about the age of 14, had an automobile accident in which he received a blow to the head. He was in a hospital for a while, and afterward he was said to be "quick to anger." He supposedly had problems in school thereafter and was taken to see a psychiatrist; then, after a time, he dropped out of school and stopped seeing the psychiatrist. "He has never been totally right since then," Alfredo told the *Post*. Other family members echoed this sentiment. In other words, it was their contention that Emmanuel's emotional problems stemmed from this accident and had nothing to do with his upbringing.

It seems likely that Emmanuel suffered from what is often called "postconcussional syndrome." It is true that personality disturbances may result from injury to the cranial contents, but as Kolb (1977) points out, "psychological factors usually participate to a varying degree." In other words, if an accident victim is already suffering from a personality disorder, then the accident is likely to worsen it. If, on the other hand, an accident victim is relatively well-adjusted before the trauma, then he will usually recover. This is apparent among soldiers in combat. Those who enter the service with emotional problems are the ones who cannot handle the stress of combat and are subject to the most severe cases of "post-traumatic stress," while those who are relatively healthy tend to resume normal lives, despite having gone through equally horrifying combat experiences.

Another factor that bears on the recovery from such an emotional disturbance has to do with how one's family responds to the situation. Again using the analogy of soldiers in combat, it has been noted that the incidence of post-traumatic stress was much lower following World War II, when returning soldiers received a hero's welcome, than it was after the war in Vietnam, when returning soldiers not only met public apathy but were also treated with disrespect and even ridicule. Similarly, if a family displays an impatient, rejecting, overprotective, or ridiculing attitude toward a child who is showing the effects of a head injury, it will serve to increase the child's anxiety and produce more disturbed behavior and a decreased capacity for learning.

In any case, from the time Emmanuel dropped out of school at the age of 15, he became increasingly antisocial. He worked at odd jobs, such as washing cars, and he continued to write and draw. "He loved to draw for little children," his brother Angel told the *Daily News*. "That was his secret world." According to Angel, Emmanuel even sold a painting once for $35. He continued to withdraw from his family, however, with the exception of his brothers. "We didn't associate with him," a stepsister, Karen Torres, told the *Daily News*. "He did his thing and we weren't close at all. He was outside the family."

He began hanging around with the Chingalings, a Bronx gang that police sources said had been "into dope and extortion for years." These sources claimed that Emmanuel was just a "hanger-on" with the Chingalings—"just a little pup" who did not actually qualify as a gang member. In 1982, when his father became the superintendent of the building where Caroline was killed, Emmanuel moved into the basement of that building. It was reported that he and the Chingalings used to prowl the hallways and harass tenants.

"They had some kind of crazy gang," one of the tenants told the *Post*. "They would kiss each other on both cheeks in some kind of expression of solidarity. There were always a lot of chains and leather."

Another tenant said, "I always felt very uncomfortable about their presence and the way these young men looked at me. It was the kind of look that makes a woman feel uncomfortable."

Another tenant said he had once paid Alex Torres, Emmanuel's father, to take care of his dog, since he was often out of town. When he asked to see his dog after several weeks, he was told by Alex that his son, Emmanuel, had killed the dog by throwing it off a bridge. Several tenants concluded that Emmanuel and his friends were "some of the scariest people I've ever seen in my life."

In joining the Chingalings, Emmanuel had apparently found a group that not only supported but encouraged antisocial and violent behavior. There is nothing like group consensus to absolve individual guilt; if everybody else is doing it, then it must be okay! So thought the Nazis during World War II; so thought the participants in the Crusades; so thought the soldiers of every battle fought in the course of our short history on this planet. When some higher authority speaks—whether it be a Hitler or the leader of a street gang—the followers will gladly follow, gladly form a consensus making the leader and themselves "right" and everyone else "wrong." They will decide that they are being victimized by some group (the white majority?) and that a particular behavior (terrorizing whites?) is therefore justified, and they will form a new value system to support whatever actions they take. So it must have been with the Chingalings, and so it must have been with Emmanuel. The gang's support seemed to fan the flames of his fury.

In 1983 he was arrested for the first time, for fare-beating on the subways. Later that year, in October, he is said to have had a fight with his father, at which time he moved out of the basement of the building on West End Avenue and back into his mother's apartment in the Bronx. His last odd job was with a traveling carnival in upstate New York during the spring and summer of 1984. Then, in July 1984, he was arrested again. Emmanuel and his brothers Edward and Angel, along with a man named Luis Martinez, were said to have attacked three other men with axe handles and chains. Edward and Angel were released without bail, but Emmanuel was required to post $1,000 bail pending a later hearing. Why he was the only one required to post bail was not explained in news reports. It appears, however, that he was once again the scapegoat.

Who was Emmanuel Torres? He was a human being who never had a chance. From the day of his birth he was as unlucky as Caroline Isenberg was lucky. He had a father who taught him violence and a mother who maintained his dependence on her while favoring her oldest son. He had brothers who teased him, calling him "Peanut." He was an outcast in his family and at school, until he dropped out. Then he became an outcast on the streets of the Bronx. He wanted to "seek out new civilizations, to explore strange new worlds, to boldly go where no man has gone before," but he was held back by the enormity of his inner pain. Unlike Caroline, whose goals were practically in her grasp, and for whom everything had come so easily, Emmanuel was a man without hope, whose goals had been trampled in the dark corners of the ghetto. His ambition had turned to despair, and his despair to rage.

THE DANCE OF DEATH

On the night of the murder, Caroline had gone to the theater. She saw a play called *Hurlyburly*, which had garnered rave reviews. She was supposed to have been accompanied by a man named Steven Rosenbaum, but when she called him earlier that evening, he backed out because of the flu. She apparently did not come straight home after the play; theaters usually let out by 11:00 P.M., and she did not arrive at her apartment building until 1:30 A.M. It is not known how she spent the time.

We do know that earlier that day she had auditioned for a role in an off-Broadway play by the Rumanian playwright Paul Eremenco. She won the role in *Married Today, Burnt Tomorrow* and was scheduled to start rehearsals shortly. It is likely, then, that she must have been quite happy that evening, and perhaps even stopped off at a bar to have a glass of champagne in celebrating her good fortune.

Emmanuel, on the other hand, was known to have been bent on revenge upon his father. At the trial, as reported in all three dailies, he said that he had been at a party that evening at his brother Edward's Bronx apartment, where he smoked a lot of marijuana and drank a lot of beer. It was reported in the *Daily News* that Emmanuel idolized his older brother. Edward, known on the streets as "Wolfman," was a respected member of the Sheridan Boys, a Bronx gang similar to the Chingalings.

Emmanuel said that he left the party feeling angry at his father, and he headed for the apartment building in which his father lived and worked in order to get revenge on him by blowing up the boiler or whatever else he could think of to do. He had had a history of "bad blood" with his father, no doubt going back to his anger at his father's having abandoned him in infancy. Psychodynamically, he was enraged at his father for not helping him "be a man." Thus, it appears that his sexual animosity had much to do with his relationship with his father and with his inability to develop healthy masculine pride.

He was not likely to have felt good on that evening—not physically, emotionally, or intellectually. Physically, because of the chronic tension due to the frustration of Eros, he would be prone to headaches, backaches, stomach problems, high blood pressure, insomnia, and other ailments. Emotionally, he would feel depressed, apathetic, bored, and at the same time driven by a low-level rage. Intellectually, he would be impatient, short-sighted, and obsessive. While his fantasies might be about other worlds, his moment-to-moment thoughts would center on the injustices done to him and how he might avenge them. Emmanuel was not a happy man when he left the party.

The building in which the murder took place was an old gray-brick structure with a limestone base and an unusual facade of bay windows and faded ornamentation. It had twenty apartments on its seven floors. When Caroline returned home, nearly all the windows were dark. She did not see Emmanuel until it was too late.

She entered the dimly lit lobby, with its faded yellow walls and dirty tile floor, and pushed the button of the self-service elevator. The elevator door opened and she stepped inside the small, 4-foot-square cubicle; it was covered with imitation-wood laminate and lit by a single dim bulb. As she turned around, Emmanuel walked in and stood in front of the sliding door. He had a knife—an illegal, 4-inch lock-blade "007"—the weapon of choice among street gangs. He had been waiting inside the lobby for some time, waiting for somebody, anybody, to "rip off." The door slid shut and he stood in front of her, the knife in his hand.

"Don't make a sound or I'll kill you," he told her. He turned to press the top elevator button and the elevator began its slow ascent to the roof.

("It's a very slow elevator," Noreen Williams, a sixth-floor resident later told the *Times*. "And if you press a floor, you can't get another floor until you stop at the first one. If you hit the roof floor, then no other floor will work.")

Emmanuel, having lived in the basement of the building for a time, must have known how the elevator operated; he knew that once he pressed the top button the elevator would go straight to the roof. Then, as he stood regarding his prey, it is very likely that his eyes popped open a bit and that a smile spread across his face.

Imagine what he must have thought and felt as he gazed at Caroline. He had wanted to rob someone, but he never expected someone like her—not at 1:30 in the morning. Standing a few inches away from him, at his mercy, was a young, white, stunningly beautiful, freckle-faced American "princess," decked out in, let us say, high-heeled shoes, a fancy dress, and a fancy coat. (What she was actually wearing that night was not reported.) He probably felt a rush of excitement as well as a knot of fear in the pit of his stomach. Perhaps he could even feel and hear his own heart pounding, and in his frenzy it might have sounded to him as though his heartbeat were amplified off the narrow walls of the elevator. Standing toe to toe, she would have been a few inches shorter than he—about 5 feet, 6 inches to his

5 feet, 8 inches—a rather thin, pale-skinned, red-haired creature who carried herself with dignity and was probably peering at him with some mixture of terror and disdain. From his point of view, he could not have asked for a more fitting target for his vengeance: If he was interested in knocking someone off a pedestal, then the higher up she was, the more satisfying it would be. He must have been very excited. In fact, he must have been out of control, running on rage. It was at this point that he probably decided he wanted more than money.

According to the version he later gave the police, he then turned to her and asked, "Will you have sex with me when we get to the roof?" And according to him she nodded her assent.

Now let us imagine what Caroline must have thought and felt as she found herself suddenly trapped in the elevator and confronted with this situation. Here was a wild-eyed, knife-wielding "black" man (she told police later that he was black, not knowing he was a dark-skinned Hispanic), shabbily dressed in old blue jeans and a corduroy coat, perhaps swaggering a bit from his night of marijuana and alcohol, threatening to do vile things to her. She must have been stunned at first, making the transition from the feeling of happiness at winning the role in the play to the feeling of terror and then outrage as she suddenly grasped the reality of her predicament. This can't be happening, she might have thought at that moment. This really can't be happening—not tonight of all nights. She too might have had a knot at the pit of her stomach, and she too might have felt her heart pounding. And if Emmanuel had indeed asked her to have sex with him as they went up in the elevator, perhaps she did nod her assent. Trapped with a leering man who had a knife at her throat, in a 4-foot-square elevator with hardly any room to breathe—and it has all happened faster than the snap of a switchblade—she would say yes to anything just to buy time. And she would think to herself, this isn't happening. This isn't happening to me! Things like this don't happen to me! And she might have asked herself questions such as, Should I have come home right after the play? Should I have gone to the play at all? Should I have checked inside the elevator before going in? And she might wonder, what do I do now?

When the elevator finally reached the top, it halted abruptly inside a small roof structure that housed the elevator shaft and a short, narrow hallway leading to the roof. "Let's go," Emmanuel said to her and he led her down the hallway to a rust-colored metal door. The door was locked by a slip-bolt, and he undid the bolt and motioned for her to step outside. She did as she was told.

Outside it was mildly cold and pitch-dark; the only light was the faint illumination from the windows of taller buildings nearby. Caroline walked out onto the green, tar-papered roof and turned around, perhaps hugging herself, perhaps casting a terrified, yet defiant eye at Emmanuel. He moved toward her with, in all probability, a slight smile on his face.

"You want to hand over your purse?" he asked her, probably in a soft menacing voice.

"No!" she answered firmly, clutching it to herself.

The smile on his face most likely broadened. He might have been both infuriated and excited by her resistance. He had a desperate need to be taken seriously, to feel some kind of power over another; yet, even as he stood there with a knife pointed at this woman, she still refused to take him seriously. However, the stronger her resistance, the bigger his thrill of victory. He would give her one more chance to surrender.

"Will you have sex with me?" he asked her.

"I will not." She stood her ground, defiant, no doubt giving him her most indignant stare, as though to tell him that it was ridiculous for him to ask her such a thing—that she would never have sex with anyone like him, and how dare he approach her in such a hostile, socially unacceptable way. She too very likely felt infuriated at this point, infuriated at being accosted so rudely. She was a woman who had always been sheltered, always been given special treatment, and who was accustomed to getting whatever she wanted. She was a woman with a Boston sensibility for social etiquette and fair play, a believer in civil rights (under other circumstances she might have championed the cause of the young man who now so rudely stood before her) who had always been taught to be kind to those less fortunate than she, to support the "correct" issues. And now this shadowy stranger from the underworld wanted to mug and rape her. She would die before she would let him lay a hand on her.

And so they stood for perhaps a moment or two, facing each other in the dark—"Peanut" and "Icky"—not knowing anything about each other, never having met before, and yet now locked in a battle of wills, a struggle of life and death in the middle of the night on a deserted rooftop in Manhattan.

Emmanuel probably mumbled something like, "Okay, if that's the way you want it, bitch." He would have been even further enraged by her "uppity" sexual rejection of him and by her tone of voice and manner, which he would see as her attempt to "put him in his place" and make him feel guilty, wrong, sick. And he would repeat once more, "If that's the way you want it!" and move toward her, slowly.

Then he took the first lunge at her with the knife. It probably happened very fast, like a snake springing out of nowhere. Caroline apparently held out her arm to stop him, while at the same time turning and backing away. The knife caught her in the upper arm and shoulder.

She began to scream. It was a piercing scream that contained all her fierce determination, terror, and outrage.

("You never heard anybody scream like that in your life," Noreen Williams told the *Times* later. "When we heard the screams, every light in this building and the next went on. All up and down the lights were flipping on, and people were looking out their windows trying to figure out where they were coming from.")

A number of tenants, including Ms. Williams and Susan Glassman, Caroline's roommate, reported that they dialed "911" and summoned the police as soon as they heard the screams. Mrs. Williams added that the screams were so loud that the police operator could hear them over the telephone. Other tenants said that they could not immediately determine where the screams were coming from, or whether someone was playing a practical joke or having a domestic quarrel.

Meanwhile, Caroline continued to back away from Emmanuel, who stalked her with a smile on his face. He stabbed her again, this time in the upper abdomen.

"Help me!" she screamed, shattering the night air. "He's stabbing me! He's killing me! I'm going to bleed to death! (All three daily newspapers reported much the same words coming from Caroline's lips at this time.)

It was at about this point that Caroline kicked off her shoes to increase her mobility. (The next day her bloody footprints would be a reminder of what had happened the night before.) She was leaning over the edge of the roof, according to Mrs. Williams, screaming, "Help me! Please help me!"

Edward Locke, a well-known jazz drummer who lived in the building, reportedly opened his window and called out, "Where are you?"

"I'm on the roof!" she called back. "I'm dying. I'm bleeding to death! Help me!"

Locke repeated his question: "Where are you?"

"929!" she called back again. "I'm on the roof! It's Caroline!"

By this time Emmanuel had stabbed her several more times in the chest and abdomen. She was in a state of absolute terror, trying to move away from him, protecting herself as best she could with her arms. This is not happening to me, she was probably thinking. She had probably dissociated herself from her body, was probably looking at the scene from outside herself and thinking, That's not really me; that's somebody else being stabbed; that's somebody else screaming; it's not me; I'm not in trouble; I'm perfectly all right. That's someone else out there and I'm fine and someone will come to save me soon.

Meanwhile, Emmanuel's frenzy would have taken a completely opposite direction; far from being detached from himself, he would feel, perhaps as never before, totally connected with himself, at one with the rage that had accumulated inside him for years—as though he were having an orgasm of rage. Now you know how I've felt all my life, he might have thought. All his jealousy, his sexual animosity, his social animosity, and the accumulated frustration of his hopes had exploded to the surface. I'm in charge now, and you must die!

Caroline staggered backwards, trying to get away, desperate, still screaming, "Help! . . . Somebody, please! . . ."

People were calling up from buildings all around. One of them, Betty Vicedomini, reportedly yelled out, "Leave her alone! Leave her alone! Leave her alone!"

"I felt completely helpless," Ms. Vicedomini told the *Post* later. "I had no idea where she was. If I knew she was on the roof, I would have run up. If you could have heard her you'd have known she was a fighter. She wasn't going to have this person violate her. The little girl was a fighter and it cost her her life."

She was a fighter but she was fighting a battle she could not win, against a maniacal man with a knife. After perhaps one or two more desperate screams, she sank to the rooftop, most likely curling up into a ball. Emmanuel stabbed her a few more times (twenty-one in all), once in the thigh and several more times in the chest and abdomen, piercing both her left lung and her liver. When he heard the police sirens he broke off the attack, leaving her there, curled up and dying, a pool of blood beneath her.

The entire attack lasted only about five minutes, but those five minutes would have an impact far beyond their time and place. Before fleeing, Emmanuel reportedly picked up Caroline's purse and took out her wallet, which, as mentioned earlier, contained about $12. He exited down an interior stairwell, running down the eight flights of stairs to the basement, hiding out for about two hours—as police searched the upper floors—in the storage room where he had once lived. The *Times* indicated that he may have taken refuge in his father's apartment later that morning and then left the building the next day.

How did he feel immediately following the murder? He probably felt relieved—relieved of the rage and the tension of holding back the rage. He would also feel a sense of self-righteous satisfaction, of vindication for what had been done to him, and a strange sort of pride at having done something so heinous; it was, from his point of view, both an act of self-assertion and a slap in the face of society, which he felt had been so callous toward him. And, of course, he would feel afraid of being apprehended by the police. He would not feel any remorse, though—not for several days. On the contrary, he would stay on a "murder high" until he was caught, even boasting to several acquaintances about what he had done.

This murder high that he experienced is not uncommon. Soldiers have reported feeling the same way after they have killed enemy soldiers, as have fighter pilots after they have shot down enemy airplanes. In fact, those who shoot the greatest number of enemies receive a hero's welcome and badges of honor to wear on their uniforms. (Emmanuel no doubt considered his victim to be an enemy, thereby justifying his act; he would therefore also expect a hero's welcome from his street acquaintances, with their street values and reverse racism, which explains why he would boast about the crime.) Similarly, deer hunters claim to have "deer fever" during and after the killing of game, and those who fish speak of a feeling of triumph after catching a big fish (as in Hemingway's *The Old Man and the Sea.*) This "high" is evidence, first, of the violence we all have repressed within us—men and women alike—which may be released when we feel it is justified or publicly sanctioned; and, second, of the fact that, in a pathological way, the extinguishing of another life can become the ultimate form of self-assertion.

Meanwhile, as Emmanuel hid in the storeroom, Caroline lay silently huddled on the rooftop, waiting for the police to find her. According to witnesses who saw her later, she seemed to take the whole event in stride, never doubting that she was going to be rescued and that she was going to be all right. Perhaps as she lay there she saw "her whole life flash before her," as the saying goes. More probably she was feeling angry, thinking, You're going to pay for this, you creep! You are absolutely going to pay for this! And also thinking, Please hurry. Oh, God, please, please hurry!

Police said later that they sped immediately to the scene, but because they had received calls from people in adjacent buildings who had reported that the screams had come from their roofs, they had to check out two other buildings before going to the correct address. The first officers to spot her did so from the roof of 925 West End Avenue. They picked out the victim with flashlights, but a 5-foot air-shaft gap stood between them.

"929!" Caroline yelled at the police, angrily. "929!"

"Wait a minute! Wait a minute!" they yelled back.

The police then hurried to Caroline's side on the roof of 929, arriving moments before ambulance and paramedic teams. Paramedics quickly bandaged her wounds and administered oxygen while she excitedly described her ordeal to the police. She told them that the man had asked her to have sex with him and she had refused, and she provided them with a description of her assailant: "He was a male black, light-skinned, with an apparently clean-shaven face and square jaw."

"Why do you say 'apparently' clean shaven?" the police asked.

"It was too dark to really see. . . . He might have had a few days' growth of beard." As it turned out, when he was captured Emmanuel *did* have a newly grown beard.

When the paramedics finally finished with her, she was placed on a stretcher. Even as she was being transported to the ambulance, she continued to talk.

"When they left for St. Luke's, she was still alive and very much coherent," said Ms. Blomquist to the *Times*. "She was talking to the police, and they were trying to quiet her down. They were trying to give her oxygen and she was bubbling with all this information. She was so willing to talk."

She is said to have continued "bubbling" information all the way to the hospital and during the time she was in the hospital emergency room. She probably would have kept talking during surgery if she had not been anesthetized.

Not only did Caroline think she was going to be all right; evidently so also did the police and the medical staff who attended her. "Up until 3:00 A.M. we thought she was going to survive her wounds," said Sergeant Terrence Quinn during a press conference on Monday. "Then, apparently, complications set in." What those complications were, he did not say.

While Caroline's lack of concern for her life seemed courageous to many, from a psychoanalytic viewpoint it may have been indicative of denial and depersonalization, both of which are normal reactions to shock, especially for a hysterical character. She seemed never to have even considered, until the last minute, the possibility that he would actually kill her, or that she could ever actually die. While he was stabbing her, and while she was being attended by paramedics and nurses in the ambulance and hospital, she never stopped talking, never stopped to consider what was really happening and what its outcome might be.

Perhaps, like many people, Caroline had never really come to grips with her own mortality, had never gone through the discomposing experience of discovering that she would have to die one day, not in the abstract but in the personal sense. Of all that we humans generally resist, the knowledge of our own mortality may well be that which we resist most strenuously. Yet at the same time, it is this very knowledge that makes us most humane, most loving, most tolerant, and most empathic—not just in a politically, religiously, or ideologically expedient way—and also causes us to respect those who would threaten us with death. Here again, it may be that Caroline's upbringing was a factor in her lack of respect for her assailant's threat to her life. Being sheltered while at the same time given the notion that she could do anything to which she set her mind might have imbued her with a false sense of security.

It was reported that Caroline was brought to the hospital in a city ambulance at 2:05 A.M. on Sunday. She was placed in the emergency room while surgeons and technicians were rounded up to perform surgery. Finally, at 2:55 A.M., she was rolled into the operating room. Anne Burton, a spokesperson for St. Luke's Hospital, told the *Times* that while Caroline was in the emergency room, "she was in shock, but she was conscious and spoke coherently."

A dispute arose during this time between police and hospital officials. Police later claimed that hospital officials told them that Caroline's condition was "critical but stable" and that she would probably survive her wounds. Hospital officials denied this. "I have found nobody" who gave that medical appraisal, Ms. Burton asserted in the *Times*. Because police thought she was going to survive, they did not attempt to question her thoroughly. Hence, only nurses and other medical staff were with Caroline during the last hour in the emergency room.

We do not know much of what she said in the emergency room in that hour. It seems likely, however, that until the very end she was still providing details about the attack and about her assailant. One of the effects of a traumatic shock is the need to talk, talk, talk, as a release of tension. In a psychological sense during that five minutes on the roof Emmanuel had transferred his rage onto Caroline; he had been humiliated by others, and now he had humiliated her. So her incessant talking was in part an attempt to release this rage, to elicit support for her cause, and to provide the facts necessary to obtain vengeance against her attacker.

It was, to be sure, the first time Caroline had ever suffered such a humiliation, and this too would undoubtedly have worsened the trauma. As her father later told *Daily News* reporters, "She was just a very unlucky woman." Lying on a stretcher and then on a bed in the emergency room, helpless, surrounded by the faces of people who probably looked at her with pity in their eyes, would have been very difficult for her. They would see themselves as lucky, and her as unlucky. This would be a view that Caroline usually had toward others, not one directed at her. It would grate against her pride.

Apparently only in the final moment did it dawn on her what had really happened. Only then did she realize the extent of her sacrifice.

"All this for $12," nurses later quoted her as saying. "I should have given him the money. I should have let him do it. I should have given in." (This quote was reported in all news accounts.)

At about 7:25 A.M., Caroline died on the operating table after 5 hours of surgery and 37 pints of transfused blood. A large team of physicians and nurses had tried their best to save her, but it was no use.

THE AFTERMATH

On the day after Caroline's murder, someone hung the following note in the elevator in the building in which she had been assaulted:

> Dear God! What else could possibly happen to be more devastating than that little girl losing her life for no reason. Remember: it could have been any one of us. Maybe, just maybe, if we had the proper security for the front door and the proper lighting for the building this tragedy could have been prevented.

These words, reported in the *Post*, served as a sort of "keynote" for the response that would follow the murder. The general theme of the aftermath was a clash between opposing religious and ideological factions, one liberal and one conservative. The liberals wanted to make of Caroline a martyr, fighter of a just cause against evil, urban violence, and sexism; however, they were opposed to capital punishment for Emmanuel and chose instead to take an understanding attitude toward him. Hence, Dr. Isenberg, who from the liberal camp, told reporters from the *Daily News*, "I haven't been thinking of capital punishment . . . I guess the justice system is going to have to wrestle with the issue of capital punishment." Asked what he was thinking, he replied, "I suppose I think that the man who murdered my little girl wasn't properly socialized."

A day later another message was tacked on the door of the elevator where it had all begun, this a poem celebrating Caroline's martyrdom, signed by "Mark Anthony." The poem, quoted in the

Daily News, seemed to be patterned after a Greek drama. Entitled "Caroline," it began with a chorus:

> O Caroline
> Caroline
> Caroline
> Caroline
>
> O Caroline
> Caroline
> Caroline
> Caroline

The three verses lamented Caroline's death in mournful tones that alluded to the belief that she had made a sac-ifice on behalf of many. One verse ended with the line, "One love stai ds to cry for all," while another concluded, "As life you gave in heaven's scent." Another verse compared her to an ancient song:

> It was a porcelain sky
> on the day you died
> rosen clouds passed us by
> an ancient song of storm and calm
> a thousand lives just in one

Similar "liberal" expressions were heard at a midnight vigil in front of Caroline's building a week after her death. "I didn't know Caroline," said Luis Reyes to the 400 people who gathered that night (as reported in the *Times*). "But I do know Caroline, because she lives in the heart of us—of anyone who has ever had a dream, whose mother ever had her child leave home."

"I heard her cry," said another speaker. "There was so much noise, but I thought there would be somebody else on the street and I didn't get out of bed. I have to live with that, and my regret."

The Williamstown Theater announced the next day that a scholarship fund would be established in Caroline's name—the Caroline Isenberg Scholarship Fund—to help new students. "Caroline started out as an apprentice at Williamstown," Bonnie Monte, an administrator for the theater group, told the *Post*. "And she would have felt that was the most worthy cause." Ms. Monte, like Ms.

Glassman, seemed to feel that doing good deeds, in this case for the arts, would erase the bitterness of Caroline's murder. She contended that Caroline "would have felt that was the most worthy cause."

And what of the conservatives? How did they respond to Caroline's murder? While liberals seemed to be ever aware of the necessity of maintaining their dignity and looking on the bright side, conservatives seemed just as zealous about expressing outrage and contempt and calling for blood. Witness, for example, the following note, which was taped to the door of Caroline's building a day after the poem was put up (as quoted in the *Daily News*):

> All your nice words of poetry and praise will not help this latest victim or any other. Why not set up a fund to help her unfortunate killer. Send him for therapy—perhaps a trip to the Bahamas would calm his murderous tendencies. Your lack of anger and outrage is almost as sick as the act itself. Shame on you!! Deep down I'm sure you are outraged—you're just too afraid people will think you're reactionaries and not liberals.

Mayor Koch, as previously noted, joined in with the conservatives, calling for capital punishment for the person who "butchered her and murdered her." Prosecutor Patrick Dugan also responded with outrage, calling the slaying "a senseless killing of a young woman" and asking for the maximum sentence.

Eleanor Rosenbaum, whose son Steven was to have gone with Caroline to see *Hurlyburly*, exclaimed to the *Post*: "As a mother, as a citizen of this city I love so much, it kills me that this kid had to come from Massachusetts to get murdered in New York. . . . All I want to say is that we walk around this city with a full sense of security, yet savages like that are around. Our young people are expiring in the prime of their lives because there are savages able to walk around on the streets."

Morton Alexander, an acting colleague of Caroline's, told the *Post*: "I do not believe in capital punishment, but I think women are vulnerable to this kind of thing. I really hope that he's castrated, so that he can never have sex again."

Finally, the *Daily News*, in an editorial on Saturday, December 8, also took the side of law and order. To its credit, however, it also noted the "public response" to the murder that "pitifully revolved around two blindly ideological extremes," one of which is characterized as "answering violence with bloody violence, vigilante justice" and the other as "treating all criminals, however bestial, as naughty, misguided children deserving succor and lollipops." The editorial concluded, "Neither perception, of course, has anything remotely to do with civilized justice—and there can be no civilization without justice."

From a psychoanalytic viewpoint, the ideologies of liberals and conservatives represent societal manifestations of the archaic ambivalence that begins in the first few months of life, during which the infant begins splitting external objects into good or evil. Neither the hard-core conservative nor the hard-core liberal can see the middle ground between these two stances—between "answering violence with bloody violence" and "treating all criminals . . . as naughty, misguided children deserving succor and lollipops." Neither appeasement and permissiveness nor punishment is the final answer to social conflict. A combination of both may be needed, along with the flexibility to know when to use one and when to use the other.

An interesting twist to the liberal-conservative conflict emerged around the issue of whether or not Caroline should have resisted her attacker. Those who supported resistance were generally feminists, and those who supported surrender were law enforcement officials. Here we have a situation in which feminists, who are usually viewed as liberals, take a conservative, "answering violence with bloody violence" position, while law enforcement officials, generally viewed as conservative, advocate appeasement. Why this twist? The answer lies in the nature of the issue—rape—and its particular meaning to feminists. For feminists, rape evokes an irrational response, grating against their female narcissism and arousing their rage at men. Law enforcement officials, meanwhile, see rape no differently than any other crime: If someone holds a gun or knife on you, don't be a fool; give up.

Not only do law enforcement officials generally support surrender, but so do statistics given out by rape crisis centers and psychiatrists. According to these statistics, as reported in *Newsweek*, only 2 to 5 percent of all sex offenders are in the highly violent category—that is, are potential killers. Proponents of surrender claim that resistance provokes violence, and that while escape or counterviolence may work at times, it is safer to go along with the attacker. Not that surrender is any guarantee that a life will be saved; however, surrender is the best bet for survival.

Indeed, Caroline may have been influenced by the feminist value system, which was typified by a quote from Betty Vicedomini, a fellow tenant of Caroline's, who told reporters, "If you could have heard her you'd have known she was a fighter. She wasn't going to have this person violate her." This woman seems to be saying that it is better to die than to let oneself be violated; to submit would be a disgrace. Apparently, in her view, one's inviolability is more important than one's life.

FINAL ANALYSIS

From a clinical viewpoint, the confrontation on the roof was between a psychopathic narcissist and a hysterical narcissist. The event itself was an eruption of primitive, infantile rage on the part of both the victim and the victimizer, the living out in the present of conflicts from the past.

Earlier in this book I quoted Kohut (1971) on the development of narcissistic rage, citing his assertion that "a traumatic alternation of faulty empathy, overempathy, and lack of empathy, which prevents the gradual withdrawal of narcissistic cathexes and the building up of tension-regulating psychic structures" leads a child to remain "fixated on the whole early narcissistic milieu" (p. 66). The question is, did Emmanuel's mother overrespond or underrespond to his needs? Was she really there for him? Or, due to her own narcissism, was she there only in body and not in spirit? Kohut points out that when a mother's responses are grossly unempathic and unreliable, the child becomes fixated on the early infantile environment. He feels narcissistically injured by his mother, who during this period is his whole world. He does not receive the kind of empathy, in the form of care and soothing, that would be required to heal the narcissistic injury, and so he "remains thus relatively defenseless vis-à-vis the effects of narcissistic injuries" (p. 65). That is, he becomes sensitive to criticism, to attacks on his self, and to attacks on narcissistic extensions of himself, such as his gender, race, belief system, or politics.

In becoming fixated, he does not make the next developmental step: internalizing his mother's soothing and learning to soothe himself. He does not learn to regulate his tension states through self-soothing and self-support; instead, he reacts with rage to his mother's lack of genuine responsiveness to his needs. He also develops a kind of grandiose pride (as though he were saying, "Who needs her? I can do it better myself; I can do it better than anybody!") in order to compensate for the feelings of powerlessness due to her faulty responsiveness. He will continue to be hypersensitive "to disturbances in the narcissistic equilibrium" throughout his life, with "a tendency to react to sources of narcissistic disturbance by mixtures of wholesale withdrawal and unforgiving rage" (p. 65).

A father can later diminish or increase the effects of early narcissistic injuries. Kohut attests that the personality of the father may, in later phases, be of decisive influence "with regard to the severity of the ensuing personality disturbance: if he, too, because of his own narcissistic fixations, is unable to respond empathically to the child's needs, then he compounds the damage" (p. 66).

For Emmanuel, we conjectured earlier that the loss of his father at an early age, due to divorce, and the additional factor of his father's somewhat belligerent personality all combined to leave Emmanuel feeling sad, guilty, angry, and fearful—and, most important, without an adequate masculine identification. During the anal-rapprochement phase, Emmanuel probably did not receive the support he needed in order to establish a healthy masculine self-esteem or to resolve his castration or oedipal complexes. His relationships with both his parents and his brothers impeded his development. He became the fulcrum of their animosity. Everywhere he turned, his masculinity was being assailed and belittled and undermined.

Kohut further points out that traumatic disturbances in the child's relationship with his parents during the oral and anal phases may interfere with the establishment of what he refers to as the "drive-controlling, drive-channeling, and drive-neutralizing basic fabric of the psychic apparatus." If such traumatic disturbances have been severe and long-lasting enough, the result is "a readiness toward the resexualizaton of drive derivatives" (p. 47), which takes the form of perverse fantasies or acts. In other words, if a child continues to feel rejected by his parents, he may not learn how to handle sexual or aggressive urges, and he may tend to sexualize all his feelings and to act them out perversely.

Signs of Emmanuel's narcissistic disturbances are evident in his short story, excerpted earlier in this chapter. For example, his feelings of grandiosity were apparent in his description of his protagonist as somebody who wanted to "seek out new civilizations, to explore strange new worlds, to boldly go where no man has gone before." His rage was indicated in his having the protagonist's father "killed in a plane crash said to be caused by a U.F.O." Other signs were his withdrawal from others—he was described as an outsider, even in his own gang—and his frequent, sometimes perverse acts of violence, such as throwing the tenant's dog off a bridge.

In fact, Emmanuel continued throughout his adolescence to display, as Kohut puts it, "a tendency to be hypersensitive to disturbances in the narcissistic equilibrium" and to react to sources of narcissistic disturbance "by mixtures of wholesale withdrawal and unforgiving rage." He was a loner in grade school and high school, and was noted for his "hot head" and for being mean and perverse. The ultimate display of his narcissism occurred on the rooftop that December morning when he met up with Caroline.

Looking at the murder scene in terms of Emmanuel's narcissistic features, we can more clearly understand why he behaved as he did. Caroline's refusal to give in to him represented yet another narcissistic blow—one of many he had accumulated since the earliest injuries at the hands of his mother, his father, and then his brothers. At that moment Caroline became a symbol of the mother who had failed to provide him with his "maturational needs" (Spotnitz 1985) and had frustrated his early sexual strivings. He wanted to annihilate the symbol before it destroyed him again. He perceived her rejection as a rejection of his very self; it not only threatened his feelings of grandiosity, but it also portended his own annihilation (which is what early feelings of infantile rage are about). He struck out at her in a perverse and violent way, like an animal who has been wounded.

And what about Caroline's narcissism? What were the narcissistic underpinnings of her behavior on the rooftop? Again, we can discern signs of narcissism throughout her childhood, but it is not so easy in her case to trace it to her beginnings. We have less information to go on.

Perhaps the primary element in her narcissism is her displacement in her mother's attention by the birth of her younger brother. Freud (1931) observed that both girls and boys are prone to dealing with the arrival of a baby brother or sister by harboring a grandiose notion. In his paper "Female Sexuality," he writes: "The little girl, just like the boy, wants to believe that she has given her mother this new child, and her reaction to the event and her behavior towards the child are the same as his. I know this sounds quite absurd, but perhaps only because the idea is such an unfamiliar one to us" (p. 238).

This phenomenon demonstrates the principle of splitting (the girl disowning her femininity) as well as of compensating for feelings of inferiority through developing narcissistic grandiosity: "I gave my mother that baby!"

Upon Caroline's displacement by her brother, depending on how her parents handled it, did she then develop a degree of hysteria? Was there a dependency on her father? Judging from the events surrounding the murder, her father seemed closer to her than her mother was. It was he who first came to her, he who referred to her as "my little girl." Perhaps she had turned to him for support upon her brother's birth.

The father, as well as the mother, can be an important influence in the development of hysteria. If a girl develops too close a tie to her father, she has difficulty letting go of him later in order to establish relationships with other men. In addition, she may feel guilty about unconscious thoughts of breaking the incest taboo, which will then have an impact on her character. As Kohut points out, the father can be decisive in diminishing or increasing the effects of early narcissistic injuries. In this case the narcissism seems to have been increased by an overprotective father.

Looking at the murder scene in terms of Caroline's female narcissism, it seems likely that her resistance to Emmanuel may have sprung from her own well of sexual animosity and her hysterical character. When Emmanuel assaulted her, demanding her money, demanding sex, holding a knife on her, he may have become a symbol of the younger brother who demanded she give up the center of attention, reviving the feelings of loss and rivalry from that earlier period. Emmanuel's penis became the despised penis of her brother, and more: It became the "bad penis" that would destroy her with its poison. Further, Emmanuel's attempt to force her to have sex went against the grain of her female grandiosity as well as her upper middle class sense of fair play; she would not allow a man, especially an impudent, lower-class man, to defeat her. Hysteria also played a part in her resistance, causing her to rail and scream with all her might, misperceiving the real danger of the situation and thinking, magically, that her screams would subdue the "beast"—as hysterical screams are wont to do—or that she would be rescued by the "knights in shining armor" from her building. That she identified herself during her ordeal by her first name, calling down, "It's Caroline," seems to indicate a grandiose and somewhat naive notion that everyone knew who "Caroline" was and would rush to her aid. New York is New York, however, and while people may yell out their windows for you, they are seldom prepared to risk their own lives for you. Thus, because of the narcissism and hysteria that clouded her perception, the grandiosity and magical thinking that caused her to misperceive the situation, and the sexual animosity toward her attacker, she was unable to respond adaptively, unable to do whatever she needed to do in order to survive. These, it seems to me, are the most likely psychodynamic elements behind her intense resistance of her attacker even after he had proved that he was serious, even after he had stabbed her in the arm the first time. She got caught up in winning rather than surviving.

Most rapists (95%) are satisfied by raping a woman. Resistance usually only serves to provoke further violence, as was the case here. Surrendering also gives the victim time to stall and consider other options, as well as the chance to maneuver the attacker into a vulnerable position.

Caroline herself later wondered if she should not have given in. Her absolute and abrupt refusal to hand her purse over, knowing that she had only $12, seemed to be an act of stubborn, hysterical defiance rather than a rational, survival-minded act. Similarly, after he had stabbed her once, twice, three times, why did she not give in? One has to admire her spirit, her will to live, and her calm in calling out exact information to rescuers; but at the same time, one must examine the situation objectively.

Not all women respond to a rapist in the same way. Response to rape depends on many variables, the most important of which is the woman's attitude toward it. Two case histories will serve to illustrate this point.

The first patient, a woman I treated for a short time, found rape to be a devastating experience. She was raped at the age of 40 by "a punk in a leather jacket," as she put it. This woman had not had a relationship with a man since high school; she felt that if she allowed a man to have sex with her, he would have complete power over her from that point on. She had a great deal of animosity toward both her parents, particularly her father, who had been an alcoholic, and she directed this animosity toward men in general. Her attitude was that she would die before she would let a man violate her; therefore, to be raped would be the ultimate destructive experience for her and would leave her in a rage for many years to come.

I treated another woman who had been raped by a man she described as "from a lower economic and racial level"; she said she had submitted to the rape not only because the man had a knife but also because she felt sorry for him. "He seemed so bitter, so lost," she said. She was a woman who had positive feelings toward her father and who was happily married, with two children, at the time of the rape. She had little animosity toward men and enjoyed intercourse. In addition, her husband and parents were very supportive. All of these factors contributed to her rapid adjustment to the rape. Within a few days she felt well enough to return to work. She reported no long-term effects.

Once again, there is a middle ground between the position of male narcissists who assume that *every* woman who is raped somehow "asks for it," and the position of female narcissists who assume that no woman ever asks for or in any way contributes to rape. There are cases in which women absolutely do not ask for it—cases in which women are assaulted in their homes by strange intruders, for example. But there are other cases in which a woman really does ask for it. One patient comes to mind. This woman, who had been sexually abused as a child, had a habit of going on hitchhiking sprees whenever she felt enraged by some disappointment with a man. She would inevitably seek out truck-drivers during these sprees, seduce them, and then fight them with all her might when they pulled over to the side of the road to do what she seemed to want them to do. So they would rape her, and she would then feel even more justified in hating men and regarding them all as "jerks."

Ultimately, the confrontation on the rooftop was just another battle in the war between the sexes. What happened that night was that two people, a man named Emmanuel and a woman named Caroline, got caught up in a narcissistic power struggle that ended in violence.

Postscript: Male and Female

Yin and yang. According to sages of old and new, all people are driven by these dualities. Lao Tzu (Bynner 1944) states:

> One who has man's wings
> And a woman's also
> Is a womb of the world
> And, being a womb of the world,
> Continually, endlessly gives birth. [p. 42]

Like magnets—each having plus and minus poles—male and female each carry poles of duality. They must approach one another correctly. Plus and minus repel plus and minus, but they attract minus and plus. The male must integrate the female and the female the male. When this does not happen, something is wrong. Kardiner (1954) notes, "When a culture uses such social machinery as tends to destroy the emotions on which social cohesion depends, and creates disastrous cleavages between the sexes so that they fly from and not toward each other, we know that a serious disintegrating force is at work" (p. 265).

The mating of male and female provides the most profound merging and integration of male and female. In this act, man and woman become one, simultaneously satisfying both Eros (the urge to create and to live most fully) and Thanatos (the urge to control, destroy, or return to the womb). When man and woman are in tune with each other, their movements, feelings, and thoughts intertwined, animosity and separatism dissolve. Each wave of masculinity meets a wave of femininity, culminating in release, in death, and in rebirth. Each feels connected and powerful in relation to the other. Each feels whole and in harmony with their dualities. Each feels fully alive.

Disharmony is destruction. Harmony is creation.

References

Abraham, K. (1925). Character-Formation on the Genital Level of Libido-Development. In *Selected Papers of Karl Abraham*, trans. by D. Bryan and A. Strachey, pp. 407–417. New York: Brunner/Mazel, 1979.

Adler, A. (1927a). Sex. In *Psychoanalysis and Women*, ed. J. B. Miller, pp. 40–50. New York: Penguin, 1977.

_____ (1927b). *Understanding Human Nature.* Trans. W. B. Wolfe. New York: Premier Books, 1957.

_____ (1929). *Problems of Neurosis: A Book of Case Histories.* Ed. P. Mairet. New York: Harper & Row, 1964.

Baker, E. F. (1967). *Man in the Trap.* New York: Macmillan.

Balint, M. (1948). On genital love. *International Journal of Psychoanalysis* 29:31–37.

Bayley, J. (1986). Unhappy families are all alike. *New York Times Book Review*, Feb. 9, pp. 14–15.

Bonaparte, M. (1953). *Female Sexuality.* New York: International Universities Press, 1956.

Bowlby, J. (1979). *The Making and Breaking of Affectional Bonds.* London: Tavistock.

235

Brownmiller, S. (1975). *Against Our Will: Men, Women and Rape.* New York: Bantam Books, 1981.

Bynner, W. (1944). *The Way of Life according to Lao Tzu.* New York: Capricorn Books, 1962.

Clower, V. L. (1979). Feminism and the new psychology of women. In *On Sexuality*, ed. T. B. Karasu and C. W. Socarides, pp. 279–316. New York: International Universities Press.

Coles, E. M. (1982). *Clinical Psychopathology: An Introduction.* London: Routledge & Kegan Paul.

Deutsch, H. (1944). *The Psychology of Women.* Vol. 1. New York: Grune & Stratton.

Dicks, H. V. (1967). *Marital Tensions: Clinical Studies towards a Psychological Theory of Interaction.* London: Routledge & Kegan Paul.

Eibl-Eibesfeldt, I. (1970). *Love and Hate: The Natural History of Behavior Patterns.* New York: Schocken Books, 1974.

Erikson, E. H. (1950). *Childhood and Society.* 2nd ed. New York: Norton, 1963.

Fenichel, O. (1945). *The Psychoanalytic Theory of Neurosis.* New York: Norton.

Ford, C. S., and Beach, F. A. (1951). *Patterns of Sexual Behavior.* New York: Harper & Row.

Freud, A. (1965). *Normality and Pathology in Childhood: Assessments of Development.* New York: International Universities Press.

Freud, S. (1909). Analysis of a phobia in a five-year-old boy. *Standard Edition* 10:3–152.

——— (1918). The taboo of virginity. *Standard Edition* 11:192–208.

——— (1920a). Beyond the pleasure principle. *Standard Edition* 18:3–66.

——— (1920b). The psychogenesis of a case of female homosexuality. *Standard Edition* 17:146–174.

——— (1921). Group psychology and the analysis of the ego. *Standard Edition* 18:67–145.

——— (1924). The dissolution of the Oedipus complex. *Standard Edition* 19:173–182.

——— (1925). Some psychical consequences of the anatomical distinction between the sexes. *Standard Edition* 19:243–260.

——— (1927a). Fetishism. *Standard Edition* 21:149–159.

——— (1927b). The future of an illusion. *Standard Edition* 21:3–58.

——— (1930). Civilization and its discontents. *Standard Edition* 21:59–148.

——— (1931). Female sexuality. *Standard Edition* 21:223–246.

——— (1933). Letter from Freud. *Standard Edition* 22:203–218.

Friedan, B. (1963). *The Feminine Mystique.* New York: Norton.

Friedman, R. M., and Lerner, L., eds. (1986). *Toward a New Psychology of Man: Psychoanalytic and Social Perspectives. Psychoanalytic Review* 73.

Fromm, E. (1951). *The Forgotten Language: An Introduction to the Understanding of Dreams, Fairy Tales, and Myths.* New York: Holt, Rinehart & Winston.

Gilder, G. F. (1973). *Sexual Suicide.* New York: Quadrangle.

Gilligan, C. (1982). *In a Different Voice: Psychological Theory and Women's Development.* Cambridge, MA: Harvard University Press.

Goldberg, S. (1973). *The Inevitability of Patriarchy.* New York: William Morrow.

Greenhouse, L. (1986). Portia faces life. *New York Times Book Review*, Feb. 23, p. 12.

Groth, A. N. (1979). *Men Who Rape: The Psychology of the Offender.* New York: Plenum.

Hoffer, E. (1963). *The True Believer.* New York: Time-Life.

Honey, M., and Broughton, J. (1985). Feminine sexuality: an interview with Janine Chasseguet-Smirgel. *Psychoanalytic Review* 4:527–548.

Horney, K. (1926). The flight from womanhood: the masculinity complex in women as viewed by men and by women. In *Psychoanalysis and Women*, ed. J. B. Miller, pp. 5–20. New York: Penguin, 1977.

_____ (1950). *Neurosis and Human Growth.* New York: Norton.

Jung, C. (1926). *Psychological Types or the Psychology of Individuation.* Trans. H. G. Baynes. New York: Harcourt Brace.

_____ (1951). *The Portable Jung.* Ed. J. Campbell. New York: Viking, 1977.

Kanefield, L. (1985). Psychoanalytic constructions of female development and women's conflicts about achievement. *Journal of the American Academy of Psychoanalysis* 13(3):347–366.

Kardiner, A. (1945). *The Psychological Frontiers of Society.* New York: Columbia University Press.

_____ (1954). *Sex and Morality.* Indianapolis: Bobbs-Merrill.

Kestenberg, J. S. (1968). Outside and inside, male and female. *Journal of the American Psychoanalytic Association* 16:456–520.

Khan, M. M. R. (1979). *Alienation in Perversions.* New York: International Universities Press.

Klein, M. (1932). *The Psychoanalysis of Children.* New York: Delacorte, 1975.

Kohut, H. (1971). *The Analysis of the Self: A Systematic Approach to the Psychoanalytic Treatment of Narcissistic Personality Disorders.* New York: International Universities Press.

Kolb, L. G. (1977). *Modern Clinical Psychiatry.* 9th ed. Philadelphia: W. B. Saunders.

Kramer, H., and Sprenger, J. (1486). *Maldeus Maleficarum*. Trans. M. Summers. London: Pushkin Press, 1928.

Laing, R. D. (1970). *Knots*. New York: Pantheon Books.

_____ (1971). *The Politics of the Family*. London: Tavistock.

Lindner, R. (1955). *The Fifty-Minute Hour*. New York: Bantam Books, 1979.

Lorenz, K. (1963). *On Aggression*. New York: Bantam Books, 1967.

Lowenstein, R. (1957). A contribution to the psychoanalytic theory of masochism. *Journal of the American Psychoanalytic Association* 5:197–234.

Mahler, M. S., Pine, F., and Bergman, A. (1975). *The Psychological Birth of the Human Infant: Symbiosis and Individuation*. London: Mansfield Library.

Malinowski, B. (1927). *The Father in Primitive Psychology*. New York: Norton.

Masson, J. M. (1984). *The Assault on Truth: Freud's Suppression of the Seduction Theory*. New York: Farrar, Straus & Giroux.

Masters, W. H., and Johnson, V. E. (1966). *Human Sexual Response*. Boston: Little, Brown.

McDougall, J. (1984). Eve's reflection: on the narcissistic and homosexual components of female sexuality. Paper presented at symposium, The Many Phases of Eve: Beyond Psychoanalytic and Feminist Stereotypes, Los Angeles, Feb. 25.

Mead, M. (1935). *Sex and Temperament in Three Primitive Societies*. New York: William Morrow.

_____ (1949). *Male and Female*. New York: William Morrow.

Miller, A. (1981). *Prisoners of Childhood*. New York: Farrar, Straus & Giroux.

_____ (1983). *For Your Own Good: Hidden Cruelty in Child-Rearing and the Roots of Violence*. New York: Farrar, Straus & Giroux.

_____ (1984). *Thou Shalt Not Be Aware: Society's Betrayal of the Child*. New York: Farrar, Straus & Giroux.

Mitchell, J. (1974). *Psychoanalysis and Feminism*. New York: Pantheon Books.

Money, J., and Ehrhardt, A. A. (1972). *Man and Woman, Boy and Girl*. Baltimore: The Johns Hopkins University Press.

Montagu, A. (1976). *The Nature of Human Aggression*. New York: Oxford University Press.

Offit, A. K. (1977). *The Sexual Self*. Philadelphia: JB Lippincott.

Rader, D. (1985). *Tennessee: Cry of the Heart*. New York: New American Library.

Reich, W. (1942). *The Function of the Orgasm*. New York: Pocket Books, 1978.

_____ (1945). *Character Analysis*. New York: Touchstone, 1972.

Ribble, M. A. (1943). *The Rights of Infants*. New York: Columbia University Press.

Roiphe, H., and Galenson, E. (1981). *Infantile Origins of Sexual Identity*. New York: International Universities Press.

Robertiello, R., and Schoenewolf, G. (1987). *101 Common Therapeutic Blunders*. Northvale, NJ: Jason Aronson.

Safer, M. (1987). The loony left. *Sixty Minutes*, CBS Broadcast, April 12.

Samuels, L. (1985). Female psychotherapists as portrayed in film, fiction and non-fiction. *Journal of the American Academy of Psychoanalysis* 13(3):367–378.

Schopenhauer, A. (1896). *The World as Will and Idea*. Trans. R. B. Haldane and J. Kemp. London: Kegan, Paul, Trench & Trübner.

Seldes, G., ed. (1960). *The Great Quotations*. New York: Pocket Books, 1967.

Sherfey, M. J. (1966). On the nature of female sexuality. In *Psychoanalysis and Women*, ed. J. B. Miller. New York: Penguin, 1977.

Shoumatoff, A. (1986). The fatal obsession of Dian Fossey. *Vanity Fair*, Sept., pp. 130–139.

Socarides, C. W. (1979). A unitary theory of sexual perversions. In *On Sexuality*, ed. T. B. Karasu and C. W. Socarides. New York: International Universities Press.

Spitz, R. A. (1965). *The First Year of Life: A Psychoanalytic Study of Normal and Deviant Development of Object Relations*. New York: International Universities Press.

Spotnitz, H. (1985). *Modern Psychoanalysis of the Schizophrenic Patient: Theory of Technique*. 2nd ed. New York: Human Sciences Press.

Stern, D. (1977). *The First Relationship: Mother and Infant*. Cambridge, MA: Harvard University Press.

Stoller, R. J. (1968). *Sex and Gender*. New York: Jason Aronson.

Tanner, L. B., ed. (1971). *Voices from Women's Liberation*. New York: Signet.

Thompson, C. (1943). Penis envy in women. In *Psychoanalysis and Women*, ed. J. B. Miller, pp. 52–57. New York: Penguin, 1977.

_____ (1950). Some effects of the derogatory attitude toward female sexuality. In *Psychoanalysis and Women*, ed. J. B. Miller, pp. 58–68. New York: Penguin, 1977.

_____ (1964). *On Women*. New York: Signet, 1971.

Turkington, C. (1986). Feminists and homosexuals oppose amendments to *DSM III*. *APA Monitor*, Feb., vol. 17/2.

Tyson, P. (1986). Male gender identity: early developmental roots. *Psychoanalytic Review* 73:4

Vilar, E. (1922). *The Manipulated Man*. New York: Farrar, Straus and Giroux.

Vogel, E. F., and Bell, N. W. (1981). The emotionally disturbed child as the family scapegoat. In *Family Therapy: Major Contributions*, ed. R. J. Green and J. L. Framo, pp. 207–234. New York: International Universities Press.

Williams, T. (1940). *A Streetcar Named Desire*. New York: Signet, 1964.

Winnicott, D. W. (1964). *Boundary and Space: An Introduction to the Work of D. W. Winnicott*. Ed. M. Davis and D. Wallbridge. London: H. Karnak, 1981.

—— (1965). *The Maturational Processes and the Facilitating Environment*. London: Hogarth Press.

Zilboorg, G. (1944). Masculine and feminine: some biological and cultural aspects. In *Psychoanalysis and Women*, ed. J. B. Miller, pp. 96–131. New York: Penguin, 1977.

Index

Abraham, K., 32, 112–113
Acting out
  and child-care centers, 110
  depression as, 107
  and penis envy, 63
Adam, 25
Adamson, J., 172
Adler, A., 6, 32–33, 84, 102
Against Our Will (Brownmiller), 77
Aggression; *see also* Thanatos
  absence of direct, 103–104
  and aging, 14
  genesis of, 8–9
  and heroes, 17
Alexander, M., 223
Ambivalence, 9, 174
  denial of, 103–104
  overcoming of, 111, 113

American Psychiatric Association, 93
Anaclitic depression, 14
Anal narcissism, 49–51, 68–69
Anal stage, 29
Animal studies, 19
Animosity, 5
  Jung's view of, 7–8
Aristotle, 83
Athletics, and war, 86–87
Augustine, St., 83

Baby-sitter, suitable, 110
Baker, E.F., 65, 80, 95
Baldridge, H., 200–201
Balint, M., 103
Basic trust, 24–25, 114
Bayley, J., 90

Beach, F. A., 121
Behrman, L., 195
Bell, N.W., 107
Bible, 5, 25, 82
Blacklisting, 91
"The Blue Angel," 67
Bonaparte, M., 31–32
Borderline narcissism, 71–72
Bowlby, J., 14, 206
Boys
  and castration complex, 30–32
  and sexual difference, 25–29
Breast
  and ambivalence toward, 9
  initial relationship with, 21–22
  splitting of, 51
Broughton, J., 92
Brownmiller, S., *Against Our Will*,
  77
Burton, A., 194
Bynner, W., 3, 233

Calvin, J., 83
Castration complex, 5–6, 26–27,
  41–46, 164
  anatomical basis of, 56
  cultural manifestation of, 28
  and Oedipus, 29–36
  overcoming fear of, 123
  precursor of, 22
Censorship, and feminism, 91, 95
Chasseguet-Smirgel, J., 92
Child-care centers, 110
Childhood
  of Dian Fossey, 171–172
  vicissitudes of, 129–148
Children
  critical periods in development of,
    17–20
  cruelty toward, 43–44, 101–104
  mother–child dyad, 20–29

narcissistic parents and, 104–107
  as scapegoats, 107
  sexual abuse of, 10, 105
  value systems and, 110
Chivalry, 115
Clitoris, 33
  self-stimulation of, 66
Clower, V.L., 82, 92, 123
Coles, E.M., 18–19
Collective unconscious, 7–8
Complementary relationships,
  121–125
Conservatives, 95–96
  reactions to murder, 223–224
Copulation, 16, 115–116
Countertransference, 155
Criminality, 116
Critical periods, 17–20

Dancing, 124
Death wish, 176
Denial, 74, 103
Densmore, D., 89
Dependence, fear of, 22–23, 30
Depression
  abandonment and, 206
  anaclitic, 14
  and relating to children, 107
Deutsch, H., 31–32
Dicks, H.V., 103–104, 106–107
Dictators, 84
Dillon, R.P., 193–194
Dominance, and submission,
  118–119
Dostoyevsky, F., 7
Double messages, 207
Duality
  in Eastern philosophy, 3–4
  of eros and thanatos, 13–17
  Freud's use of, 4
Dugan, P., 196, 223

Egalitarianism, 119–121
  misguided, 116–117
Ego
  collective, 99
  fragile, 56
  infantile, 20
Ehrhardt, A.A., 28, 35
Eibl-Eibesfeldt, I., 76, 87, 114–115
Einstein, A., 85
Electra complex, 59–65
Elizabeth I, Queen of England, 83
Emotional cripples, 106
Empathy, traumatic alteration of,
  20–21
Eremenco, P., 201
Erikson, E.H., 8, 24–25, 113
Eros, 4, 9, 13–17
  collective frustration of, 85
Etiology, 13–39
Eve, 5, 25, 82–83
Exhibitionists, 53

Fairy tales, narcissism in, 109–110
Family
  beginning of, 84
  disintegration of, 106
  sexual animosity in, 101–110
Fantasy, of getting a penis, 63–64
The Father (Strindberg), 41
Fathers
  of borderlines, 72
  castration fear of, 44–45
  and daughters, 35
  fear of women in, 38
  girls' feminine strivings and, 61,
    64
  of hysterics, 68
  incestuous behavior of, 38–39
  of lesbians, 72
  of masculine-aggressives, 66–67
  of psychopaths, 52

role of, 37
sadomasochistic, 69
and separate identity, 44
and sexual difference, 26–27
Female masochism, 31, 69
  versus receptivity, 33, 36
Female narcissism, 59–77
  attitudes of, 108–109
Female sexual magnetism, 75–76
The Feminine Mystique (Friedan), 88
Femininity, valuation of, 64
Feminism, 5, 88–91
  attack on Freud, 6–7, 35–36,
    91–95
  and censorship, 91, 95
  in conflict, 95–99
  and masculinism, 79–82
  penis envy and, 30, 66
  and rape, 224–225
Feminist Therapy Institute, 93
Fenichel, O., 32, 50, 111
Fetishists, 53
The Fifty-Minute Hour (Lindner),
  130
Fliess, W., 6
Ford, C.S., 121
Fossey, D., 169–180
  Gorillas in the Mist, 165
Freud, A., 6, 63
Freud, S., 8, 12, 14, 53, 56, 61–63,
  99, 104, 121, 123
  dual-instinct theory of, 4
  on female moral development,
    5–6, 31–33
  "Female Sexuality," 228
  feminist attack on, 6–7, 35–36,
    91–95
  letter to Einstein, 85
  Little Hans case of, 42
  and Oedipus, 29
  seduction theory of, 92–93

Three Essays on the Theory of Sexuality, 6
Friedan, B., *The Feminine Mystique*, 88
Friedman, R.M., 94
Fromm, E., 109

Galenson, E., 18, 26–28, 32, 35, 37, 44, 61–63
Gender identity, establishment of, 25–29, 44
Gender roles, 10–11
Genitality, 111–114
Germany, Nazi, 86
Gibbons, K., 199
Gilder, G., 122–123
Gilligan, C., 6, 32–35, 60, 91, 95
Girls
    and castration complex, 30–32
    separation task of, 60
    and sexual difference, 25–29, 60
    sexual organ of, 63–64
Glassman, S., 199, 215
Goldberg, S., 118
"Gone With the Wind," 68
Goodall, J., 170, 173
"Good-enough mothering," 21
Gorillas in the Mist (Fossey), 175
Grandiosity, 34, 160, 161
Gratitude, 15
Greenhouse, L., 90–91
Groth, A.N., 207

Hansel and Gretel (Humperdinck), 109
Harmonic couple, 111–125
Hatred, unreasonable, 81
Helen of Troy, 87
Heroes, and aggression, 17, 85
Hindu Code of Manu, 83
Hitler, A., 43–44

Hoffer, E., 81
Holding environment, 21
Homicide, 14–15
Homosexual fantasy, 164
Homosexuality, 10
    female, 23–24, 72–73, 89
    male, 53, 57
    rise in, 81
    and social unrest, 96–98
Honey, M., 92
Horney, K., 6, 32–33, 46
Hypnotic induction, 104–105, 149
Hysterical narcissism, 67–68, 181–182

I-Ching, 3
Id, collective, 99
Identification
    adult, 80
    with the aggressor, 66
Ideology
    and fanaticism, 95–96
    sexual, 80
Illusions
    counter-, 166
    created by family, 166
    therapist's, 167
Incest, 38–39
    psychological, 161
Infant
    and the breast, 9, 36
    depression's effect on, 107
Initiation rites, 116–117
Interpretation, 94
    intolerance of, 154
Isenberg, C. 193–196
    death of, 210–225
    before the murder, 196–202
    narcissism of, 227–229
Isenberg, E., 197–198
Isenberg, P.L., 196–197, 201, 221

Jerome, St., 83
Jesus, 177
Johnson, V.E., 121–122
Journal of the American Academy of Psychoanalysis, 35
Jung, C., 7–8, 103, 113

Kanefield, L., 35, 91
Kardiner, A., 81, 96–97, 117, 233
Karisoke Research Center (Rwanda, Africa), 169–171
Kennedy, J.F., 47, 114
Kestenberg, J.S., 63, 117
Khan, M.M.R., 8, 23–24, 38
Klein, M., 8–9, 15–16, 21–22, 51, 63, 174
Knots (Laing), 130
Koch, E., 195–196, 223
Koedt, A., 89
Kohut, H., 8–9, 20–21, 225–228
Kolb, L.G., 208
Kramer, H., 83

Laing, R.D., 104, 149
  Knots, 130
Lampl de Groot, J., 32
Lao Tzu, 3, 12, 99, 233
Leakey, L., 173
Lerner, L., 94
Liberals, 95–96
  reactions to murder, 221–223
Liberated women, 123
Liberation, 98–99
Lindner, R., 52
  The Fifty-Minute Hour, 130
Little Red Riding Hood, 109
Locke, E., 216
Loners, 160, 161
Lorenz, K., 114–115
Love
  first act of, 36
    and gratitude, 15
    natural capacity for, 112
Lowenstein, R., 8
Luther, M., 83, 177

Mahler, M., 8, 18, 25–26, 30, 32, 35, 42, 62–63, 190
Male dominance, 118–119
Male narcissism, 41–57
  attitude of, 107–108
Malinowski, B., 87
Malleus Maleficarum (Kramer and Sprenger), 83
Mandell, E., 201
Marasmus, 14
Marks, J., 199
Marmor, J., 32
Marriage
  basis of, 123
  separatism of, 124–125
Martyrdom, 177–180
Masculine-aggressive narcissism, 65–67
Masculinism, 5, 82–84
  in conflict, 95–99
  and feminism, 79–82
  and war, 85–88
Masochism, 8
  female, 31, 33, 36, 69
  and victimology, 10
Mass movements, psychology of, 81
Masson, J.M., 92
Masters, W.H., 121–122
Masturbation
  cessation of, 62–63
  clitoral, 60
  precocious, 23–24
  punishment for, 61
Mating behavior, 119–120
  of "higher animals," 114–115
  of human species, 115–116

McDougall, J., 61, 63
McGuire, W., 162
McKinley, W., 86
Mead, M., 24, 42, 87, 95, 116–117
Men
    exclusion of, 35
    fear of, 76–77
    "fragile egos" of, 56
    moral development of, 6, 30–33
Miller, A., 43–44, 71, 104–105
Mitchell, J., 33
Moltke, H. von, 86
Money, J., 28, 35
Monitor (American Psychology
    Association), 93
Montagu, A., 19–20, 87
Monte, B., 222–223
Moral development, 5–6, 30–33
Morgan, R., 88
Mother
    absentee, 117–118
    and anal narcissists, 69
    borderline, 72
    castrating, 38–39
    and child, 20–29, 36–37
    dread of being killed by, 61
    fear of fusion with, 53
    "good-enough," 21
    hostile ambivalence toward, 61
    incestuous behavior of, 38
    intrusive, 66
    of lesbians, 72
    love of, 15
    narcissism of, 64
    penis envy of, 44
    prestige of, 10–11
    of psychopath, 52
    reinforcement of penis envy by,
        38
    surrogate, 190
Motor retardation, 14

Moulton, R., 32
Muhammad, 83
Mussolini, B., 86

Narcissism, 9
    and adult identification, 80
    anal, 49–51, 68–69
    borderline, 71–72
    in fairy tales, 109–110
    father's, 64
    female, 59–77, 108–109
    homosexual, 72–73
    hysterical, 67–68, 181–182
    male, 41–57, 107–108
    masculine–aggressive, 65–67
    mother's, 64
    oral, 51–52, 70–71
    passive, 48–49
    pathological, 20
    perverse, 53
    phallic, 47–48, 181–182
    psychopathic, 52
    psychotic, 53–54, 73
    and social ills, 98–99
Narcissistic parents, 104–107
Narcissistic rage, 160, 161
National Geographic Society, 174
New Guinea, 24
Newsweek, 194, 224
New York Daily News, 198–201,
        203–204, 208–209, 211,
        220–224
New York Newsday, 101
New York Post, 195–198, 201–202,
        208–209, 221, 223
New York Times, 193, 201, 219–220
New York Times Book Review, 90

Obsessive–compulsive character,
        50
Oedipal

guilt, 164
  sexual joining, negative, 164
  situation, 163
Oedipus complex, 29–36
  resolution of, 45–46
Offit, A.K., 123
Oral narcissism, 51–52, 70–71
Oral-sadistic phase, 24–25
Organic diseases, 16
Orgasm
  function of, 112–113
  inability to achieve, 52, 66
  and reproduction, 122

Pandora's box, 82
Paranoid–schizoid position, 174
Parents, narcissistic, 104–107
Passive–aggressive, 162
Passive narcissism, 48–49
Pathology, and thanatos, 16
Patriarchy, 120–121
  decay of, 117–118
Paul, St., 83
Pedophiles, 53
Penis envy, 5–6, 30–32, 44, 156–157
  female narcissism and, 59–65
  feminist view of, 33–34
  maternal reinforcement of, 38
  overcoming, 123–124
  predisposition to, 22
Perverse narcissism, 53
Perverse sexual practices, 23–24
Phallic narcissism, 47–48, 181–182
"Phallic woman," 65–67
Plato, 83
Poisonous pedagogy, 104
Postconcussional syndrome, 208
Post-traumatic stress, 208
Power, and thanatos, 15
Pregnancy, transmission of traits
  during, 17–18

Primary anxious
  overpermissiveness, 52
Projection, 74
Psychoanalysis, feminist use of, 7
Psychoanalytic community,
  polarization of, 32
Psychoanalytic Review, 92, 94
Psychopathic narcissism, 52
Psychosis, 161
Psychotic narcissism, 53–54, 73
Pygmalion (Shaw), 108

Rage
  gender, 46
  and mass movements, 81
Rape
  obsession with, 7
  reactions to, 224–225, 229–231
Rapprochement stage, 18, 25–26,
    37, 60
Redstockings Manifesto, 88
Reich, W., 65, 112
Relationships, complementary,
    121–125
Religion
  degradation of women in, 82–83
  and martyrdom, 177–180
Repetition compulsion, 50
  and martyrdom, 179
Resistance, joining, 157
Ribble, M.A., 8, 18
Roiphe, H., 181, 26–28, 32, 35, 37,
    44, 61–63
Roles, gender, 10–11, 34
Rosenbaum, E., 201, 223

Sadomasochism, 8, 163
  and anal narcissism, 49–51, 68–69
Safer, M., 95
Samuels, L., "Female
    Psychotherapists as Portrayed

in Film, Fiction, and
    Nonfiction," 93
Santos, A., 203
Saudi Arabia, 120
Scapegoating, 82, 89–90, 107, 206,
    210
Schopenhauer, A., 11
Seduction theory, abandonment of,
    92–93
Seldes, G., 86
Sensory deprivation, 21
Separation-individuation, 190
    for girls, 60
    failure to pass through, 53
    rapprochement stage of, 18,
        25–26, 37
Sex crimes, 10
"Sexism," 89
Sexual animosity, 3–12, 163–164
    etiology of, 13–39
    in family life, 101–110
    and sadomasochism, 8
    in society, 79–99
    transmission of, 107–110
Sexual difference, discovery of,
        25–29, 62–63, 77
Sexual functioning
    healthy, 112–113
    and male dominance, 115–116
Sexual harassment, 67
Sexuality
    frustration of, 123
    meaning of, 122
    perverse, 23–24
Sexual magnetism, female, 75–76
Sexual passion, 11
Sexual responses, 122
Sherfey, M.J., 32–34
Shoumatoff, A., 169–175
60 Minutes, 95
Socarides, C.W., 28–29, 38, 53

"Social injustice," 34
Society
    hunter–gatherer, 120
    sexual animosity in, 79–99
Socrates, 167
Spitz, R.A., 9, 14, 18, 24, 52, 98,
        106, 110, 117–118
Splitting, 51, 164, 218
Spotnitz, H., 8, 20–21, 37, 227
Sprenger, J., 83
Stern, D., 18
Stewart, K., 170
Stoller, R.J., 28
A Streetcar Named Desire (Williams),
        130, 181–192
Strindberg, A., The Father, 41
Submission, dominance and,
        118–119
Suicide, 14–15
Superego
    borderline, 71
    collective, 99
    formation of, 30–32
Swit, L., 199

Tanner, L.B., 88
Tao Te Ching, 3
Teasing, as communication, 166
Thanatos, 4, 9, 13–17
    masculinism and feminism as
        expression of, 79–80
Theory, dual-instinct, 4
Therapeutic alliance, 158
Therapist, training of, 11
Thompson, C., 6, 32–34, 82, 123
Tolstoy, L., 90
Tolstoy, S., 90
Torres, A., 208
Torres, E., 193, 195–196, 210–218
    before the murder, 202–210
    narcissism of, 225–227

Torres, K., 209
Transference, 155–157
  impaired capacity for, 106
  mass negative, 94
Transitional objects
  addictive substances as, 51, 70
  vibrator as, 151–152
Transsexuals, 53
Transvestites, 53
Traumatic impingements, 21
Turkington, C., 93
Tyson, P., 44–45

Undue excitation, 21

Vagina dentata, 52
Values
  decay of, 106
  in fairy tales and on television,
    109–110
Vanity Fair, 159
Vicedomini, B., 216
Victimology, 10, 177–180
Vilar, E., 49
Vogel, E.F., 107

Voltaire, 202–203
Voyeurs, 53

War, masculinism and, 85–88
Weber, B., 171, 174
Williams, N., 200, 215–216
Williams, T., *A Streetcar Named
    Desire*, 130, 181–192
Winnicott, D.W., 21–23, 30, 41,
    83–84, 107
Womb envy, 42–43
  mitigation of, 56
Woman, as cursed object, 164, 167
Women
  fear of, 22–23, 30, 41–43, 59,
    83–84
  liberated, 123
  moral development of, 5–6, 30–33
  religious degradation of, 82–83
Workplace, male narcissism in,
    56–57

Zhukov, G., 86
Zilboorg, G., 32, 84
Zoroaster, 83